'There are few people in our world who embody optimism like Ping Fu. Anyone who struggles with adversity or believes that their success and happiness are conditional on their circumstances needs to hear Ping's story. She shows us how the human spirit can endure amazing hardship to find happiness, joy and astounding success. More important, Ping shows us how being devoted to others is what carries us forward. Ping is such an inspiration to me and everyone she meets'
Simon Sinek, author of *Start With Why*

'Resilience is the most essential element of life and business today, and there is no more shining role model for resilience (and grace and humility and a whole bunch of other qualities) than Ping Fu. ...e story of how she fled China under precarious circumstances, made ...ew life in the United States, and built a vibrant company should be ...quired reading' Chip Conley, founder of Joie de Vivre Hospitality and author of *Peak* and *Emotional Equations*

'Ping Fu's life story is the stuff of heroic novels. Not only has she ...umphed over adversity most of us can scarcely imagine, but she has ...anaged to draw out of her experience a wealth of practical business ...essons. Those lessons, which she presents in *Bend, Not Break*, have a...owed her to emerge as a leading entrepreneur in a technology that is transforming the world of manufacturing, with far-reaching implications ...or global competition in the twenty-first century' Bo Burlingham, ...or-at-large of *Inc. Magazine* and author of *Small Giants: Companies That Choose to Be Great Instead of Big*

ABOUT THE AUTHORS

Ping Fu is the founder and CEO of Geomagic, a 3D digital reality solution company. She earned an MS in computer science at the University of Illinois and worked at the National Center for Supercomputing Applications and AT&T Bell labs. She is a member of President Obama's National Council on Innovation and Entrepreneurship and a board member of Long Now Foundation. She lives in Chapel Hill, North Carolina.

MeiMei Fox is an author and book editor who also blogs regularly for the *Huffington Post*.

Bend, Not Break

A Life in Two Worlds

Ping Fu

with MeiMei Fox

PORTFOLIO
PENGUIN

Penguin   , USA
Penguin Group   ada M4P 2Y3

Penguin Irel   Books Ltd)
Penguin   stralia

Penguin Books   110 017, India
Pengu   land

Pe
1

Penguin   gland

www.penguin.com

First published in the United States of America by Portfolio/Penguin,
a member of Penguin Group (USA) Inc. 2012
First published in Great Britain by Portfolio Penguin 2013
003

Copyright © Ping Fu, 2012

The moral right of the authors has been asserted

Photograph credits
Insert page 6 (below): White House photograph
7 (top): Gregory K. George, Jr., Geomagic Inc.
7 (left middle): Shaan Hurley of Autodesk
7 (left below): Photo by Eva Kolenko, design by Scott Summit
8 (top): Jonathan Fredin
8 (below): Tom Simon, Geomagic, Inc.
Other photographs courtesy of Ping Fu

Printed in Great Britain by Clays Ltd, St Ives plc

A CIP catalogue record for this book is available from the British Library

ISBN: 978–0–670–92201–7

www.greenpenguin.co.uk

MIX
Paper from
responsible sources
FSC   FSC™ C018179
www.fsc.org

Penguin Books is committed to a sustainable
future for our business, our readers and our planet.
This book is made from Forest Stewardship
Council™ certified paper.

ALWAYS LEARNING   **PEARSON**

I dedicate this book to
Xixi Edelsbrunner and Liyun Tang, my daughter and mother,
and to the memory of my father and Shanghai Mama and Papa.

CONTENTS

AUTHOR'S NOTE

I HAVE TRIED my best to remember and describe the events and people in my life. Mostly, I have used real names, although some names have been altered to protect privacy. For simplicity, I have sometimes used spellings in English that correspond to the Chinese pinyin system. Many details happened more than forty years ago and I've tried as much as possible to verify the facts.

Bend,
Not
Break

ONE

Three
Friends
of
Winter

FRESH OFF THE PLANE: 1984

WHEN I WAS twenty-five years old, the Chinese government quietly deported me. I was terrified to leave my homeland. But the alternative was exile to a remote place in China—or worse.

On January 14, 1984, my parents, aunts and uncles, cousins, and siblings gathered at the Shanghai International Airport to send me off for my flight to San Francisco. I'll never forget that cold, wet afternoon.

As the embarking process began, my family stood in a tight circle outside the passport checkpoint, shuffling our feet and avoiding eye contact. We made small talk about the weather, the clothes we wore, and the farewell banquet they had hosted the night before—anything to distract us from our imminent parting.

Hesitating for a moment before she spoke, my Shanghai Mama, the woman who raised me, broached the subject on everyone's mind. "Ping-Ping," she said, her tongue tripping as she called me by my family nickname, "I made you a dish so you won't get hungry on the long flight." Her whole body trembled as she reached into her bag and passed me a round tin pan tightly covered in foil, still warm. I lifted a corner of the foil and inhaled. The sharp, sweet scent of duck with soy sauce wafted up to my nostrils, a poignant reminder of my happy childhood years in Shanghai. I reached my hand out to clasp hers, giving it a gentle squeeze.

I glanced around; nearly everyone in our group was crying. My younger sister, Hong, grabbed at my shirt to mop the tears from her face, the way she had done as a little girl. I couldn't bring myself to utter any words of comfort for fear that I, too, would break down sobbing.

Only Nanjing Mother and Father, my birth parents, kept their gaze steady. "You will be fine, Ping-Ping," Nanjing Mother said, clearing her throat. "I know you will be able to handle whatever comes your way."

I waited until the last possible minute to go. "It's time," I said, making an effort to keep my voice from catching. My family members began to cry the way people do at funerals, as if I would disappear from their lives forever. They knew that since I was in trouble with the authorities, we might never see one another again or even be allowed to communicate. Resolutely, I kept my eyes dry as I walked down the ramp and away from everything that I had ever known.

As I settled into my seat aboard the aircraft, the vent blasted warm air at my forehead. It occurred to me that this was my first experience of temperature-controlled air. I had never flown in an airplane, though I had spent most of my childhood sliding down aircraft wings at an abandoned airfield and dreaming of becoming an astronaut. I had never traveled anywhere outside of China. The farthest I had been from Nanjing, the city of my birth, was Suzhou University, where I had studied journalism and literature. But that was not why I felt apprehensive about the journey that lay ahead. Because of my writing and other activities, I was no longer welcome in my homeland, yet I knew little about America. I had no home, no friends, and no sense of what awaited me there. I didn't have a single spare dollar in my pocket or speak more than three words of English.

When we were airborne, the flight attendant came by, wheeling a cart. She was an American with blond hair, blue eyes, and a warm smile. In English, she asked me if I wanted something to eat or drink. I didn't understand her since I knew how to say only "Hello," "Thank you," and "Help," but I guessed at her intention. I presumed that the refreshments would cost money, so I waved my hand in a gesture that said no, hugging Shanghai Mama's tin pan even tighter on my lap. Then I pointed toward the cocktail napkins piled high at the edge of the cart, and the stewardess wordlessly handed me a large stack.

For hours, I scribbled Chinese characters onto the thin squares of paper, placing one after another at the corner of my tray like miniature flags of surrender. I did not intend to share these notes; journaling had proved comforting to me since I was a child. The act of recording my thoughts gave the illusion of having a conversation with a trusted friend, when in truth I now had none.

⌒

I landed in San Francisco fourteen hours later, jet-lagged and emotionally drained. The airport amazed me. It glittered like a jewel with its multiple-story-tall windows and sparkling cleanliness.

As soon as I had cleared immigration, I sought out the ticket counter. I was en route to Albuquerque, where I was registered to study English as a second language at the University of New Mexico. Although I had exactly eighty dollars in traveler's checks to pay for the connecting flight, the airline staff refused to issue me a ticket. I couldn't understand why; that had been the price when I had checked in Shanghai.

Bless San Francisco—there was a Mandarin-speaking agent behind the counter who understood my problem. In China, the government sets prices, so ticket prices rarely changed. But here in America, prices changed frequently, she explained. "The ticket price has increased since you left Shanghai. You are five dollars short."

I didn't have five dollars, a credit card, or a number to call for help. As I stood there silently, an American man waiting behind me in line asked us what the problem was. When the desk agent explained my predicament, he took a five-dollar bill out of his wallet.

"Here you go," he said, flashing an easy smile. The ticket agent translated.

"Thank you," I replied in English, surprised that a stranger would help me. The gesture may not have meant much to him, but it meant the world to me. My first impression of Americans—and one that endures to this day—was that they are warm, giving people. The experience offered me this life lesson: "When in doubt, always err on the side of generosity." It is a value that I have held dear to my heart ever since.

⌒

When I got to Albuquerque, I found myself stranded once again. My father had given me the name of Mr. Sheng, a former student of his who was studying at the University of New Mexico and had helped my family to get me accepted there. I called him collect several times, but the phone rang endlessly. I waited, hoping eventually

I'd reach this stranger who was my only U.S. contact. I had nowhere else to turn. (Later, I learned that Mr. Sheng had graduated
from UNM a few weeks before I arrived and was touring America
before returning to China.)

As I sat on the curb outside the luggage claim with my one large,
tattered bag, I watched the cars coming and going. The popping
sound of car trunks opening unnerved me. No one seemed to notice me; they were all too busy leaving the airport or coming here
to pick up their loved ones. It reminded me of the day, when I was
eight years old, that I left Shanghai by train and arrived at the
Nanjing station alone. The feelings of loss hit me hard, and I began
to cry.

A car pulled up in front of me sometime later. When I looked up
with hazy eyes, I saw a Chinese man sitting in the driver's seat. He
rolled down the window slowly.

"Do you need help?" the man asked, speaking in Mandarin with
a thick accent that I couldn't place. Yes, I said, I needed a ride to the
University of New Mexico campus. "Get in," he said, waving his
hand toward the passenger seat. "I'll take you there."

Another generous American! And not only that, there were
Chinese-speaking people everywhere here. I couldn't believe my luck.

We drove off in his beat-up car across a vast and desolate desert
plain that resembled a postapocalyptic landscape. My limited im-
pressions of America had come entirely from Chinese state-run television, which I had watched from time to time, huddled in groups
with my classmates and neighbors around someone's black-and-
white TV. Mostly, I knew that the Chinese dominated the Americans in Ping-Pong. Still, I had expected to be living in a city like the
dense metropolises of Nanjing and Shanghai where I had grown up,
not a place like this.

"Do you mind if we stop by my house?" the man asked. "I need
to check in on my kids before I can drop you off at the university."

I nodded. A few minutes later, we drove into the Albuquerque center city, where the cluttered, uniform housing complexes looked not unlike those in Nanjing. At least here were signs of familiarity. But unlike in any Chinese urban center, the streets were empty. The only people I saw were homeless with dirty sleeping bags and signs that looked like they were selling themselves or their children. I began anxiously tapping my fingers against my knee. The man pulled up in front of an apartment compound with high windows covered by metal bars. It reminded me of a Chinese prison. Later, I found out it was government-subsidized housing for refugees, and the man was a Vietnamese refugee of Chinese descent.

"Please come inside and meet my children for a minute," the man offered.

I climbed out of the passenger seat and followed him. Although the surroundings made me a little uneasy, I had no reason to feel suspicious. He seemed like a caring father and had been so kind to me.

As soon as I stepped inside, he handed me a box of cookies and stammered, "My wife just walked out on me. I need someone to look after the children for a few hours because I have to go to work." Then he dashed out of the small apartment. I heard him lock the front door from the outside with a padlock.

I turned around and saw two young boys, perhaps three and four years old, and a baby girl with wide, watery eyes. They stared at me with their hands reaching out and feet glued to the ground, desperate for attention but too scared to approach me.

"Mama, Mama," they cried out. *Mama* means "mother" in Chinese as it does in much of the rest of the world.

"No, no, I am not your mother," I said in Mandarin. But they didn't understand.

"Mama, mama," they continued in unison, voices reaching a fever pitch.

For a few frantic moments, I ignored the children and searched the dingy apartment for a back door or a window whose bars I could slide my petite frame through—any hope of escape. I found none. I saw no telephone, either, though even if I had, I wouldn't have known to dial 911. I was a prisoner.

The strain of the past few days caught up with me and I sank onto the cool concrete of the living room floor. My body frozen, all I could hear was the pounding of my heart. The plain gray walls were closing in on me. The faces of the children were fading. I felt like I was going to pass out.

Then the toddler came up to me and took my hand. She placed her face next to mine, eyes innocent as a bunny rabbit's and skin soft as finely ground flour. I had a great deal of experience caring for children, so I gathered up the energy to care for these three. I doled out the cookies, washed their dirty faces, and let them ride on my back for a game of horsey, which I'd been fond of playing as a child. When I got worn out, I would fall to the ground. They would laugh and call out strange words. It didn't matter that I didn't understand; I assumed they wanted me to repeat the game, time and time again.

Hours passed and the sky grew dark, but the children's father did not return. I wondered how long I might be held captive, hoping that the man was working a late shift and would come home soon. I put the children to sleep in the bedroom, which had only one bed. The living room and kitchen shared the same space. Next to the dining table were two chairs and a hard bench, no couch. I was too tired to care. I wound up spending my first night in America as I had passed many in China: sleeping on a concrete floor, cold, exhausted, hungry, and miserable.

The next morning, the children quickly finished the cookies. The two boys became cranky, crying and patting their tummies. I found a box of macaroni and cheese in the apartment's near-empty cupboards, but I had no idea how to prepare it properly. So I boiled the noodles and we ate them plain, without the cheese that lay hidden in its metal envelope.

By midmorning, with no sign of the father's return, I started to wonder if something had happened to him. Through an open barred window, I began shouting one of the few English words I knew: "Help." The children joined in with me, thinking we were playing another game. But the passersby—and there weren't many—did nothing.

The next day I tried again. My voice grew louder and more desperate with each passing hour, as we all became hungrier and I lost hope that my captor would ever return to set us free.

Finally, on the third day, we heard shouts from just outside, followed by pounding on the apartment door. "Help, help!" I screamed. Moments later, police busted the door open. At last, a neighbor had heard us and called the cops. They loaded us into a paddy wagon and took us downtown to the police station.

As soon as they had found a Chinese interpreter, two burly policemen began to interrogate me. "Do you know your kidnapper? Why did you get into a stranger's car? How did you end up inside his house? Who can we call about the children? Do you have any family or friends we can call to verify your identity? Did the man hurt you?"

My answers came out as hysterical semi-nonsense. Not only was I sleep deprived and ravenous, but also I had a well-developed suspicion of authority figures. In China, no one trusted the police, and we never wanted our names appearing on official paperwork—that almost always brought lifelong troubles. Was I now considered a criminal by the American government, I wondered? Would I be punished? Would the Chinese government find out that I'd gotten into trouble on my very first day in the United States of America? If so, would they go after my family in China for revenge?

The police tried to get me to press kidnapping charges against the Vietnamese man. I refused. I simply begged them to set me free. Eventually they gave up on me and put a call into UNM on my behalf. They got directions for where on campus to take me: the International Student Center.

I arrived at the University of New Mexico in a squad car.

Although I had made up my mind to leave my life in China behind, those days of captivity that followed my arrival in the United States had drawn me back into painful memories of my childhood. Ones that I had tried hard to forget.

MOTHER: 1966

WHEN I WAS little, I thought dragonflies chose to hover just above my family's garden because they liked to admire its beauty. I was the baby of the family, younger by several years than my sister and four brothers, and we lived together in a grand Shanghai home with our parents, whom I called Shanghai Mama and Papa. We liked to catch the magnificent humming red-orange dragonflies in a net. We would compare the colors of their wings, debating which was most beautiful.

I assumed that Shanghai was the center of the earth, partly because of my grandfather's historic maps etched with many shipping lines that fanned out from the Bund, partly because of the city's sheer enormity and traffic, and partly because it was the only home I knew. We lived on a tree-lined lane in a neighborhood of "little mansions" built by entrepreneurs of the early twentieth century, when Shanghai was known as the "Paris of the East."

Our family house was peaceful rather than showy, a three-story and three-section villa connecting to a courtyard with a front gate that opened onto the main street of our neighborhood. Surrounding the complex, a stone wall decorated with an ornate iron fence shielded the serene interior from the unpredictable outside world.

Curved, handcrafted iron and stone balconies adorned the south

facade, letting in warm light on sunny days and offering a pan-
oramic view. Standing there, you could glean something of our lives
in the early 1960s: the imposing headquarters of the Soviet Friendship Society looming large amid the boutiques and businesses that
lined the city's famous Nanjing Road. Chairman Mao's most radical reforms had yet to fully penetrate China's most cosmopolitan
city then; a Hong Kong tailor still made the Western suits that my
brothers wore to school. Streetcar Number 24 passed nearby, and
my family and I often took it into the heart of the old city, surrounded by swarms of bicyclists commuting to work or school, past
ancient bazaars and old ladies selling flowers.

The front of our house held a traditional Chinese courtyard with
a well that offered us crystal clear drinking water. In the backyard,
a lovely garden filled with exotic species of flowers, wooden pago-
das, and winding stone paths offered itself up to our imagination.
This was my father's scholar garden, a modest version of the sym-
bolic landscapes developed centuries earlier by the educated elite of
China, places they went to contemplate and restore their serenity
when Europe was still in the Dark Ages. Shanghai Papa taught me
that the garden contained plants for each season, and that there was
a reason for each plant.

"There are three friends of winter: the pine tree, the plum blossom, and bamboo," Shanghai Papa once told me. "Pine trees are
strong. They remain happy and green throughout the year. In the
unbearable heat of summer and the severe cold of winter, they stand
unperturbed." He plucked a branch and offered it to me. I inhaled
the sharp odor.

"The crimson petals of the plum blossom gleam brilliantly
against the white snow," he continued, pointing to a tree covered in
magenta flowers. "The ability to bloom in the midst of misfortune
suggests dignity and forbearance under harsh circumstances."

Shanghai Papa then walked over to a grove of bamboo. "This is
the third friend of winter. Bamboo is flexible, bending with the

wind but never breaking, capable of adapting to any circumstance. It suggests resilience, meaning that we have the ability to bounce back from even the most difficult times."

I nodded, reaching out to grab a stalk of bamboo and bending it toward me until its leaves tickled my nose. Shanghai Papa smiled and continued. "The Taoists understand that there can be no summer without winter, no ups without downs, no growth without decay. Your ability to thrive depends, in the end, on your attitude to your life circumstances. When you are like the three friends of winter, you take everything in stride with grace, putting forth energy when it is needed, yet always staying calm inwardly." He asked me to memorize that and other Taoist sayings, and was proud when I could recite them in front of our frequent houseguests.

It was said that Shanghai Papa's hair was completely silver by the time he was thirty, a confirmation of his wisdom. For a while, I thought that if I painted my hair white I would become wise like him. He was a man of influence. When he spoke, each phrase unfolded like a precious gift. Yet he also had a way of making others laugh, and was unafraid to make jokes at his own expense.

Shanghai Papa ran a factory that made thread. When he came home at night, he would enter the front gate and call out, "Sweetheart, I'm home!" Shanghai Mama would come running, her footsteps quick and light. I liked to stick my head out from the second-floor balcony to spy on them in the courtyard below, hugging and kissing. Then, when they came walking up the stairs inside the house hand in hand, I would jump on them. They made a game of fighting to see who could catch me first. I never once saw them raise their voices with each other or with us. Theirs was the happiest marriage I have ever known.

Shanghai Mama was the embodiment of Chinese womanhood, dimpled and pretty with large, gentle eyes and soft skin. She made every visitor, including her own children, feel as though it were a great pleasure that we stayed in her home. I loved her tender embraces. Every morning, she would buy three jasmine flower buds from the market. One she pinned to her blouse. The other two she gave to me and my sister, whom I called Jie Jie (meaning "big sister"), so that we always carried a sweet fragrance with us.

While my older siblings were off at school, I would spend afternoons with Shanghai Mama in the kitchen. She said that food must appeal to all five senses: aroma, color, texture, taste, and love. I'd hang on to her legs amid the sizzle and steam and chopping sounds as she prepared the traditional dinners we enjoyed each night: four appetizers, one soup, and eight main courses. My favorite dish was crabmeat with ginkgo nuts in mint mango sauce.

Shanghai Mama loved all six children dearly, and since I was the youngest, I was still small enough to cuddle and kiss. She used to call me her "pearl in the hand," a Chinese phrase used to refer to that which is most delicate and precious, something that must be kept close to safeguard it from harm. She gave me the nickname that the rest of my family later adopted: Ping-Ping, which means "Little Apple." At night, though I had a small canopy bed of my own, she would let me fall asleep in a corner of her and Papa's large rosewood bed.

It was in the library that I taught myself to write a phonetic form of Chinese known as pinyin at an early age. It is also where Shanghai Papa and his father, my grandfather, cultivated in me a lasting appreciation of ideas—which they said, like books, required proper care. They would easily forgive me if I left a scroll out on the floor; I was just a small child. But returning it to the wrong cubicle was a more serious infraction.

My brothers teased me that I was a bookworm, but I wasn't always reading. I also enjoyed the library because it was at tree level and I could look out the windows past the heavy drapes embroidered with cranes, symbolizing peace, to catch a glimpse of the sparrows as they darted in and out of our garden at sunset. I saved kernels of rice for the birds, my wild golden pets, and dreamed of growing wings so that I could fly with them through the clouds and even higher, to the moon. It was said that a woman with a long flowing robe lived there, and I longed to pay her a visit.

I wanted so much to fly that I wished for it on my eighth birthday, in May of 1966. Shanghai Mama brought out a square cake decorated with green latticework on the sides and covered with roses made of yellow cream. It looked like our garden! I blew hard, but two of the candles stayed lit.

"You won't get your wish," taunted Brother Four, before Shanghai Mama shushed him and told me I could try again. But my brother was right.

When I look back on that birthday dinner, I see the ink print of a perfect childhood. It was as a member of that family, within those nurturing, loving, and intellectually inspiring arms, that I assumed I would grow up. I don't know how I could have coped with what happened next if I hadn't first known the beauty that flows from a child's simple expectation of love.

That spring, rain fell in torrents, washing away the spectacularly colored flowers in our garden and the tranquillity of our neighborhood. I didn't know at the time that the Cultural Revolution was just beginning, and no one in my family anticipated that it would last for the next ten years. It would prove to be the darkest period in modern Chinese history: thirty-six million people were persecuted, and three million were killed or maimed. Chairman Mao was consolidating his grip as the leader of the People's Republic of China with an ultra-left-wing, anti-intellectual, pro-labor version of Communism fueled by his often out-of-control army of fanatical young people, the Red Guard. In order to seize power, he had elevated an existing student movement to the level of a nationwide campaign. Mao called on not only the youth but also the masses of workers, peasants, and soldiers to carry out the task of reforming China by ridding it of corrupting capitalist and intellectual influences.

Many young Chinese at the time were enthusiastic about the prospect of becoming politically influential at such a young age. With "Little Red Books" filled with Chairman Mao's quotations in their hands, squads of Red Guards formed and began to go from house to house looking for potential elements of corruption, which often included their own family members. The accusations against their opponents frequently seemed ridiculous to outsiders, yet the punishments the Red Guard exacted could be exceptionally cruel.

I was too young to understand the political surges that were changing our lives, but I remember noticing strange things happening around that time.

First, a friendly German man who lived across the street from us left without saying good-bye, as if the rain had washed him away. I had liked him. He used to give me horsey rides on his back, one after another, until he ran out of breath and put me down, huffing and muttering, "*Kaputt! Kaputt!*"

I went into his empty house after I found out that he'd gone. The door was unlocked, yet the furniture remained untouched. I saw his favorite armchair, its sagging cushions permanently indented from where he used to sit. It was like looking at a photographic negative, a shadow of a presence. The air seemed thin without the sounds of his Chinese, thickened by a German accent, and his resounding laughter.

I walked back to our house and found Shanghai Mama. I asked her where the German man had gone. She told me that he was a "foreign devil" and that I should put him out of my mind. The unusual sharpness in her voice scared me so much that I didn't dare ask any questions about him again.

Shanghai Mama came home with bad news one afternoon not long after that. She had lost her position as head of our neighborhood committee because she wasn't a member of the Communist

Party. Being part of a well-educated, relatively wealthy merchant-class family was rapidly falling out of favor.

Communist flags unfurled furiously throughout the city. Pieces of propaganda sailed through the streets like autumn leaves, calling everyone to join the revolution. Posters with big black characters soon covered the real estate of every enclosing wall around our neighborhood. I grew particularly fearful of those with thick red lines painted over a person's name. One of my brothers explained that these people had been identified as enemies of the state. I overheard them telling one another stories of neighbors being tortured to death. The graphic details made me feel so ill that I had to cover my ears.

Learning itself came to be labeled "counterrevolutionary." I was in first grade that spring when Mao closed down all the schools in China. Everyone, old and young, was required to get up each morning and stand outside to salute a picture of Chairman Mao that hung at the end of the lane. From there, the older children headed off to study sessions, during which they recited quotes from Mao's Little Red Book. I was still young enough to stay home.

One day, a frenzy of excitement swept the country as Mao eliminated train fares and invited millions of Chinese to travel to Beijing to see him speak in the People's Square. My brothers were excited and applied to make the trip. But Mao's army was conducting background checks that extended back for three generations. If you received verification that your family tree was "clean"—that you were descended from three generations of workers, farmers, or soldiers—then you were given a red band to put on your arm, a moss green military uniform, a cap with a single red star, and the status that went along with being a Red Guard.

"We're dirty," my brothers complained over dinner when they were denied.

"See, you should have listened to Mama and bathed every day," I teased. Shanghai Mama often chased after my mud-stained brothers at bedtime, trying to get them to wash up.

"You don't understand," my third brother said, shaking his head.

"Well, I'm just glad we are all home safe," Shanghai Papa spoke firmly, urging us to eat our dinner. That may have been one of our last meals together as a family.

Communist Party meetings were held in homes all over the city. Later that week, our iron gates swung open and people poured into our courtyard. Shanghai Papa escorted them into the ballroom on the ground floor. Some were neighbors, but most of them I didn't recognize. At first, my brothers, sister, and I took it all for fun, buzzing about like bees. Then the talking started. It went on and on as people dozed off sitting in our sofas or propped up against the walls.

I lost interest until Shanghai Papa took the microphone in his hand and started talking. I cannot remember his words, but I know that he was saying something in his wise and careful manner about himself and our family.

"Revisionist!" someone in the audience shouted at Shanghai Papa rudely.

The room went quiet. Shanghai Papa searched the room until his eyes locked onto the person who had spoken out against him. I was shocked when Papa thanked him, saying he was grateful for the man's feedback. Shanghai Mama immediately found me and led me upstairs to my room, telling me this conversation wasn't meant for my little ears.

Red Guards appeared at the doorway to our home the next day, commanding my brothers to go with them. They were being "sent up to the mountains or down to the countryside," a Communist Chinese expression that soon became synonymous with forced labor and a hefty dose of physical and psychological abuse. Shanghai Papa was arrested. Only then did I become frightened for the first time.

I never imagined that they might come after me next.

It was later that summer. I was sitting on the floor of my grandfather's library. A column of small drawers, like the ones in traditional Chinese medicine cabinets, extended floor to ceiling from the library's mahogany wall. Numbered and meticulously stacked in these drawers were picture books, stories illustrated in fine ink on long and narrow sheets of rice paper protected by silk covers. Shanghai Papa said they were special because they were hand drawn, with only a few copies made of each edition. I knew how to open and close the accordion folds carefully so as not to damage the books. I loved to touch the beautiful pictures and trace my index finger over the dense and delicate black ink strokes.

Outside, the streets of Shanghai, which were often foggy during the summer, wore a thick coat of hazy drizzle. I paged through a story about the Monkey King, the infamous trickster of Chinese mythology who could fly thousands of miles across the clouds. I imagined the Monkey King hopping off the page and, with a naughty grin, handing me a peach he had stolen.

Suddenly, I heard a crash echoing from the courtyard below. Next came the heavy beating of boots entering our home, and then voices from the living room on the ground floor. Soon I could hear shouting, then my mother's voice, soft but broken. She and I were the only ones home.

I threw my book onto the floor and ran to the library door. The sound of my mother's pleading was almost buried under quarrelsome shouts, the smashing of broken glass, and the cracking of furniture.

"Where is she?" a young male voice demanded. "Where did you hide her?"

"She—she is so little . . ." my mother murmured, breaking into sobs.

I rushed out of the library to the top of the staircase and poked my head through the banister to see what was happening.

"She's upstairs!" a teenage boy cried, spotting me and pointing me out to the others.

Oh, no—they want to catch me, I thought. My legs barely obeyed my panicked mind as I scampered for a hiding place. I ran directly back into the library, the safest and most comforting place I'd ever known.

But there was no escape. The invaders made their way up the stairs too quickly—four boys and one girl, all teenagers, all members of Mao's Red Guard. They wore matching oversized moss green uniforms, red armbands, and olive-colored caps adorned with a simple red star. Two of them held lit cigarettes between their fingers. They backed me into a corner of the library and surrounded me in a half circle.

The boy who had spotted me spoke first. "You are not a resident of Shanghai. You can't live here." He stepped forward to grab me by the shoulders. "Come on—follow us," he said close to my ear, adopting a gentler tone. "We will take you to Nanjing. It is the city of your registry residence because you were born there."

I felt more and more confused. No one had ever told me that I'd been born in Nanjing. I had lived in this house my entire life and didn't know any other home. I took a step back, and the female guard slammed me backward into a mahogany cabinet.

"Come with us this minute," the girl ordered, grabbing my right arm with a firm grip, her face flush with excitement. Then her eyes narrowed even further. "Let me tell you," she said, turning her head toward my mama, who had followed the guards upstairs. "This woman is not your mother."

"No, no, no! That's not true," I said. "She *is* my mama, she is my mama!" I kicked my feet and squirmed in the girl's grip until she handed me back to the boy who had spotted me first.

I lifted my head to look at him. He was quite handsome in his uniform, as tall as my oldest brother. The red star on his cap was slightly bent and scratched. I immediately thought of him as "Bent Star."

Bent Star tapped the ashes off his cigarette and stuck it into the right side of his mouth. Then he lifted me up with one hand, roughly grabbing the back of my T-shirt by the neck the way butchers handle slaughtered chickens. I reached my hands out to Mama. But the other three boys pushed her even farther away.

"Let me go," I said as I struggled. "Mama, save me, save me!" I called out to her, my arms waving.

Bent Star dropped me onto the wooden floor and took another drag from his cigarette. Ashes fell from the air, a spark singeing my ankle before dying out. He then grabbed my hand and pulled me through the library door to the top of the stairs. His strides were long, like a giraffe's, so I had to scramble to keep up with him in order to avoid being dragged across the floor.

"Don't be stupid," he said. "You are lucky that we're taking you to your real mother."

"But she *is* my real mother," I replied, pointing back to where Mama stood at the library door, hands over her mouth to muffle her cries. "Please, let me go, let me go! You're hurting me!"

"Shut up or I'll hit you," he hissed, his big palm rising in the air. I could see, though, that he was like a barking dog that is not really going to bite. He was only trying to appear tough in front of the others. My brothers behaved the same way. I wished that they were home. They would not have allowed anyone to hurt me.

"Ping-Ping, stop fighting," my mama said, raising her voice to stop my protests. "He is right—I did not give birth to you. Nanjing Mother is your real mother."

"No, no, no! *You* are my mother. You told me so many times. I'll be good. Don't let them take me away—please!" Tears gushed down my face and blinded my eyes. How could my mama say such a thing? Only a few weeks ago, I was playing in the kitchen while she cooked dinner and she had told me that I was her favorite child. My mama only uttered a small cry. Her hands shook furiously, and her almond-shaped eyes filled with tears.

"She's lying!" I screamed.

The girl guard walked over and slapped me twice on the face, hard.

"What are you doing that for, Lin?" Bent Star asked, placing his arm in front of my face to shield it from any further blows. Lin threw her head back in disgust. Bent Star tossed aside his cigarette butt, picked me up with both arms, and carried me downstairs. The others cheered as they marched down the stairs behind us.

"Mama, please take me back. I'll be good—I promise. Please!" I wailed, as the guards carried me out the villa's front door.

The last glimpse I had was Shanghai Mama standing behind the iron gate, waving, her hands stretched toward me while she spilled out a few halting words. "Ping-Ping, be . . . be good. Ping-Ping . . . be a . . . a brave girl . . ."

Bent Star pushed me quickly away from the house, while Lin gave me another slap. "Keep quiet," she hissed. They loaded me into an empty black military van. Ten minutes later, we arrived at our destination.

Shanghai Train Station West was jammed to the breaking point with people carrying babies, baskets, and suitcases. I had never seen it so busy before. Bent Star grabbed my hand and pulled me out of the van. His eyes wandered around as if he were confused.

"Over there!" Lin said, pointing to an approaching train. I watched the hot steel creature grunt and lurch into the station. Sparks of burning coal swirled out of the engine pipe until they faded into the damp gray air.

As we walked closer to the train, the scene grew even more chaotic. The cars were already packed full when the train pulled in, yet more people struggled to get on board anyway, pushing their way through doors and climbing in windows. Arms, legs, and bottoms stuck out from every possible opening. I noticed several other groups of Red Guards on the platform as well. Some were boarding the train themselves; others were pushing unwilling passengers with tear-streaked faces.

Bent Star watched the scene for a few moments as he tried to figure out how to load me onto the train. I noticed that we stood in front of car number five. Copying the other Red Guards, the gangly teenager picked me up and heaved me through the nearest window like a sack of rice. I was struggling to find my footing in the crowded compartment when I heard him call out my name.

"Ping, catch!" Bent Star said, throwing his own wool sweater in after me. "Put it on before you get sick," he ordered. Then he turned and disappeared into the sea of people.

I found myself crammed into a tiny space on the floor surrounded by strong odors of cigarette smoke, urine, and sweat, fighting for breathing room with strangers far larger than I. Family members screamed for each other and babies cried, creating a symphony of suffering. I began to weep.

An old man noticed me and asked if I was traveling alone. When I nodded, he offered me a wedge of seat between himself and the window. I felt a breeze as the train began to move. The fresh air, the view of the deep green rice fields, and the swaying motion of the train offered me some small comfort.

Smashed into my seat corner, I sorted through the puzzling events that had just taken place. I tried to tell myself that Mama had said those hurtful things about not being my real mother only because the Red Guards had been threatening me and she had been afraid that they would hurt me if she didn't lie. But the truth of the matter was, there had been hints before that I'd been adopted. I remembered a time when my older sister had complained that my brothers were giving me a longer sedan chair ride in their arms than they were giving their "real" sister. I had run inside the house crying. Mama had assured me that she was my real mother.

"Ping-Ping," she had said, stroking my hair, "you're so special that you needed two mothers to give birth to you."

Nanjing Mother, Shanghai Mama's sister, had been a part of my life for as long as I could remember. I had often wondered why Shanghai Mama had worked so hard to encourage me to form a bond with Nanjing Mother and write letters to her. My nanny had even taken me on this very train to visit Nanjing a few times, though it had been a while since our last trip. I had also found it strange that Shanghai Mama had always asked me to call her sister "Nanjing Mother," as opposed to "Auntie." Still, it had never occurred to me that Nanjing Mother might be my real mother. Now I finally faced the undeniable truth: Nanjing Mother *must* be my birth mother.

I remembered Nanjing Mother as a serious person. She had an efficient, close-cropped hairdo that she kept perfectly blow-dried. Short and thin with a round face and sloping shoulders that made her face seem even rounder, she nonetheless stood very erect. During my visits, she always hurried off to work early in the morning and arrived home late. She carried with her at all times a dark wooden abacus, each bead shining from use. At night, I would fall asleep to the sound of the abacus clicking in a pleasant consistent rhythm. Once she told me proudly that she had won the Nanjing city abacus championship.

Nanjing Mother often asked me questions to test my knowledge of basic math, such as, "Two plus two equals?" If I knew the answer, another question would follow. "Two times three equals?" This would go on for a while until I didn't know an answer. "You'll know next time," she'd say.

In Shanghai, we always had a table full of fragrant homemade dishes for dinner. Mama was a wonderful chef. Papa would share his stories of the day, while my brothers interjected their jokes, making me laugh so hard that my tummy ached. Nanjing Mother, on

the other hand, didn't like to cook. She often went out to get dinner. I accompanied her a couple of times. We waited in a long line
until we reached the window of a large cafeteria. Servers scooped
the food out from vast metal containers. It didn't look or smell ap-
pealing, and it often contained big chunks of pig fat that I couldn't
swallow. When I spit them out, it would infuriate Nanjing Mother.
"You are wasting food," she'd complain. We never talked or laughed
at the dinner table. Nanjing Mother didn't seem to enjoy the food
or her time with me.

Nanjing Mother's husband, whom I now realized was probably
my birth father, was even shorter than she was, but I couldn't picture his face. I just remembered Nanjing Father getting up early
each morning to fetch fresh food from the market and make me
sesame pancakes with soymilk for breakfast.

"Don't say you like it," Nanjing Mother warned. "You will get
the same breakfast every day if you do."

They had a two-bedroom flat on the second floor of an apartment building with an old-fashioned Chinese roof and patchy, dis-
colored brick walls. The building housed members of the faculty of
the Nanjing University of Aeronautics and Astronautics, or NUAA,
where Nanjing Father taught engineering. They had a cute little
daughter named Hong, four years younger than I was. The last time
I'd seen her, she was learning how to use the potty by herself.

I didn't dislike my Nanjing parents; I just didn't know them.
They hadn't raised me, and I couldn't think of them as my real parents. But I took comfort in knowing that at least I wouldn't be alone
when I got to Nanjing. I was going to live with them and visit my
Shanghai Mama and Papa, instead of the other way around.

In the seat opposite me, a woman nursed her baby girl. Faces
filled with love, they seemed oblivious to the cacophony surrounding them. It made me miss Shanghai Mama even more.

Four hours later, the train came to a squeaking halt at Nanjing Station, where the scene was almost identical to the one I'd witnessed in Shanghai. People fought their way off the train and onto the packed platform, sending their sacks flying through the windows. Fights broke out. Women, their clothes and children wrapped tightly in bundles under their arms, dashed out of sight.

I felt beads of sweat form on my forehead and the palms of my hands. I wondered if everyone except for me knew where to go and what to do. The kind old man who had shared his seat with me had already left; I was alone.

I sat motionless on my seat, trying to make myself invisible. Streetcar Number 24, which stopped in front of our Shanghai house, traveled in a loop. Shanghai Mama always told me that if I ever got lost, I only needed to stay on the same streetcar until it brought me back home. It occurred to me that the train probably worked the same way. If no one found me here, I could simply stay put, and this train would take me back to Shanghai, where I would be reunited with my mama.

"Ping Fu! Ping Fu!" The sound of my name being called by two voices—one male and one female—jolted me to attention.

"I'm here! I'm here!" I answered instinctively, thinking this must be my Nanjing parents coming to fetch me. I poked my head out the train window and waved my hand furiously. But the afternoon sun blinded me so that all I could make out rushing across the platform toward me were two silhouettes.

As the figures came stomping onto the train, I was horrified to discover that these were not my Nanjing parents after all, but two new Red Guards. How had they known where to find me? Bent Star must have notified them that I was in car number five. I glanced around for an escape route, but it was too late. The girl already had her hand on my shoulder and was shaking me.

"Why the hell did you stay on the train, you idiot? Get off this minute," she commanded in a high-pitched voice. I decided to call her "Squeaky."

"She wanted a free round-trip," the boy guard joked, not realizing just how close he was to the truth. It looked as if he had broken or dislocated his nose at some point, so I labeled him "Crank Nose."

Crank Nose and Squeaky led me to a car and drove me through the city. I had learned just about everything I knew of Nanjing from my Shanghai Papa. He had told me that the city was known for its prime location on the Yangtze River and for attracting intellectuals as well as artists. Nanjing means "Southern Capital." The city had earned this name because it served as the capital of ten dynasties in ancient China. Papa's tales of its rich history, plus the presence of Nanjing Mother and Father, made the city mystical in my childhood mind.

A dark period in Nanjing's recent history had lent the city a newfound and unwelcome notoriety. In December 1937, the Japanese army occupied Nanjing for six weeks. The city erupted in violence, becoming the scene of one of the biggest massacres in modern history. An estimated three hundred thousand Chinese civilians were slaughtered, with mass beheadings, live burials, burnings, and other forms of torture. More than twenty thousand women were raped and many were then killed. A third of the city's buildings were damaged by fire, and countless shops, stores, and residences were looted and sacked. Blood ran through the boulevards; corpses floated on rivers and littered the streets and alleys. Children, the elderly, even nuns—no one could escape the savagery of the Japanese army. When I was nine or ten, I learned that the Rape of Nanjing Memorial Day falls on May 30, my birthday. The coincidence unsettles me to this day, making my birthday both a cause for celebration and an opportunity for grave reflection on humankind's potential for cruelty.

Nanjing had recovered somewhat in the decades that followed

the Japanese occupation, but I recalled from my previous visits that it was still nowhere near the glamorous, cosmopolitan city that Shanghai was. As we drove through the streets that day, I saw that it was not even as pleasant as I had remembered; it seemed more like a war zone. Military tanks rolled down the tree-lined roads. Gunshots rang out like bad omens. Bloodstains dotted the sidewalks, serving as warning signs. The streets were almost empty of citizens except for a few people dressed in blue-and-gray Mao-style jackets riding bicycles silently with their heads down. But everywhere, I saw Red Guards with their matching military uniforms, caps, and red armbands. It was clear that these young people were running the show.

Without a word, Crank Nose and Squeaky dropped me off at the front gate of the Nanjing University of Aeronautics and Astronautics. I was relieved to recognize the place from previous visits: this was where Nanjing Father was a professor. I got out of the car excitedly, hoping to catch site of my birth parents. My two Red Guard escorts darted away in their vehicle, leaving me behind with nothing more than the stink of their black exhaust.

Once I took in the scene, the situation seemed hopeless. Armed military personnel unloaded from tanks and trucks lining the road in front of the main entrance to the university. Behind the military line they had formed, a crowd of thousands pushed at one another and yelled at the Red Guards. Trucks jammed with more people passed by. Chaos filled the air, and confusion shone forth from the face of every citizen. Still eager to find Nanjing Mother and Father, I squeezed between people's legs and made my way to the front of the crowd, right up against the university gates.

Suddenly, I heard my nickname being called by a thin and familiar voice. Standing on my tiptoes and stretching my neck long to make myself taller, I struggled to determine where the sound was coming from.

"Ping-Ping!" the voice called again, enabling me to home in on one of the trucks where Red Guards were loading up citizens. Standing there in the truck bed were my Nanjing parents. They furiously nudged their bodies through the crowd to get closer to the edge of the truck bed so that they could wave to me. Their faces were flushed red and drawn tight.

I kept pushing my way toward them through the crowd, but their truck pulled away too quickly. All I caught were a few glimpses of Nanjing Mother, with Nanjing Father's head popping up over her shoulder.

"Ping-Ping, take care of your sister," I heard Nanjing Mother shout as the truck drove off in a cloud of dust.

At their disappearance, I felt numb. My shoulders shook as I doubled over on myself, scared and confused.

That was the first time I felt the falling sensation that was to become so familiar to me over the years. I was falling, falling, and there was no one to catch me. There was no one left here who knew me, and no one to care for me. I got sick to my stomach, nearly vomiting onto the shoes of the people surrounding me.

If only my eighth birthday wish had come true, I thought. If only I could fly. I'd soar like a bird up into the heavens, out of this nightmare, and back home to Shanghai, to my loving mama and siblings and our peaceful home.

The next thing I knew, Red Guards grabbed me and pushed me into a line with other disheveled kids. We walked across the street to the student dormitory area, where a pair of two-story gray concrete buildings stood parallel; not far from them were a scum-filled water canal and a long brick wall. A trail of garbage brought my attention to a soccer field on the west side. This would be my home and neighborhood for the next ten years.

In the early 1960s, the government provided Chinese students and faculty with standard housing on campus. But everything changed with the Cultural Revolution. Receiving an education suddenly was considered an activity of the bourgeois elite, and teachers were declared enemies of the state. Most people with an intellectual background—merchants, doctors, lawyers, bureaucrats, professors, and students—were killed or carted off to the countryside for re-education. I later found out that, before my arrival in Nanjing, my parents' two-bedroom faculty flat had been confiscated along with everything in it.

Now that Mao had decided to require everyone in China to return to the city of their birth—even children unaccompanied by their parents—the university student dormitories were being converted into housing for families or individuals who had been relocated, like me. Several Red Guards sat at a table calling out names and assigning room numbers. I waited until they called "Ping Fu," and I approached the table.

I was handed papers that I couldn't read—the characters were too sophisticated for me. A big, official red stamp decorated the top of each page. Along with several dozen other children who either wept or wore blank expressions, I was escorted up to the second floor of the dormitory. At the top of the stairs, I gazed, terrified, down a long, dark hallway illuminated by a single lightbulb that hung by a wire from its socket. Identical rooms lined each side. The door hinges all were smashed, leaving the doors hanging at a slant.

Room 202 was near the stairs. "This is yours," a Red Guard escort told me. "You are forbidden from talking to anyone but your sister." I didn't have time to register what he'd said before he pushed open the creaking door to reveal a four-year-old girl sitting in the middle of a trash-littered room. She was wailing for her mama. A circle of shiny cement surrounded her on the filthy floor. She had flailed there for so long that she had polished it, like a halo, with her clothes, tears, and sweat.

"Mama!" she cried out, reaching her hands out to me.

I recognized her vaguely as Hong. When I had seen my Nanjing parents' little girl during previous visits, I had thought of her as my cousin. Now I realized that Hong was my sister. Still, I wasn't her mother!

"I'm your *jie jie*—your big sister," I said as I approached her cautiously. "I am not your mama."

The guard left us there. I told Hong to stop screaming, but she wouldn't listen. Exhausted, I threw myself onto the floor next to her, and we cried "*Mama, Mama*" in unison, but for different mothers. I don't know how long we stayed that way.

When I couldn't stand her screams any longer, I pulled Hong into an embrace and tried to quiet her. She sagged into my arms like a dirty puppet. I examined her face closely for the first time. Bubbles of snot blew out of her nostrils. Her cheeks were muddy, and her eyes swollen and bloodshot. Her voice had gone raw, but she wouldn't stop crying. I panicked, thinking that if she kept going at this rate, she might cause herself permanent damage.

What would Shanghai Mama do? I asked myself. I looked around the room, where all I saw was trash—mostly paper, a few notebooks, some broken pencils, a few rags. A smashed table lamp with a broken lightbulb sat not too far from Hong. There was no sink, but there was a faucet sticking out of the wall with a bucket underneath it. I was excited to find an old half-empty box of powdered laundry detergent nearby. I poured water into the bucket, dumped in some of the detergent, and dipped a filthy rag into the mixture, hoping to clean Hong's face and cool her down. Bubbles floated up into the room, and Hong chased after them, murmuring, "Bubbles, bubbles . . ." Magically, she burst into giggles.

Night fell, and our room was engulfed in darkness. There was no food, but neither of us was hungry; we were too grief-stricken. There was also no bed. I found an old sheet in the corner, folded it in half, and spread it over the shiny spot Hong had made. I lay down next to her and tried to wrap the top half over us, but the sheet wasn't wide enough. So I turned around, placing my head at Hong's feet. We lay there, upside-down sisters each absorbed by our own agony.

It probably didn't strike me then, but in the course of one day I had not only lost the mother I loved and the mother who had given birth to me; I had also become a mother myself.

That first night, I felt an acute sense of loss and confusion. I had no food, no friends, no family other than my helpless baby sister, and no clue as to when, if ever, my birth parents or my Shanghai parents might come to my rescue. Everything I had known and loved was gone. The beautiful house and its scholar garden, the aroma of Shanghai Mama's delicious dinner wafting throughout our home, the silky feeling of my skin as it touched the sheets on my Shanghai parents' bed, the echo of my siblings' laughter. The days ahead held only a hideous dorm room, the stench of humans living in close quarters, the sting of a cold concrete floor, and my newfound sister's howling sobs.

I wanted to run away, but I was fearful of being caught and tortured by the Red Guards, who seemed to know more about me than I knew about myself. Nor could I imagine leaving Hong alone in this awful place. I felt trapped. I couldn't turn off what I saw, heard, smelled, or touched. Even the humid summer air felt oppressive, as though it couldn't escape through our open window. I lay awake for hours, staring out into the darkness. Eventually, Hong's breathing fell into the soft, regular pattern of deep sleep.

I crept to the window, where a tiny shard of light illuminated a section of the floor. With a piece of newspaper and a bit of charcoal I found among the trash, I began to scribble a letter. I don't know why, but I began with Nanjing Mother. Perhaps I thought it would be easier for her to find me since she was originally from this city. I wrote:

Dear Nanjing Mother,

Shanghai Mama always asked me to write letters to you, but she addressed the envelopes for me, so I don't know where to send this. At home, we put letters in that little blue mailbox on the front gate, and the mailman came every day. I don't think I can find a mailbox here. It is all very confusing.

Can't you tell me how to make Hong stop crying? She cries a lot. Sometimes she calls me Mom, sometimes big sister. She is crying all the time.

Why don't you come back? I don't remember you very much. Shanghai Mama told me that you gave birth to me. Is that true? I have so many questions. When do you come home?

Then I etched a letter to the parents who were most dear to my heart, Shanghai Mama and Papa:

Dear Mama and Papa,

Where are you? When are you coming to get me?

Hong is sleeping now. She cried a lot. I made soap bubbles for her, a lot of bubbles. She laughed and jumped after them. I will make more bubbles when she cries again. She is very loud when she screams!

I want to go back to Shanghai, to be with you. You told me before many times that you bore me. Now you say you didn't. I don't believe you. Tell me you are my real mama.

Tell me, tell me, tell me. It is not fair.

I hate this place. Come get me and bring me home as soon as you can, Mama.

XOXO

Ping-Ping

I awoke to loudspeakers in the hallway blaring the song that had become the People's Republic of China's anthem, "The East Is Red." The East was Red and Mao was our Sun, the one who would bring fortune to us all.

"I have to go pee-pee," Hong informed me in her baby voice.

I had no idea where the bathrooms were, but the little creature seemed to know the way. She took my hand and we ventured outside. There were people in the corridor, their faces no more distinguishable in the dim light than pancakes. Many seemed to be Red Guards who had taken up residence with their families; others were orphaned children like me. I avoided their eyes as we made our way to the end of the hall, where there was a common lavatory.

The stink shocked tears back into my eyes even before we went inside. Instead of Western-style commodes or traditional Chinese squat toilets, there was only a long, open U-shaped concrete trough. Sewage floated inside, in danger of overflowing. A line of strangers squatted over it, dropping waste in front of me from their bare bottoms.

When we returned to our room, Hong resumed her crying. I looked around for something to distract her, but the room was barren. I dumped the rest of the detergent into the bucket and blew more bubbles at her. She giggled for a while as I stared out the window, trying not to cry and set her off again.

Looking out the window, I could see the dirty water of the canal I'd noticed the day before and hundreds of rusty bicycles. Close by stood another concrete dormitory like ours. Countless lines of laundry crisscrossed the short span between the two buildings: soggy gray pants and green uniforms, garments stitched from bedsheets, and nylon underpants in all colors of the rainbow. I knew underclothes had to be dried in the sun to sanitize them, but in Shanghai we hung our things in private. Here, as evidenced by the toilets and the laundry lines, there was no privacy. That, I came to understand, was why the doors hung so oddly: the hinges had been systematically broken so the doors could never be locked.

I desperately needed to find drinking water and food for myself and Hong. I eyed the faucet sticking out of the wall, but I knew that water had to be boiled before it was safe to drink. The problem was, I had no idea how or where to do it. I had eaten nothing since the morning before, and I longed to be back in the kitchen with my mama, delighting in a simple bowl of rice congee.

Hidden among the litter in our room, I found some rancid pickles, a small amount of rice in a jar, and a few pieces of discarded cookware. The Red Guard had told me not to speak to anyone other than my sister, and I was shy around strangers anyway, so I was reluctant to ask for help. I went out into the hall to observe what others were doing. It turned out that what I had thought were pipes outside each door were actually small coal-burning stoves. I had never been allowed to play with fire, but I brought some coal from a common bin as others were doing, stuffed it in the stove with some bits of newspaper, and lit a match. I tried again and again, but the flame went out each time.

An old man watched me for a while. Finally, he brought over a live coal from his stove and, without speaking a word, showed me the way to light a fire with it. I bowed my head in gratitude and boiled water to drink. Then I boiled more water and put the rice that I'd found into the pot. After we had finished our meager meal, Hong said she was still hungry. But there was no more food.

I learned later that week that each of us got rations from the Communist government. We could collect food stamps from the neighborhood community office and exchange these for products at the community store. The government told us how much we could fetch each month—for instance, ten kilos of rice, one bar of soap, a quarter kilo of salt, one bottle of soy sauce, a half kilo of meat, one bottle of cooking oil, ten eggs, and so on.

But for now, there were no food coupons and there was no mealtime. Hong was too young to understand, but I had gotten the impression that there were no bedtimes, no playtimes, no evening bath times, no good-night kisses, and no one other than the Red Guards to tell us what to do. Still, I couldn't begin to comprehend what living alone with my four-year-old sister really would mean.

From that moment on, I would never again be a child at my parents' side, under their protection and guidance. The boat on the long river of life was in my hands alone.

I thought of the three friends of winter: pine tree, plum blossom, and bamboo. Strength, courage, and resilience. I would need to keep all of them close by my side from now on. I could sense that a long winter lay ahead.

TWO

Behind Every Closed Door Is an Open Space

NOBODY: 1966–1967

HONG'S ENDLESS CRYING made my ears hurt. I was hungry and exhausted from crying myself. Shadowy figures moved like paper puppets through the dormitory corridors. Angry shouts from Red Guards just a few years older than I, yet infinitely more powerful, pierced the thick concrete walls. Nightmares became only more disturbing after I awoke and found them to be real. I was separated from my parents and older siblings, and I had no outlet for my frustration and anger. This place was the reality I had to face now. There was no escape and no one to rescue me.

Memories of those first days at the Nanjing dormitory form a hazy picture in my mind. Somewhere around the third day, an announcement came over the loudspeakers calling all the "children of black elements" out to the common area for a "bitter meal." A Red Guard came by our room to collect us. As we continued down the hall gathering others, he used his rifle butt with casual cruelty to strike at the laggards and sleepyheads.

From the field near our building, the Red Guards ordered the forty or fifty kids from our dormitory to march in military formation, ten to a row, into the soccer field just to the west. I realized then that we were not alone: additional lines of young people streamed in from other parts of the NUAA campus. There must have been a hundred of us all together, all children of black elements, most without parents because the Communist authorities had sent them away for reeducation.

Although Shanghai, similar to San Francisco in its weather patterns, had been cool and rainy when I left there in late June, the heat in Nanjing was oppressive. The Chinese called the city one of the "three hot stoves" of the country because of its infamously high summer temperatures and humidity. Sweat stung my eyes, but I kept my expression impassive, fighting the urge to run and dive into the nearby canal to cool off.

Red Guards took turns lecturing us from a podium on the field. We had been labeled "black elements," they told us. We were not even worthy of being treated as people because we were the bastard outcasts of educated, affluent parents. Black has a bad connotation in Chinese culture—it is the color of evil and death, a color worn at funerals. Being marked "black" meant that we had been born guilty for the crimes committed by our parents and ancestors, and that we must suffer for their corruption and greed.

Unlike us, the Red Guards were descended from generations of workers, peasants, and soldiers, and so their blood was good. It was red, the most favored color in China. Red is the color of celebration and happiness, a color worn at weddings. It also was known as Mao's color, the iconic symbol of the Communist revolution and hope.

We black elements had led privileged lives, while they had had nothing, the Red Guards ranted. We had lived in big houses and had plenty to eat, while their families had starved. Our parents and grandparents were responsible for depriving millions upon millions of workers and peasants of a decent living.

Now it was our turn to pay the price, they declared. Chairman Mao had called for the reeducation of all black elements. We were extremely lucky that our supreme leader was giving us a chance to reform. We had better do what we were told and keep our behavior in check.

So that is why I am here, I thought. For the first time since I had been taken away from my Shanghai parents and shipped to Nanjing, something made sense. I *had* grown up with all those blessings, while others were suffering. I felt a tinge of shame for my family's guilt, and for the delicious food and comfortable home that I had taken for granted throughout my life.

There was a big pot on the field into which the Red Guards began dumping dirt, animal dung, pieces of tree trunk, and anything else they could scoop off the ground. One of them scraped a sheet of yellow mold off a tree trunk and flung it into the pot with an evil cackle.

"This was what our ancestors ate," a female guard said loudly. "Our parents, grandparents, and great-grandparents suffered because your selfish families deprived them of good food. Today you will eat this bitter meal to remember our families' suffering." I watched her carefully as she spoke. I didn't see any signs of suffering on her face, only the glimpse of a devilish smile.

As we lined up to be served, I noticed a young girl in the army of Red Guards whose face seemed familiar. She was about my age, but far taller and more muscular than I was. I realized that I had seen her before on my visits to my Nanjing parents. I had played with some of the other kids who lived on campus during those times, but never with this girl because the other kids had warned me away, saying that she was mean. She had a long, square face and a pronounced chin, and some of the other kids had called her "horse face." Zhang—her name was Zhang, I remembered.

Zhang was begging her mother, who was a Communist Party leader, to let her serve us. Her mother handed her a ladle. I watched as she took the ladle in one hand, scooped out the mixture, and slammed it onto a boy's plate. He wasn't holding the plate tightly enough, and his bitter meal spilled onto the ground. A Red Guard hit him hard. Zhang's eyebrows shot up, and then she giggled with pleasure. She could make a game of this.

When I arrived at the front of the line, I held my plate securely in both hands in anticipation. I couldn't help but feel a sense of victory when Zhang failed to make me drop my food as she smacked her ladle down with extra vigor. She squinted her eyes at me as I quickly sneaked away to hide among the other children seated on the field.

The meal tasted sandy and repugnant. I was hungry but afraid of getting sick or stuck with splinters from the wood, so I spit my first mouthful out. All around me, other black elements were doing the same, while moaning about how terrible the food tasted. I knew to keep my mouth shut. The more the loudest kids complained, the more fun the Red Guards seemed to have forcing many of them to clean their plates. The Red Guards looked cheerful, as though they'd just won a championship.

When I returned to my dormitory room, I saw that someone had moved the cooking pot from the stovetop outside our door onto the floor. When I crouched down to put it back in its place, the lid slipped off. My jaw dropped. "Wow!" I exclaimed. Sitting inside were two delicious-looking steamed buns wrapped in a piece of brown paper. They were still warm, and just looking at them made my mouth water. I thought someone must have left the buns at the wrong door by accident, but I grabbed them quickly anyway. I wasn't about to let them go.

"Hong-Hong, I found food. We have two steamed buns!" I cried out as I brought the treasures into the room. The starving little girl reached her hands out, and I handed her one. She finished it before I had even fetched a cup of water for her from the kettle outside the door.

"More, more," Hong demanded. I gave her the other bun. As I watched her gobble it down, my stomach made a loud rumbling sound, my mouth watered, and I felt a rush of hunger. But what else could I do? I was an older sister with responsibility for my younger sister; I had to care for her, as Chinese tradition demanded. Besides, I would rather endure my own hunger pangs than watch Hong suffer. I recalled a poem that Shanghai Papa had taught me:

> Weeding under the summer sun,
> It is sweat that waters the thirsty ground.
> Be sure to value the food for our meals,
> As every grain sings a hardworking song.

I had never paid attention to the meaning of the poem before, although I could recite it from memory. Now every word echoed in my mind along with the noises coming from my stomach. I understood what it meant to truly appreciate a meal.

The next day, I awoke to discover our pot filled with cooked rice and vegetables. A few days after that, a few eggs and a cucumber magically appeared. It wasn't much sustenance for two growing girls, but it made a huge difference. For many years, I would occasionally find prepared or uncooked foods at our door. The food was usually left in the wee hours of the morning, before dawn. I often tried to spy and find out who was helping us in secret, but I never caught sight of anyone. It was another lifetime before I finally discovered our benefactor's identity.

These gifts of food made me feel a little safer. Here was a sign that, even in the worst of circumstances, there were people willing to watch out for us and even risk their lives. I vowed that I would be like our anonymous donor and do my best to help others, including Hong. I reasoned that I didn't have a choice about having been born a black element, but I could choose to be good. I could be kind to strangers, bear my suffering without complaint, and learn from Mao's teachings. In this way, perhaps I could be forgiven for the bad things that my ancestors had done.

Zhang had somehow gotten ahold of one of my childhood dolls. It was, in fact, my favorite doll from Nanjing Mother, who had brought it home from a business trip to Hong Kong, which at the time was a British colony. Nanjing Mother would unwrap the doll from its special protective packaging only when I visited.

I used to love playing with this extraordinary little person. Unlike Chinese dolls, Mei, as I called her—the name means "beauty" in Mandarin—had blue eyes and blond hair. It wasn't ordinary nylon doll's hair, either; Mei's hair would stay curled in perfect spirals if you wrapped it around your fingers. She would stare at me lovingly with eyes wide open when sitting up, and then softly close her eyes when I cradled her in my arms and sang her to sleep. I had a small trunk of clothes for Mei, and I would change her often, tying and untying her tiny shoes with great care.

I had last visited Nanjing at Chinese New Year, in early February of 1966, before the fervor of the Cultural Revolution had fully taken hold of China. Nanjing Mother decided it would be best to get rid of this representation of the "foreign devils" that Mao blamed for polluting our country. Nanjing Mother made me say good-bye to Mei, then tossed her into a bin at a collection site designated for garbage. I was so sad, feeling as though I'd lost a best friend.

One afternoon not long after that first bitter meal, I was gazing into the common area from my dorm room window when I saw Zhang sitting in the dirt playing with Mei. She or her red parents must have fished my favorite doll out of the collection center's bin. The moment I saw Zhang crudely dangling *my* Mei by her legs, I became infuriated. Mei's delicate features were covered in dirt, her elegant clothes torn. She must be suffering terribly, I thought. I could feel her in my heart.

I wanted that doll back so much it hurt more than my hunger pangs. It wasn't fair. I had lost everything. I had no parents, no belongings, no home, nothing. If only, I thought, I could just have this one thing to call my own . . .

Only there was nothing I could do. Zhang was from a red family. Everyone knew her and her mother, who held a critical role in distributing food stamps to residents on campus. They had the power. I was from a family of black elements with no parents to look out for me, and I had no rights. This much had become clear to me in just a few days.

I formulated a plan: I would follow Zhang around whenever I had the chance, waiting for her to put the doll down and forget about her for a moment. Then I would snatch my Mei and hide her in my room. Only Zhang was too careful. She remained constantly vigilant, especially when she brought Mei out of her apartment to play with when I was around. She could see the envy in my eyes, and she wasn't about to let me win.

⌒

"Down with the black elements! Down with the black elements!" the crowd chanted ferociously, eager for a spectacle.

To help us reform, we children of black elements were ushered into a large public auditorium jam-packed with people to learn from an adult "struggle session." I felt like a chicken with its feathers stuck in the wire coop, trapped and terrified. The crowd included many people now occupying the campus, as well as hundreds of peasants and workers from nearby communes who had come to see the show.

A smell of rot from the Red Guards' heavy boots triggered my first onset of a migraine headache, which would continue to plague me for life. We kids sat watching people walk onstage one at a time to "verbally struggle" with their pasts. They would criticize professors, administrators, students—anyone who represented Mao's black elements. I was reminded of Shanghai Papa's talk in our home when someone had shouted, "Revisionist!"

The struggle session grew more and more abusive and intimidating. People denounced their ancestors in the worst possible language, and then made vows to reform in front of Mao's portrait. If they didn't behave to the Red Guards' standards, they were struck.

One day, it was the children's turn.

My legs began to tremble as I listened to the endless taunts and jeers from the crowd, the repeated chants of "Black element!" I was the third or fourth person to be called onstage. Before me was a sea of angry, curious, and frightened faces. Red Guards hung a sign around my neck made from a piece of chalkboard they'd taken from one of the classrooms at the university. It had my name and the crimes of my bourgeois family printed on it. The chalkboard was so heavy that the wires cut into my neck. I was forced to assume the "airplane position": arms held out straight on either side of my body like wings. My limbs shook so uncontrollably that I felt as though I were standing on a plank floating in a tank of water.

I could not think of what to say. For that, I received a heavy blow to the head from a tall Red Guard. Blood flowed from my nose and from my neck where the chain was cutting into my flesh.

I had to think on my feet. I repeated some of the same sentences the black elements who had gone before me had used. "My parents are bad people," I said. Then I took my criticism further: "No, they are not people; they are animals. They take money from the poor. They should be punished and I should be punished." My voice was flat and mechanical.

The Red Guard slapped me again, knocking me to the floor this time. I heard Hong yelp from somewhere offstage. The tall man then wiped his hand on his pants. "You are not sincere!" he bellowed. "You must dig deeper into your crimes."

I managed to stand up. Suddenly, I recalled something I'd seen one of the adults do during his struggle session: I started slapping my own face with my hands, left and then right, harder and harder, until I tasted blood in my mouth.

"I am nobody!" I shouted out as loud as I could. "I don't deserve even to live. Anybody can step on me and squash me like a bug. I am nobody—I am not worth the dirt beneath your feet!"

They let me go.

That was not the first or the last time I was forced to publically humiliate my family and myself. Eventually, I started to believe what I said onstage. I *was* nobody. I became unquestioningly submissive to the abuse I received. I gave up on craving affection, such as what I had received from Shanghai Mama. I became indifferent to suffering, to the sunrise and sunset.

During those first few months, Red Guards gave us "remember the bitterness" meals and lectures nearly every other day. But we received more teachings at these sessions than food, and I learned for the first time what starvation really felt like. My empty stomach growled and gurgled—I was amazed that it could make so much noise.

After a few weeks, I actually began to look forward to the sessions because at least they filled me up. Sometimes, my stomach would get so bloated that it seemed as though I were pregnant. Other times, the meal would make me sick and my body quickly would empty itself out, leaving me even hungrier than I had been a few hours before.

In Nanjing, residents referred to summer as "the season of yellow mold." It would rain nonstop for days, leaving the air thick and damp. Mold would grow more quickly than spiders scampering from the light, clinging to every wall and surface. During this season, days passed while the Red Guards fed us nothing, nor were we able to attain our rations from the store. It occurred to me that it might not be an accident that there was no food; they might be starving us deliberately. My German neighbor in Shanghai had told me once about how German soldiers had taken millions of Jews like him out of their homes during World War II and forced them to live in "ghettos" before burning them up in ovens. Is that why we had been brought here to live in this ghetto? Was mass extinction awaiting us? Were they going to starve us first, or put us straight into the ovens and burn us alive?

The Red Guards were mostly in their late teens, and they ruled us with a combination of *Lord of the Flies* brutality and Orwellian exercises in thought control. We could do whatever we wanted, and they could do whatever they wanted to us.

On one occasion, the Red Guards gathered us to watch a teacher be thrown head first into a deep well, and another quartered by four horsemen on the soccer field. Later, they beat to death an older boy for a prank he had pulled involving a cat because the Chinese word for cat, *mao*, has the same pinyin spelling as Chairman Mao's name, differing only by a subtle tone change. Crime and punishment were meted out haphazardly, so no one among us black elements ever felt safe.

That summer was so hot in Nanjing that Hong and I sometimes

went to bed naked on sheets of newspapers spread out across our cement floor. One morning, Hong burst out laughing, pointing at my back. Our sweat had imprinted our bodies with inverted images of Chairman Mao from yesterday's official news. Hong was too young to understand the consequences, and so was giddy with joy at the trick. But I was fearful that we could be executed for making a parody of our supreme leader. I had to dress us both in long shirts in spite of the stifling heat. Worried that Hong naively would show off her body art, I watched her carefully all day long until we had sweated ourselves clean.

Our time was occupied by study sessions, in which we did nothing but recite slogans from Mao's Little Red Book, and struggle sessions, in which we denounced ourselves and ate bitter meals. Otherwise we had most of our time free. Along with the other orphaned children of black elements, I would play chase in the dormitory hallways late into the night. We would light fires on our coal stoves just for fun.

One day, several boys came up to me in the hallway outside my room and said, "Let's go play on the old airplanes." Hong wanted to come with us, but I insisted that she stay in our room because she was too young. I threatened to tie her to the window frame with a torn piece of sheet and not feed her dinner if she disobeyed. To this day, Hong still remembers how much it upset her that I wouldn't let her play outside with us.

The boys led me across campus to a warehouse filled with abandoned Chinese-manufactured airplanes. As we slid down the emergency chutes and onto the silver wings, it felt like the greatest playground ever built. I stood inside one of those huge empty carcasses and wondered, How do such small wings carry such large planes into the sky?

Most children of black elements older than I had gone to normal schools for a few years before the Cultural Revolution started, and they took pleasure in showing off their knowledge when we played.

I was able to pick up some basic math and science concepts over the years. I remember a particularly smart boy posing an interesting question one day.

"Ping," he said, "do you know the fastest way to add the numbers one to one hundred?"

I had known how to add and subtract since the age of three, since I had lived in a household with five older siblings who loved to teach me things, and Nanjing Mother had regularly quizzed me in math. But I didn't know the answer, so I shook my head.

The boy was very proud to share his trick with me. "First, you add one plus ninety-nine, then two plus ninety-eight, then three plus ninety-seven, and so on. That's how you get to five thousand fifty." His clever solution fascinated me.

I remember many other challenging questions posed by the older children, including this one: "If one bike has two people on it, and another bike has one person on it, and both bikes are rolling downhill, which one will go faster?" I answered with glee, "The lighter one!" The others told me that I was wrong: the two bikes should travel at the same speed. But why, they couldn't explain. So they got on their bikes and tried it. Contrary to both our expectations, the bike with two people on it rolled down the hill faster.

Later that day, we went to ask a man who swept the street outside our dorm every morning for an explanation. We knew from our struggle sessions that he had been a physics teacher prior to the Cultural Revolution. The "wise man," as we later secretly referred to him, didn't have a simple explanation. He picked up two rocks, one smaller and one bigger, and took us up to the seventh floor of a building he was cleaning. Following his instructions, we threw the two rocks out the window and watched them hit the ground at the same time. He explained to us that the reason things with different weights fall at the same speed is that gravitational force and inertial mass are equal for all objects. The boys had been right, then: in theory, the two bikes should have crossed the finish line at the same time. But in reality, things were more complicated. We had to take into account air resistance, friction, and rotational forces. That's why the heavier bicycle had won the race. I didn't understand everything the teacher said, but it fueled my curiosity about how things work.

As we roamed across the NUAA campus discovering walled-off libraries and a stone bridge composed of five magnificent dragons, my imagination also ran free. The intricate carvings on the Five Dragon Bridge reminded me of those on my Shanghai parents' rosewood bed. I imagined that one day I might learn to be a craftswoman.

Although I enjoyed playing with them, I was careful not to become too friendly with any of the other children of black elements. The Red Guards had warned us that if we spent much time together, they would accuse us of conspiracy and exact whatever punishment they saw fit.

The dorm was a noisy place. Every night, Hong's breathing bubbled like a kettle that needed tending; she suffered from allergies. Outside, through half-closed doors, waves of our neighbors' cacophonous snores resonated. Beyond the campus, machine guns fired. I learned to block out these noises—it was as though I could make myself deaf. I can still shut down my hearing at will to this day.

Mega speakers perpetually echoed through the dormitory corridors and from the trees outside its windows, reminding us of our crimes and about the class struggle. Every day, the campus was papered with new flyers, Communist propaganda. Posters went up with faces of black elements, their supposed crimes listed underneath.

I had been living at NUAA for a few months when I saw Nanjing Father's name with a big red X over it. He was listed as a "historical counterrevolutionary" and "American spy." That was why he had been sent away for reeducation. What exactly had he done? I was curious to know, but I didn't dare to ask. What about Nanjing Mother? I didn't know what had happened to her, either, or whether she was considered a counterrevolutionary. I didn't see her name on any posters.

By that time, I had thoroughly cleared the trash out of Room 202, scrubbed the walls and floor clean, and begun forming a makeshift homestead for Hong and me. For a bed, I found a thin, stained single mattress next to the trash collection site. Sometimes as I wandered around campus, I would come across a chair with a missing leg or other discarded small household items, which I'd bring back to our dorm room. But I thought of what I still considered to be my "real home" constantly: Shanghai Mama's smile when she woke me up in the morning; the bustling familiarity of mealtimes; feeding my little finches from the library balcony; watching my brothers run with enthusiasm out the door to school together; aromatic steam rising from the stove as my mother cooked all afternoon; the way my forefinger fit roundly into the whorl of a vine carved into my parents' bed frame; the crinkling sound of rice paper welcoming the ink from my grandfather's calligraphy brush; Shanghai Papa's joyful *clip-clipping* in the garden. I encased these memories in my mind and filed them away like the scrolls that my grandfather kept carefully stowed in his library cabinets.

I knew that I wasn't supposed to remember my parents or think good thoughts about them. The Red Guards had ordered me during those long, hot bitterness sessions to forget my past and reform my ways by learning from workers, farmers, and soldiers. I was eager to make my black blood flow red. Yet it seemed I couldn't help myself.

Some nights when I couldn't sleep, I would get up, as I had that very first night, and record my confusing thoughts in letters to my parents, both Shanghai and Nanjing. Eventually these letters, which I learned I could not send because they frequently were checked by the authorities and used as proof of counterrevolutionary thinking, formed a sort of journal. I'd collect propaganda flyers to use as paper, scribbling my thoughts in a combination of my elementary school Chinese characters and phonetic pinyin.

One evening I wrote:

Dear Shanghai Papa and Mama,

Are you nice people or bad people? I can't imagine that you are bad people because we were such a happy family. I love you very much.

But how come you didn't tell me there were poor people? Why did you make the peasant people starve? Why did you taint me with your black blood?

Another night, I wrote a poem:

LOST
Wrong city, all a mess
Don't trust my guess
Mother's face, fading in the distance
Hunger
I am at a loss.

When I was finished writing, I would turn the papers upside down and put them under a stack of untouched flyers. If you read it right side up, it was a history of Communist teachings saved by a dutiful student. But if you turned the pages over, you would discover my secret journal of daily happenings and reflections on my situation. Even though I was terrified of what might happen to me if anyone ever discovered this, I didn't want to burn the papers or throw them away. I had to share my suffering, confusion, and sense of loss with somebody, and the journal was the only one I could trust.

One day, while the Red Guards were conducting one of their routine searches of our rooms, they found my journal.

"What is this?" a pudgy, unpredictable eighteen-year-old named Ming asked, eyebrows arched. I could feel my blood pressure rising, but I said nothing. I watched as he continued to read, turning one page after another, seemingly in slow motion. I felt utterly naked before him. He surely saw on the back sides of those sheets of propaganda my questions about why I was here, my longings to return to Shanghai and my former life, my doubts about the Red Guards themselves—dozens of traitorous thoughts that easily could have warranted having me killed. Yet his face remained impassive.

"You black elements are all the same," Ming said. Then he walked out of my room carrying my journal in his hand.

I remained there, frozen in fear. My mind raced, imagining what might follow. Would I lose all the writings and be publicly humiliated? Worse, would the Red Guards torture and beat me? Might they even kill me? What would happen to Hong if I died? Who would take care of her? A few minutes later, Ming returned. The Red Guards would be building a bonfire at noon, he told me, and I was expected to be there to watch my frivolous pages burn before a crowd.

I spent the next hour huddled in a corner of my room, shaking. At the appointed hour, I lurched like a drunk, unable to control my movements, down to the common area of our dormitory. There were several large fire pits on the NUAA campus, which had been built a few years earlier to burn scrap metal for steel production during the Great Leap Forward—China's effort to compete with Western countries on industrial power. One of these pits was located next to our building. I saw that the Red Guards had built a fire with wood chips and coal in the pit for the sole purpose of publicly burning my journal.

Several dozen people stood gathered around the fire. They had been summoned to witness my humiliation. Some looked at me with accusing eyes, others with compassion and sadness. We all were so accustomed to the ridicule, tempestuousness, and unjustifiable brutality of the Red Guards that I'm certain some of the onlookers couldn't help but feel relief. At least, this time, they were not the victims. Others surely saw me as a weak, corrupt, hopeless person who deserved to be punished.

"Here goes your journal," Ming said loudly as soon as he saw me walking toward the pit. He burned it slowly, one page at a time, passing some pages to other Red Guards to burn. They laughed and spit into the pit as they tossed the papers into the fire.

The familiar hand scribbles that had become my best and only friends flickered and darkened into ashes. I felt a deep pain in my chest and couldn't make a sound. I was allowed no voice in this world. Even the silent conversation between my head and the page had been taken away from me in a violent fashion. I'll just end it myself, here and now, I thought, and leapt toward the flames. But someone grabbed hold of my arm from behind so vigorously that his fingernails cut into my flesh.

"It is easier to be shot than to die a slow death by fire," a male voice whispered in my ear. I don't know who it was that stopped me from destroying myself. I didn't turn around to see.

After all the pages were burned, Ming walked over to stand beside me. I knew he would shoot me then and there if I dared to utter a word of protest or even make eye contact. "Listen up," Ming said, pointing at me with his index finger and ordering me to face the crowd. "Remember this always; let it burn into your memories: This is a Cultural Revolution. That means no writing stupid counterrevolutionary stories. This is your final warning. You will stop writing unless you write for the Party. Otherwise, you will burn just like these pages." We were dismissed.

In truth, I was lucky. For some reason I'll never know, Ming had chosen to let me off easy, and I suffered no further punishment. But after that day, I became a different person, one who no longer clung to anything or anyone. I broke out in hives every time I touched a pencil and stopped writing. I grew even more introverted. My ears filled only with silence. My eyes saw only flames. All that was left behind was a body resembling me.

Winter descended with its bitter winds. When I had to, I rose early and walked, shivering, through freezing rain to attend study sessions. Otherwise, I generally stayed inside the room, caring for Hong and our household. I hardened to the cold, retreating further and further inward.

Then, one icy day in February 1967, a most unexpected warm breeze blew into Nanjing. I received a letter from my Shanghai Mama. I recognized her handwriting at once on the envelope. I couldn't believe that the mail office had allowed this letter to come through to me without being confiscated by the Red Guards. Worried that it might be taken away, I hurriedly tore the envelope open and read:

> My dear Little Apple,
>
> After you left, I was ill for many weeks. Sitting on the bed, I am thinking about you now. How do you get by every day? Are you cold? Are you hungry? I am so sorry that I couldn't take care of you anymore. I was terrified of the way you discovered that I was not your birth mother. I saw the pain in your beautiful eyes; it ripped my heart into pieces.
>
> I still have your things in my room. That little red dress of yours, I hug it to sleep every night. I love you so dearly, my Little Apple. Please don't hate your Shanghai Mama.

Your brothers are all settled down in the countryside, each in a different place. The youngest is all the way in the north, in a place that borders Russia. I am so worried about him, as I am worried about you. How can a thirteen-year-old boy survive such harsh conditions by himself? Your big sister is at home. She works at a factory nearby.

Take good care of yourself and your little sister Hong. Your Nanjing Mother and Father are in the countryside paying loyalty to Chairman Mao and devoting their lives to the Communist cause. They will come home when they are reformed.

My Little Apple, be good and take care.

Many kisses and hugs,
Shanghai Mama

My eyes filled with tears of both joy and sorrow. I read the letter over and over again, each time feeling more alive. The sound of Hong's giggles crept back into my ears. I was able to hope once more. I might see my Shanghai Mama again someday.

Sometimes in life, out of the clear blue sky comes a vicious storm. We must seek out the shelter of a cave in order to survive. We might feel as though we'll never escape the dark crevasse. But there is always hope. Just when I felt like giving up, a stranger would leave food at my threshold or a letter from my Shanghai Mama would arrive. I clung to such moments of grace, no matter how small, as proof that behind every closed door, there lies an open space.

BECOMING AMERICAN: 1984–1988

MY INITIAL PERIOD of settling in at the University of New Mexico was easier than I had anticipated. After the police dropped me off at the campus, friendly staff from the International Student Center, including some native Chinese speakers, helped me to establish my new life. They signed me up for English as a second language (ESL) classes and placed me temporarily in an apartment with two American sisters who were studying law. I could live there rent free until I got my feet on the ground.

The gregarious sisters and I communicated through facial expressions and full-body gestures, like a game of charades. They knew I was desperate for money, so they connected me with one of their professors, an Iranian man who had recently divorced and was in need of a babysitter. I couldn't speak English, didn't understand American culture, couldn't drive, and had never written a check. But here was one thing I knew how to do.

The very next day, I started my new job. As I walked into the professor's apartment, I saw dishes piled up in the kitchen sink, heaps of dirty laundry, and toys strewn across the floor. I cleaned the house thoroughly and played with the professor's five-year-old daughter for seven hours. When the professor returned home, he asked me how much I wanted to be paid. I hadn't yet figured out the American system of prices and payments, so I just shook my head. He handed me a one-dollar bill. It didn't seem like enough.

When I walked back into our apartment, I showed my roommates the money. They didn't understand. So I drew two clocks onto a piece of paper: one showing the time I had started, the other showing the time I had finished. Then I drew an equal sign and placed my dollar bill next to it.

The sisters pointed at the dollar bill and drew their eyes wide in surprise. They shook their heads, their faces turning purple with indignation. "No, no," they said. They called the professor at once and scolded him for giving me so little money. They made him come over and pay me ten dollars per hour. I learned later that he had told them it was all a mistake; he'd thought I didn't want to be paid. But the sisters didn't believe such nonsense.

I prepared an authentic Chinese meal for the sisters to thank them for their hospitality. Although they smiled politely and made little humming sounds of contentment as they ate, I got the impression that they didn't like it very much. I soon discovered that "Chinese food" was Americanized here—sugary red fabrications of sweet-and-sour pork, pot stickers that got dumped straight from the freezer into deep fryers—so unlike Shanghai Mama's fresh shrimp with lotus seeds and grilled pork belly with red cabbage.

A few days later, I went to work cleaning for a kind Japanese woman who owned a futon shop. She introduced me to several families in search of housekeepers. I worked hard and took extra care with their delicate items. Even though I couldn't communicate with them verbally, I understood that they were happy with my work—they grinned widely when I entered their homes and referred me to their friends. I made five dollars an hour cleaning houses, and soon I had more clients than I had time.

Within a month, between housekeeping and babysitting, I was earning enough money to strike out on my own. I moved into a run-down house with four other Chinese students. Rent was just sixty dollars a month, which we split five ways. Still, I could barely afford UNM's out-of-state tuition. Some days, I ate nothing but bananas because they were cheap, nutritious, and relatively filling.

One night, I dreamed that I was drowning. I awoke to water splashing on my face: a desert downpour had found its way through the cracks in the roof. I ran into the bathroom to grab a towel and screamed. There, in the bathtub, were hundreds of cockroaches, a black army on the march. The loneliness that had set in when I left China deepened. Was I destined to grow old in this run-down house without ever seeing my family again?

I needed to make sufficient money to cover UNM's pricey out-of-state tuition and living expenses. When I asked around, people told me that I could earn more money as a waitress. But I didn't speak English well enough yet, so I took a job busing tables at a Chinese restaurant in a shopping mall. It paid as little as housekeeping, but the owner promised me that I could advance to waitressing when my English improved.

I identified with the African American and Mexican workers who clocked in every day, cleaning the restrooms and washing dishes with me: we were all struggling to climb our way out of poverty. I loved the rich tapestry of cultures and ethnicities in the United States: Japanese, Chinese, Italian, German, Iranian, Brazilian, South African, Latino, Australian, and so on. In China, there was very little diversity except in the border regions. Nearly everyone in the country's highly populated eastern area where I had grown up was Han Chinese.

People's upward mobility and freedom of choice in America were the envy of the world. I'd never experienced that, and found it to be intoxicating. At the same time, I was surprised by how limited people's thinking could be. It seemed to me that some Americans had a very narrow view of life, even though their society was so much more open than China's. In China, we didn't believe the propaganda that the government fed us on a daily basis. In America, I realized that propaganda still existed, only it was far subtler. It came from the media companies and advertisers rather than directly from the government. It was clever, with a lot of science behind it. People could end up brainwashed without even being aware of it. We didn't have free speech in China, but we were free thinkers. In America, I sometimes wondered if the opposite was true. I found people's sense of superiority when it came to foreign policy unsettling: they seemed so certain that the American way was the right way. I also observed how influenced women were by their female role models in magazines and Hollywood movies: being sexy was more important than being wise.

I knew that I had to master English in order to excel in America, but learning a new language was not an easy task at the age of twenty-five. Jane, my first English teacher, was a classic beauty with dark hair and eyes as wide as an owl's. On the first day of class, she gave us a placement test. I could hardly answer a single question, even though I was permitted to use my Chinese-English dictionary. An hour passed by, and Jane came by our desks to collect our test papers. Next we would have an oral exam, she explained, a test of our ability to speak. She then wrote on the blackboard, "Take a break."

I took out my dictionary, but even after having looked up each of the words, I still couldn't make sense of this curious phrase. What does she want us to break, I wondered—our pencils? I watched as other students walked out of the classroom, which only puzzled me more. Why don't people stay for the next part of the exam? Soon I was the only person remaining in the classroom. Jane approached my desk and gently explained the American idiom. There were dozens of other such embarrassing occasions that I still remember.

Marcy was another of my English teachers. She was finishing her PhD in journalism and had taken a part-time job at the local TV station. Like a fashion plate, Marcy changed her clothes two or three times a day, and her hairdo nearly as often.

A single mother, Marcy had quite an influence on my early life in America. She invited me to live with her in her orderly, comfortable two-bedroom apartment, offering me free room and board in exchange for occasional babysitting. I was thrilled to get out of my leaky, shared house. As I wished, Marcy practiced English with me tirelessly every chance she got.

One day in class, Marcy announced excitedly that she would be appearing on TV in a few moments. We all hovered around the television set in our classroom to watch. But all that appeared onscreen were glimpses of Marcy's hand holding the station's microphone. The next day, she told us that the director had cut her out of the piece because she had "held the microphone like an ice cream cone."

Although I had majored in literature in college, watching Marcy struggle to find a job in spite of possessing the intellect, good looks, and savvy required to succeed as a journalist validated my choice to find a new field of study. Not only did I have insufficient English skills to pursue an advanced literary degree, but also earning such a degree would not make it any easier for me to find a secure, well-paying job.

After about three months of busing tables, I was promoted to waitress as promised. I memorized the menu, including the names of the sodas, beers, and wines we offered, all of which were unfamiliar to me. The job turned out to be a great fit. Even my ineptitude at English proved valuable. I came up with a simple shorthand system for taking orders, using the initials of the foods and their numerical order on the menu to indicate what my customers wanted—B1 was the first beer on the list, RW5 was the fifth red wine on the list, and so on. With this system, I was able to serve people more quickly than the other waitresses. I also figured out how to plan out in my head routes, like the Chinese shipping lines etched on my grandfather's maps of old, for picking up and distributing my orders with maximum efficiency. The owner told me that I was a natural and gave me more tables to wait, which meant more tips.

With no savings to buy a car and little public transportation available in Albuquerque, I continued to commute to work every day on a bicycle I had bought for ten dollars at a yard sale. When one of my colleagues, a young African American waitress named Aba, found out that I was riding alone through the city an hour each way, sometimes after midnight, she offered me a ride to and from work.

"Not just tomorrow," she told me. "*Every* day." I was appreciative of her offer.

Aba was stunning enough to be a model, with a warm personality that felt like a ray of sunshine directed right at you. Everyone loved being served by her, and regulars would request her section. As we became friends, Aba noticed that the hostess would often seat people who were known not to tip well in my section. Aba offered to speak to the manager on my behalf. The hostess immediately started giving me better tippers, and soon I was making enough money to put aside some savings each month. In China, I had grown up with no right to complain and had never learned how to be assertive. Watching Aba, I marveled that in America people could ask for fair treatment and respect.

Aba and I grew close. In general, I tucked China away, not speaking about it or dwelling on the past. I had to build a new life in the United States, and I didn't want to waste time clinging to memories of my family or wallowing in the hardships of my youth. But as my English improved, I shared bits and pieces of my China story with Aba, and listened to her tales of racism and discrimination in America.

"I'm black, too," I told her on our drive to work one day. "The Communists say they have red blood because they were born poor. I have black blood because I was born into an educated merchant-class family."

Aba gazed thoughtfully at the road. "Hmm. I wonder which is worse: to be born with black blood or black skin?"

We had many discussions about civil rights. It was Aba who first showed me a tape of Martin Luther King Jr.'s "I Have a Dream" speech. His message inspired me to pursue my own dreams.

I missed cities and was eager to see more of America, so I used the first few hundred dollars I saved to buy a plane ticket to New York City for a three-day vacation. I had never bowed to statues of the Buddha or pictures of my ancestors in China, as people did prior to the Cultural Revolution; Mao had forbidden it. But in New York, I bowed to the Statue of Liberty, the "mother of exiles," and begged her to protect me.

⌒

A year later, after I had further honed my waitressing and English skills, asked a classmate to teach me how to drive, and purchased a beat-up used car, I went to work at a fancy Chinese restaurant that had just opened in Santa Fe. Americans were accustomed to Chinese food being cheap, fast, and no-frills. But this restaurant's owner, a famously flamboyant reporter from Taiwan, had different ideas. He brought in chefs from five-star hotels and made a point of pampering his guests. I was thrilled to get the job, though I was not comfortable with the work uniform, a tight-fitting *qipao*, or traditional Chinese dress, with an unusually high slit up the leg.

Santa Fe was an artistic city, and many Hollywood stars had second homes there. Linda Evans, John Wayne, and Miles Davis all came to our restaurant. I didn't know who any of these people were, so my boss often assigned me to wait on them, knowing that I wouldn't get starstruck or ask for autographs.

One night, a large, muscular man with dark hair and an asymmetrical face came into our restaurant. The boss told me to serve him.

I approached the table. "What would you like to drink?" I asked.

The man said nothing, but startled me by reaching around and grabbing my rear end with his enormous right hand. Without hesitating for a second, I slapped him on the cheek, hard. Then I gasped. What had I done? Surely the boss would fire me for such insolent behavior.

The man sat quietly for a heartbeat, staring me straight in the eyes. Then he laughed and said, "Do it again."

I raced back to the kitchen, still convinced, with my Chinese mentality, that I would lose my job. But everyone who had witnessed the event was cheering. "Ping, you slapped Rambo!" they squealed with delight. Even the boss, who had followed me to the back room, was chuckling. The customer, they told me, was Sylvester Stallone, a famous action hero.

In a matter of weeks, business was booming. I kept my tips in a jumbo-sized Coke cup, stuffing coins and bills in through the plastic lid. One night, I filled the cup to overflowing. Each time I pushed another bill inside, the lid would threaten to pop off. The moment came when the built-up pressure was too great—the plastic cup exploded, propelling wads of cash up into the air. Dollar bills drifted to the ground like fall leaves. Everyone in the back room laughed, saying that clearly I made too much money for my own good.

Suddenly, I felt liberated and independent. For the first time, I knew that I had enough money to not just survive, but thrive. The pressure of scarcity to which I had grown accustomed since the age of eight finally lifted. The thought came: I will never eat another banana for lunch again.

Even later in life, when I became a skilled professional, knowing that I could always be a waitress gave me an immense sense of reassurance. If I ever selected the wrong job or career, I could always afford to go searching for a better opportunity while serving tables. I was able to pursue my passions with peace of mind.

Waitressing proved the ideal transition into my new life in America. It was choosing to study computer science that switched the trajectory of my journey, both personally and professionally.

After completing the English as a foreign language course in a year, I was able to pass the TOEFL (Test of English as a Foreign Language) and enroll as a full-time graduate student at UNM. I knew by then that I didn't want to study literature, but what should I pursue? A few classmates suggested that I check out computer science. I had never heard of it. An equally clueless American student told me that it was a man-made language that people used to make stuff. Her description intrigued me because I had enjoyed learning how to make things while working at factories in China.

Computer programming was a new field of study in the early eighties, and there were almost no women interested in it. I was accepted as a computer science master's student even though I had no prior course work in the subject. Nearly everyone was starting from scratch, just like me, which helped me keep up.

In my first CS class, the professor explained that computer language was based on binary numbers. I could remember, when I was very young and he was still a professor of aeronautical engineering, Nanjing Father showing me early computer punch cards printed with zeros and ones. I had chosen a field of study that was not entirely foreign to me.

At the computer lab, I came face-to-face with a modern computer for the first time. Terrified that I might break it, I barely touched the keys. The student sitting next to me laughed. "Don't worry. You can pound away on that thing—it won't break," he said. He typed fast, slamming the keys so hard that it sounded as though he were playing drums.

Calculus class was mandatory. I could follow most subjects if professors taught them from the beginning, but in this course, a great deal of mathematical knowledge was presumed. I had learned some math in an unstructured way throughout the years—from my older siblings in Shanghai, Nanjing Mother, older children at NUAA, counting money to manage my household, and doing calculations while working at factories during my teenage years. But when the professor put fractions on the chalkboard, I stared blankly at the strange notation, which I had not seen before. I stopped him after class.

"What does that mean?" I asked, pointing at the chalkboard.

The professor looked puzzled. "Can you be more specific?"

I placed my index finger on a fraction. "That. What does it mean when you put one number, then a slash, then another number under it?"

"You don't know fractions?" he asked, squinting his eyes at me.

"No," I replied, feeling shorter even than my five-foot frame.

The professor was blunt. "Well, you need to go back to high school." He must have wondered how I had been accepted into the master's degree program in the first place.

I went to the city library and started thumbing through math textbooks. I didn't find fractions in the high school math book, nor did I find them in the middle school texts. Finally I found them in the second-grade math textbook. Even high school math was too advanced for me. I ended up checking out the entire arithmetic curriculum from first grade on. I knew how to add, subtract, multiply, and divide. But other than that, some basic concepts such as fractions, long division, square roots, and logarithms were unfamiliar to me.

I plunged into the textbooks, studying them in every spare hour that I had. I'd also ask other students to tutor me. "You don't need to know much," they counseled. "As long as you get the basic concepts, then you can use a scientific calculator to do the actual calculations."

I found myself falling in love with math, geometry in particular. The poetry of shapes and formulas mesmerized me. Above all, I reveled in the opportunity to learn, as I had enjoyed only four years of formal education at Suzhou University in China. I earned a C on the calculus midterm. But by the end of the term, I was doing so well on the exams that my professor called me out in class. "Is your brother the famous winner of the math Olympics? His last name is also Fu," he said with a smile.

My face blushed pink. Rarely before had I been praised in public.

Programming was fun and addictive for me. Sometimes our homework was assigned as group projects. Even though I was not the strongest programmer, I discovered that I was often good at software design. Programming is as much art as science: software design is about structure and flow, just like literature. It came naturally to me.

In a computer logic class, the assignment was to design an intelligent traffic light control system, one that would respond based on approaching cars from each direction. Typically, students created a highly technical logic flow on paper. I had a different idea, and convinced my group to go along with me. We went to Radio Shack, where we bought resistors, capacitors, transformers, and soldering materials. Then we went to a toy store and bought a Hot Wheels set with racetracks and a traffic light. Together, our team built an actual intelligent traffic light control, which we demonstrated with the toy cars. The professor gave us an A-plus.

From then on, it was easy for me to recruit teammates. The engineers were gifted at solving problems, while my creativity helped with the design. We asked many whys: Why do we need to solve this problem? Why is this relevant in the real world? It was so much fun to work as a team. We would celebrate together if a project turned out well; I'd bring Coca-Cola and M&Ms. I was still shy then, often sitting quietly in class and rarely taking the presenter's role. However, I was assertive in our assignments, going above and beyond the professor's requirements and driving our team to achieve excellence. Years later, I would find this approach written about in business management textbooks: it was a leadership style known as "servant leadership."

The Chinese government was growing more lax about allowing its citizens contact with America, and I was thrilled to be able to get occasional letters from home. Hong wrote to tell me that she was depressed without me and wanted to join me in the United States. By the time she arrived, eighteen months after I did, I had a rented apartment, two jobs, a blue 1973 Opel, and a full academic load. I got her a job at a Chinese restaurant and invited other students over to make a party out of teaching her how to mix drinks like fuzzy navels and screwdrivers.

"Say '*gracias*' to the fry cook when you pick up your food," I told her.

Hong hated America at first, and complained that I had failed to tell her the truth about how hard life was going to be. When she came home from work hurt by the injustice of a boss who made her clean up beer that someone else had spilled, I let her have it. I wasn't her mother anymore, and she was nearly as grown up as I was. "So what if it's not your fault? No job is too small and every job has some problems! It's your life. America is what you make it." If she couldn't take it, I told her, I'd buy her a ticket back to Shanghai.

As it turned out, Hong adjusted quickly and stayed on to earn a master's degree in architecture at UNM. I was the one who left.

~

I was talking with one of my computer science professors at UNM, Henry Shapiro, one day over lunch. He felt that Chinese students shut themselves out of American life. "You guys come over here, get your master's degrees in two years, and then work in cubicles without ever knowing what you're missing in the outside world," he said.

"What should I do if I don't want to live a life like that?" I asked.

He replied, "Well, do an undergraduate degree. Mingle with the American students. Have you ever taken a class on the American

Constitution? Learn more about this country and live the life of a typical American college student."

I nodded, thinking about what he had said and what I needed to do.

"Go to a better school if you do that," he added.

Professor Shapiro could not have guessed that I would take his advice literally. Many years later, he told me he must have been in a bad mood that day to say such nonsense.

Less than one year away from completing my master's degree in computer science, I dropped out of the University of New Mexico. Hong had met a few friends at school and was happy with her studies. She decided not to come with me. I packed up my few belongings in my Opel and drove off west.

I chose a school in a city that had been described as having eternal spring: San Diego. As I cruised along Highway 101, the sparkling blue ocean on one side and beautifully blossoming flowers on the other, I thought, This is paradise.

I walked into the admissions office at the University of California at San Diego (UCSD) and told the middle-aged woman behind the desk that I had come to study there as an undergraduate in the computer science program. The admissions officer peered at me over the top of her glasses, asked my name, and then disappeared into a separate room. "I couldn't find your application," she said when she returned to the desk.

"I didn't apply yet," I said lightly, not knowing anything about the American college transfer student application process. "I can do it now."

The admissions officer looked surprised. "I'm sorry, miss. It's the middle of spring quarter. You wouldn't be able to enroll until the fall. Anyway, there is no guarantee you'll be accepted."

"I thought this was a free country," I said.

"Yeah," she said. "Free to reject you."

Like a deflated balloon, I drifted away from campus and down toward the beach at La Jolla to contemplate my next move. Rent was far more expensive here than it was in Albuquerque. I supposed that I would find a waitressing job while I applied to UCSD. I stood facing the ocean for a long time, mesmerized by the rhythmic power of the waves.

A handsome thirty-something man walking along the sand approached me and asked if I'd like to walk with him. I said yes. As we strolled down the beach together, I told him how I had gotten here and about the rejection from UCSD.

"You should kill that professor," the man said, shaking his head in disbelief. Then he gave me a bright smile and a fatherly handshake, using both of his hands. He introduced himself as Lane Sharman, and explained that he was the owner of a computer software company, Resource Systems Group. He gave me his card and told me to stop by if I needed a job.

I spent the night at the Red Roof Inn and showed up at Lane's office the next morning. It occupied one big room with a floor-to-ceiling window overlooking the ocean, waves crashing onto a wide and unspoiled glittering white sand beach. Lane told me that he had worked for NCR, a renowned computer company. But he loved to surf every morning, and missed out on it far too often at that job, so he started his own database software business. He offered me a job as a computer programmer at fifteen dollars an hour. I enthusiastically accepted.

That spring and summer, I audited four classes and got all As. I was admitted to UCSD in the fall. I managed to transfer enough credits from UNM and Suzhou University to start as a junior. While I rapidly pursued my undergraduate degree in computer science, taking five classes per quarter, I also became fluent in database software systems by working at Lane's company. I befriended the two talented, sweet, and nerdy computer programmers that Lane already had working for him, who taught me a great deal.

Lane asked one day if any of us would be willing to work nights. We would earn double our usual hourly rate, he said, and get paid for every hour that we were on call, regardless of whether a service request came in. I immediately volunteered. Not only could I make more money working the night shifts, but also I would have the time to take any classes that I wanted to during the day.

For the next two years, I answered calls in the middle of the night, mostly from legal clerks working at law firms that handled time-critical court cases. I would drive to the clients' offices during the wee hours and fix their hardware or software problems, which sometimes meant simply rebooting their system. By the time I graduated, I was earning close to eighty thousand dollars a year.

⌒

While I was in San Diego, Nanjing Mother wrote to me every month. Her letters were my windows to China's further political opening and economic development. Hong and I talked on the phone sometimes, but not too frequently. She told me how she was making friends at UNM and had developed a crush on an American classmate. I visited her in Albuquerque in the fall and bought her a microwave. She sold it a few months later when she was short of money.

I worked all the time, either for Lane or on homework. One day, Lane asked me if I would like to go out to lunch. "No," I said. "I prefer to work." He asked me again the next day. Again I said no.

"What do you like for lunch, then?" Lane asked.

"Instant noodles."

Lane shook his head. "Ping, you need to learn to live a little, have some fun." I ignored his advice and continued to work. From then on, Lane kept the kitchen stocked with instant noodles.

I valued my time working for Lane Sharman immensely. The experience offered me my first taste of entrepreneurship. I watched Lane deal with difficult clients. I traveled with him to San Francisco to pitch to venture capital firms, and observed how he kept going even after having the door slammed in his face. I saw him cope with a crisis when the bank froze his assets. In an ironic twist of fate, for a short time he had to borrow money from me and even drive my car. We had a terrific relationship based on camaraderie and mutual respect.

And yet, when I graduated from UCSD in March 1988, I told Lane that I was quitting his company to join Bell Labs. I wanted to work for a large, well-established, prestigious American business. I was still Chinese at heart, and in China working for a state-owned enterprise was considered a privilege for the individual and a source of pride for the family. A secure job was called an "iron bowl," meaning that you could always count on being able to put food on the table. I had a dozen job offers, including ones from Arthur Andersen, Honeywell, IBM, HP, Xerox, and AT&T Bell Laboratories. Most recruiters loved that I had a few years of real work experience under my belt in addition to a prized CS degree. I chose Bell Labs because it was world famous for its groundbreaking innovations and home to many Nobel Prize winners. The company also offered to pay 60 percent of my salary, full tuition, and room and board if I pursued a PhD.

Lane did everything he could to talk me out of my decision, including warning me that big companies aren't nearly as interesting places to work as start-ups. When I refused to reconsider, he said, "If you stay, I'll give you 5 percent of the company." I had no idea what a generous offer this was. Above all, given how hard I had worked to put myself through school, I felt I simply couldn't refuse the Bell Labs opportunity because it had offered to pay for my PhD. Lane and I parted on the best of terms.

Six months later, Lane called. He had sold his company to AT&T, the parent company of Bell Labs. I finally understood what 5 percent meant: millions.

That summer, before I moved to Illinois to begin working at Bell Labs, I asked Hong if she would like to travel around Europe with me. She said yes. I bought us Eurail passes, and we embarked on an amazing adventure, finally operating more as siblings than as a mother-daughter duo. We stayed flexible and made up our itinerary as we went.

When we arrived in Vienna at night, we couldn't find a single hotel with vacancy. We wandered the streets with our guidebook and an increasing sense of desperation, getting turned down by one place after another. Finally, a woman we asked for help pointed to a building across the street.

"There's no sign for it, but you'll find a great bed-and-breakfast over there. Take the elevator to the fifth floor," she said in English marked by a thick German accent.

Hong and I followed the stranger's instructions, arriving moments later at a beautifully renovated apartment with bright lights, clean furniture, and large windows. The Hungarian owner greeted us warmly, and the room rate was a steal.

Later that night, I woke up and looked out the window. I thought surely I must have been dreaming: extending herself upward from the rooftop across the street, as if she were about to soar up into the heavens, was a beautiful naked woman with smooth, fair skin. I rubbed my eyes and realized that in fact she was a sculpture, carefully illuminated to appear real. The sight of her reminded me of the wish I had made on my eighth birthday, that I could fly like the finches and dragonflies that darted so gracefully above our Shanghai garden. I had endured many hardships during my youth, including one incident that nearly had destroyed my spirit. But here I was at long last—about to take flight.

THREE

I
Am
Precious

BROKEN SHOE: 1968–1970

ZHANG HAD MADE my misery her pleasure since I'd first arrived to live at the NUAA campus. I could not believe my bad luck when I was ten and she was assigned to sit next to me during our regular study sessions.

One day, out of pure spite, Zhang started a rumor that she had seen a boy our age named Fong in my room washing my bra. Everyone knew this to be physically impossible because there weren't any washing basins in the dormitory; we washed our clothes outside in a common area. Another day, Zhang told our classmates that when Fong walked by, I would reach inside my pants and touch myself. As unlikely as Zhang's stories were, the other children, starved for entertainment and gossip, would add their "oil and vinegar"—a Chinese phrase for rumormongering—and the tales would grow.

I knew why the mischievous Zhang had chosen the epithet "Fong's concubine" for me. I had met Fong on my occasional visits to Nanjing as a child. He was the same age as me and his family lived next door. Hong hadn't been born yet at the time, so Fong was my playmate. We had chased each other in the yard, running until our faces were caked with dust and sweat, laughing until our bellies ached.

When the two of us were about three years old, my family joined Fong's family and many others from the neighborhood for an open-air movie on the NUAA campus soccer field. Everyone arrived at these popular events an hour early and laid down their bamboo mats on the grass to claim their spots. Fong's family settled in next to my own. His parents talked with my Nanjing parents and their other neighbors while Fong and I sat on our mats getting bored.

Fong looked over at me and bragged, "I have something you don't." It was common in those days for proud Chinese parents to show off their young boys' genitals to family members and friends in order to prove that they had a son, which was considered vastly preferable to a daughter. Fong must have picked up on this behavior. He pointed to his pants and said, "If you show me yours, I'll show you mine." I played along. I had older siblings in Shanghai, so I knew roughly that boys' parts were different from girls', but I wasn't sure exactly how. Fong yanked down his pants and underpants, quickly flashing me. Too young to understand that what I was about to do was taboo, and oblivious to the dozens of adults who sat chatting on their mats around us, I accommodated by pulling up my shirt and flashing Fong my bare, flat chest. "Shame on you," I heard some adults teasing us, but they were all laughing.

I probably wouldn't even have remembered the incident except that when I came to live full-time at NUAA, neighbors who recalled our antics years earlier started teasing me by calling me "Fong's concubine." I didn't know what the word "concubine" meant, but I came to understand that I had done something shameful in glancing at Fong's private parts and showing him my chest in public. Zhang surely must have heard the story and nickname from her parents.

For several months, Zhang's childish taunts and rumors frustrated and annoyed me in the classroom. Little did I know that a torment far worse lurked just around the next corner.

The old Nanjing city wall stretched like a serpent along one side of the NUAA campus, passing very close to the dormitory where I lived. Next to the wall, a canal flowed, carrying water into the city. During sticky summer days, many of the children enjoyed splashing our feet in the canal's cool waters.

Hong, age six, had a dangerous penchant for courting trouble. I often found myself having to save her. One lazy, hot summer afternoon, as I lay resting in our room, I heard the voices of several children screaming from outside, "Hong is in the river! Hong is in the river!" One of them called to me, "Ping, your sister is drowning!"

As though my feet were on fire, I tore out the door, down the stairs, and across the street to the canal, where I found Hong frantically dog-paddling to keep herself afloat. I had never learned how to swim, but I jumped in immediately. Fortunately, even though it was too deep for Hong, the water was shallow enough for me to stand up in.

I wrapped my arms around Hong and dragged her out of the canal. As we gasped for breath, sopping wet and muddy on the canal's edge, I noticed a group of about ten teenage boys standing nearby. They laughed as though they were watching a comedy routine, pointing at us and shouting taunts such as, "Paddle like the dog that you are."

Avoiding eye contact with the menacing gang, I took Hong by the hand and pulled her as fast as I could toward our dormitory. The wet clothes hugged my body tightly. I felt naked. The boys kept up with us, pushing and shouting every step of the way. After what felt like an eternity, we finally got within ten feet of the back doorway. I shoved Hong forward with all my might. "Run, Hong, run!" I whispered in her ear. She raced into the building without looking back.

Hong was saved, but I was not. The gang blocked me from entering the dorm, their faces twisted into ferocious snarls. Several of the older boys picked me up and carried me to the nearby soccer field, the site of many a bitter meal.

"Beat her!" one of the boys cried as he dropped me onto the ground at their feet. "Beat Fong's dirty little concubine." The teenagers began kicking me like a soccer ball. "Get her, beat her! She's a filthy girl." I curled in on myself, attempting to protect my head, face, and stomach from the sharp blows. One of the boys kicked me so hard that I flew into the air and landed on another boy's steel-tipped worker's boots. I heard a crack like a tree branch splitting and felt a sharp pain in my tailbone.

Then, suddenly, the beating turned into something else—something I couldn't quite grasp. "Take off her clothes," someone ordered. I fought with all my might, but I found that I could no longer move my legs; all I could do was flail at my attackers with my arms. They easily grabbed hold of my hands and feet to hold me steady as I tried desperately to squirm my way to freedom. "Take off her clothes," the command sounded again. One of the boys who wasn't pinning me down took a knife out of his pocket.

I'd been attacked by a pack of hungry wolves. Darkness closed over my eyes and stars danced before me, like when I suffered from migraines. I could not hear. I could not scream. For a few nightmarish moments, all I could do was feel the boys cutting my clothes off, the knife ripping into my armpit and my bare stomach, and the pain of something blunt pressing between my legs. I lost consciousness.

The next thing I remember, I woke up in the NUAA health clinic. A kind nurse told me that I had sustained "deep cuts, a broken tailbone, and internal injuries." It had taken more than forty stitches to close the wounds. I carry the scars to this day.

I did not understand what had happened to me or why, and I wouldn't for several years. We received no sex education in China, and I had no parents or guardians to explain to me that I had been gang-raped. I thought the boys had beaten me up badly, which was cruel, but I didn't realize that what they'd done had brought deep shame upon me. I never for a moment guessed that I might be blamed for what had taken place. After that day, Zhang spread word that I had a new nickname, "broken shoe"—a shameful, denigrating expression implying that you are so worn down from overuse that you're no longer worth a penny.

At age ten, I was a ruined woman.

Memories of the time immediately following the beating and rape flutter like butterflies at the edges of my consciousness. I can, however, vividly recall the sensation of falling, which I had experienced for the first time upon my arrival at NUAA. I was tumbling through space, and I heard the wind whistle past my ears as I fell. No mother to comfort me, no father or older brother to defend my honor, no therapist or teacher to help me process what had happened, and no friend on whose empathetic shoulder I could cry. I felt unwanted, dirty, and unworthy. My dreams felt like memories as my memories faded into dreams—senses fractured, real people and places shaded themselves apart. At times, I considered suicide. The only thing that kept me from taking my own life was a sense of responsibility for my sister.

Hong didn't know exactly what had happened. She understood only that the gang of boys had attacked me. Even though she had witnessed violence before, I saw fear in her eyes when staff brought me back from the health clinic with a pile of torn and bloody clothes. They told her that I was hurt and needed rest. My sister watched me carefully for a while, then touched my face gently with her hands. I tried to smile to comfort her, but I couldn't make the muscles at the corners of my mouth turn upward. A few hours later, she tried to get me up, but stopped when she saw that moving caused me pain. That night, she came home with warm buns and stir-fried greens, which she had sweet-talked a neighbor into giving her, and insisted that I eat first. Later, in an attempt to cheer me up, she made soap bubbles and blew them at me, as I once had done to entertain her.

During those weeks of recovery, I did not have to attend study sessions, so I lay listlessly in my room. Tears streamed down my face like running water, too numerous to wipe away. As they dried, they tightened my skin. I tasted the salt and silence on my lips. I could not lash out in anger and frustration—doing so would only cause harm and bring more shame upon my family and me. I had no choice but to bury my feelings as I had buried so many other wounds over the past three years, deep underground in a dark and lonely place. A void.

It gave me some comfort to call to mind the Taoist teaching Shanghai Papa had asked me to memorize years earlier about the three friends of winter. The image of the pine tree, evergreen in winter and always standing straight, reminded me to be strong. The plum tree was my favorite. I loved to see its crimson red blossoms lying bright against the crisp white snow the morning after a storm. One winter day, watching me marvel at the delicate flowers in our scholar garden, Papa said, "This is what courage looks like: to blossom when none others dare because they could easily die from the cold. Courage is the heart refusing to fear." I hadn't really understood his words then, but I did now. Then there was bamboo, the most popular plant in the region where I grew up. Shanghai Papa had said that I must be like bamboo, bending from the prevailing wind, but never breaking. Perhaps he had predicted then that something terrible would happen to me, and had had the foresight to instill in me the values that I would need to overcome atrocities.

When I was very young, like most Chinese children, I was taught that revealing my emotions was a sign of weakness. But during this recovery time, I couldn't help but expose my vulnerability to others. I never would have guessed it, and I didn't understand why, but I discovered that showing people my pain led some of them to become kinder and more compassionate toward me. For those few weeks when I was most depressed, neighbors would stop by my room to check on me, offering to do our shopping or wash our clothes. Others generously provided Hong and me with food, sacrificing their own meager supplies.

I also chose to respond to the difficult circumstances by acting with kindness to everyone, including those who ridiculed me. Shanghai Papa had taught me to always treat people the way I liked to be treated. I reasoned that if I were giving to others, they might have a harder time attacking me so vociferously. I even adopted this approach in dealing with Zhang.

I had discovered that "broken shoe" was a label customarily given to prostitutes and promiscuous women. Teasing me with it seemed to be some children's favorite form of entertainment. One of our leaders, Ms. Lu, rearranged the study sessions to move a few of the boys who'd bullied me the most to a different class. But for some reason, Zhang stayed seated at the desk next to mine, tormenting me daily.

I saw how Zhang struggled in our study sessions. We routinely were assigned to write essays about what we had learned from Mao's

Little Red Book. We read our writings out loud to each other every week. Sometimes Communist leaders attended to observe us, causing a big fuss. The best essays would be posted on the wall for everyone to see. This was a badge of honor, especially if the Communist leaders ended up quoting the work in their speeches. Zhang got in trouble several times because she couldn't write; nothing she read aloud for the class made any sense. In spite of her family's red blood and her own position as a youth leader of the Red Guard, she became known as a bad student.

One day, I offered to write Zhang's study assignment for her. She seemed suspicious at first, but accepted. The next morning, I handed Zhang the essay I'd written, and she turned it in as her own work. I had carefully crafted a poem with a propaganda-like tone to it. The teacher liked the essay so much that she called Zhang up to the front of the classroom to praise her for her excellent work. She asked Zhang to recite the poem aloud, right then and there. Zhang cleared her throat and read my words from the page with gusto:

> Listen! The Communist drum is beating like rain drops of a
>   storm hitting a pond.
> Look! The Communist flag is flying like blood drops of a hero
>   floating on the ground.

The class burst into applause when Zhang finished. No one questioned whether or not she had written the poem. She smiled at me and grinned with pride at our classmates.

After that, Zhang's taunting remarks grew less frequent and less hurtful. She asked me to complete other assignments for her over the coming months. When I offered to teach her how to write them herself, she refused at first. I rationalized with her, "What if I'm not here to do your work for you one day? You'll be in big trouble if you suddenly stop turning in good reports. Let me teach you how to write." Eventually, Zhang accepted my tutoring. When she did, her tormenting of me ceased once and for all.

I gradually felt better and no longer dreaded going to study sessions. Over time, I found that showing vulnerability and being kind to others helped me to become more social, less timid and inwardly focused. I developed a greater sensitivity toward my own and others' feelings. As the caretaker at home and helpmate at school, I earned others' respect for being "good," in spite of the rumors and nicknames that had spread to the contrary. I also paid more attention to the goodness in those around me, including neighbors, teachers, classmates, Zhang, and a few of the other Red Guards. One of them even became my protector.

I met Li at my second military training camp—grueling events all youth were forced to attend at regular intervals throughout the Cultural Revolution. We were eleven years old. The soldiers made us march for miles through the countryside in the pouring rain, day after day, with little more than rice porridge for sustenance. My boots, hand-me-downs from the military camp, didn't fit properly. The shredded back of the left boot rubbed my heel until several blisters the size of thumbnails erupted. After several days, the skin peeled off in a single giant sheet, like wonton dough, exposing an angry red patch of skin. I had no ointments or bandages, but I did not ask for any. I knew better than to complain or be needy.

I noticed a beautiful, tall, slim, oval-faced Red Guard girl about my age watching me closely as I tended my wound, attempting to wash out the dirt with water from my canteen. I wondered if she was going to make fun of me—here I was, the "broken shoe," stuck wearing one. I was tempted to make the joke at my own expense. But the soft lines around the girl's wide eyes and the bright smile on her face showed warmth and compassion. Her gentle nature radiated from her like a pink halo, reminding me of Shanghai Mama.

I smiled. The girl approached me confidently, yet paused for a moment to gesture toward my mat before taking a seat. She was asking my permission, I realized with a start. Never before had a Red Guard treated me so politely.

"I like you," the girl said in the direct, openhearted manner that I came to love and admire her for. "I want to be your friend."

I wanted to reach out and touch her hand. But after years of struggle sessions and reeducation, I knew better. I shook my head and glanced back down at my wound, picking bits of dirt out of it with my fingernail. "We can't be friends," I explained. "I'm the child of black elements, and you are the reddest of the red. I would taint you with my black blood."

The girl grinned proudly and stated without a hint of fear, "Oh, my family is five generations of red. I'm not worried. My name is Li. What's yours?"

And that was that: I had my first best friend.

Until that day, I had been a loner at NUAA. I had formed casual ties with a few other black elements, but we lived in terror of being punished if we spent too much time together; the Red Guards had told us that we might be accused of conspiring against the Communist cause. Li was not only of red blood, but also very idealistic, often talking about how she wanted to be "Mao's loyal soldier." She was right: there was no danger in my friendship with her.

Soon Li and I were joined at the hip, like Siamese twins who couldn't be more different. Her worker family was so poor that she, like me, had only rice and a few pickled vegetables for lunch, and her clothes were clearly hand-me-downs. But Li had grown up doing physical labor, so she was physically fit and stronger than I was.

I was short and skinny, and more emotionally fragile. Li talked all the time, making friends with other kids every day, it seemed to me, telling jokes and laughing robustly. I was quiet and reserved, afraid of talking to strangers. Yet Li accepted me as I was. What's more, her red blood loaned me status that I never could have attained on my own. For the first time since I'd left my Shanghai home, I could relax into the comfort of another person standing strong beside me.

Even though we were the same age, Li treated me like her little sister. She loved to wrap her arms around me, sheltering me from criticism and showering me with praise. Once, when a group of kids including a few Red Guards began their familiar chant of "broken shoe, broken shoe" as I walked by, Li stepped in.

"Stop that," she commanded. "You mustn't say such things about Ping. They aren't true." I couldn't believe it: Li had the power to say no. I marveled at her authority, the way many Chinese people stood in awe of Chairman Mao—she was my hero.

On free days, we would take long bicycle rides across the old city of Nanjing, visiting the green areas and sometimes wandering as far as Sun Yat-sen Park. We talked about friendship and the meaning of life, boys and fights with family members. Finally I had someone with whom I could share my private thoughts, and I rejoiced daily in this gift. However, given Li's enthusiasm for the Communist cause, I was careful never to utter a word of critique against our government or complain about what had happened to my family in front of her.

One roasting Nanjing summer day, I passed out from heatstroke during a marathon race the Red Guards were forcing us to run. Li helped carry me home to her apartment. I woke up to her mother leaning over me to wipe the sweat from my brow. Her face mirrored the strength and compassion I found so attractive in Li. She pressed a cool stone into the palm of my hand.

"My daughter has told me how brave you are," Li Mama said.

I gazed at the stone she had given me. It was captivating, with streaks in all the colors of the rainbow and a translucent milky white base. "It's called a rainflower stone," Li Mama told me, her melodic voice making me sleepy, as though she were singing me a lullaby. "It is agate made strong and polished smooth by millions of years of tumbling along the riverbed with other stones. You can find rainflower stones all around Nanjing. The red in the stones symbolizes the blood that has been shed by the people's heroes in times of war."

I sunk into the deepest sleep I could remember since I had left Shanghai. Li Mama's story comforted me. When I left the Lis' home a few hours later, I slipped the stone into my pocket.

That stone became my most precious belonging, inspiring my lifelong passion for collecting rocks and stones whenever I travel. Li Mama's gift was one of the few items I carried with me when I left China for America over a decade later. I would touch the stone to calm my nerves when I felt anxious or lonely. It served as a reminder, then and now, of beauty in a world where so much around us is rough and crude.

My life took another turn for the better shortly after my twelfth birthday. By then, I knew how to forage, grow, and cook my own vegetables, raise chickens, spin silk thread, build radios, march in military formation, remove leeches, operate milling machines, harvest rice, navigate huge cities without a map, and survive in the wilderness. But what little formal academic education we received included almost no science, literature, or art.

In Shanghai as a young girl, I had loved the library more than any other room in our house. During the Cultural Revolution, Chinese citizens were forbidden from reading anything other than Mao or selected propaganda. The Communist education was designed to encourage group thinking and blind loyalty. Anyone with an independent mind who suggested an original or, even worse, contrary opinion was bound to get in trouble. Fortunately, Mao wrote many books and was, in my opinion, a good writer. Still, I was eager to read other authors.

Then, in the summer of 1970, an amiable middle-aged man with a glass eye, short black hair, and a tattered satchel appeared at the door of Room 202. Initially I was wary of this stranger with his one eye always pointing straight ahead.

"I am your uncle, and my name is Wan. Everyone calls me W," he said, introducing himself and reaching out to shake my hand with a twinkling smile that reminded me of Shanghai Papa's. I kept my hand on the door, blocking the man from entering the room. I had never heard about him from my parents in Shanghai or in Nanjing.

The man reached into his satchel, pulled out an envelope, and handed it to me. "Here is a letter from your aunt in Shanghai to me. Why don't you read it?" I opened the envelope, instantly recognizing Shanghai Mama's handwriting on the outside. As I read the letter, I started to relax a little. Addressing him as W, Mama told him how her family had been separated and sent to the four corners of China to "honor Chairman Mao," and asked after his health and well-being.

Uncle W explained that we were distantly related. He had come to visit Nanjing Mother while on his annual leave from Tianjin, the city where he had been sent into exile. He showed me a picture of himself in a park with my uncle and aunt from Tianjin, whom I had met before. They were seated together on a bench under a huge magnolia tree, wearing serious expressions and Mao jackets. I relaxed, deciding that I could trust this stranger.

Uncle W had an easy way about him, and I appreciated how he talked to me like an adult. I told him that my mother was not home, but invited him inside. I gestured toward the only chair, which had just three legs. He leaned it against the wall for stability while I looked around for some refreshments to offer him, as any good Chinese host would.

"I'm so sorry," I said, gazing forlornly at our small bag of moldy rice. "All I can offer you is tea."

Uncle W's lips turned upward at the corners. "Please, don't apologize. I don't expect much." His smile then doubled in size. "But wait," he said, reaching for his satchel, which he had placed on the floor next to him. "I have something for you."

Uncle W pulled out a small packet of rice candies wrapped in beautiful transparent paper printed with a fruit and flower decoration. He handed the bag to me with a wink. I hadn't been offered such a treat since the start of the Cultural Revolution. "Thank you!" I exclaimed, tearing open the package and unwrapping one of the sugary delights with as much restraint as I could muster. When the candy melted on my tongue, I felt as though I'd been transported to another world, one far kinder and gentler than my own.

After preparing and serving the tea, I seated myself on the concrete floor on the opposite side of the room from Uncle W. I was craving adult attention after being on my own with Hong for the past four years. Strangely—or maybe not, given the circumstances of our lives back then—this man, fortyish, and I, a near teenager, settled instantly into a comfortable friendship. It felt as though we had known each other for years. Uncle W told me a few stories about my relatives and his adventures in the countryside, and I listened closely, delighted to have a grown-up as a friend.

Hong returned home an hour or two later, and Uncle W greeted her with a gentle hello. Then he asked if we would mind if he stayed with us for a few days. He had the rest of the week off and no place else to go. Hong eagerly agreed; she was more outgoing than I and loved having visitors. I fixed us a simple meal of rice and vegetables for dinner, using the coal stove in the hallway, while Hong set our makeshift table using a wooden stool that I had found in a collection bin.

"Sit," Hong ordered when the meal was served, pointing to the concrete floor. Uncle W toppled out of his three-legged chair, causing Hong to giggle in her contagious fashion. It seemed to me that he had done this on purpose, to amuse Hong, and I laughed with them both.

After we had eaten, Uncle W asked us if we would like to hear a story. I had been making up bedtime stories for Hong ever since I had arrived in Nanjing, so we welcomed the idea. Hong and I climbed onto our single mattress and gazed expectantly at Uncle W.

"Have you read any authors from other countries? Non-Chinese authors translated into Chinese?" Uncle W asked, as he slid a ragged paperback with an unfamiliar title out of his satchel. Our jaws fell and our eyes shot wide open when we caught a glimpse of the forbidden treasure: a foreign novel. I couldn't help from reaching out to touch its wrinkled cover, which contained a picture of a handsome white man holding in his arms a dark-haired beauty in a crimson dress. "This is a love story, and it takes place in America," Uncle W said, as he thumbed open the book. "It's called *Gone with the Wind*."

Before reading from the novel, Uncle W gave us a bit of context. The story was about a man and a woman who fell in love but could never find a way to be happy together. This was at a time when Americans were fighting over whether people should be allowed to own slaves, he explained. To me, the battle sounded like the Chinese Civil War, with Mao's Communist troops battling Chiang Kai-shek's army: a fight for the freedom of the worker. But the love story was completely foreign territory. The only connection I could find to this aspect of the tale was recalling Shanghai Mama and Papa's joy at seeing each other when he returned home from work each day.

At times, Uncle W read passages directly from the book. At other times, he summarized several pages of text. Hong and I listened with rapt attention as our minds were opened to a whole new world—one where feelings and opinions were expressed openly without fear of repercussions. Eventually, our sleepiness got the better of us, and we fell into a peaceful slumber.

I had recently been assigned to a job at a nearby factory, and the next morning I rose early to walk to work. Hong went to a study session with kids her own age. That evening, I raced home to our dorm room. When I found that Uncle W had prepared dinner for us, I nearly wept. It had been so long since anyone had taken care of me.

"It's called Soup of Chicken Soup," Uncle W said. I squinted into the pot, where I saw nothing but a few greens floating in water. The rich grassy smell tantalized me. I gave Uncle W a skeptical look.

"Don't you know what Soup of Chicken Soup is?" Uncle W teased, raising his eyebrows. I shook my head. "It comes from the olden days, when cooks used to prepare chicken soup for the emperor. They weren't allowed to have any for themselves, so they would take just a spoonful of the broth and use this as a base for their own soup."

I grinned and dipped my spoon into the pot. The broth's savory flavors tickled my taste buds, setting off fireworks in my mouth. It reminded me of Shanghai Mama's cooking. "It's delicious," I said. "How did you make it?"

Uncle W explained that he had picked the vegetables, wild Chinese spinach, from where they grew like weeds on the abandoned soccer field and along the old Nanjing city wall. He had mixed them with water and a bit of MSG. "It isn't even Soup of Chicken Soup, really." He laughed, a deep rumble starting from his belly and rising up to his throat. "More like Soup of Weed Soup!"

I laughed along with Uncle W. As I did, my entire body relaxed. All at once, I could breathe more deeply and smile more broadly. I sensed that now I had a new friend and confidant, an adult I could trust. There were so many questions locked inside my head that wanted to be answered.

For the next several days, we followed the same pattern. In the morning, I would go to my factory job and Hong would go to her study sessions. When we returned home in the evening, we would enjoy a simple meal prepared by Uncle W, then race to bed so that we could listen to him read from *Gone with the Wind*.

One afternoon, I came home early. Hong was still out, and Uncle W and I fell into a deep conversation. "Why don't we talk about you?" he asked earnestly, after sharing a few stories of his life prior to the Cultural Revolution. "Tell me more of what life has been like for you."

The floodgates opened. Here was the invitation that I had been longing to receive—from a parent, a teacher, a neighbor, or any adult, really, whom I felt I could trust. I spilled my tales like grains of rice from an overstuffed bag, scattering them everywhere with reckless abandon. I hadn't dared mention many of these things even to Li; she was just a child like me, after all, and so red-blooded that I feared what she might think. I shared with Uncle W the story of being taken away from my Shanghai family; of my shock when, instead of finding my birth mother in Nanjing, I had become mother to Hong; and of the crimes I had pinned on my parents during struggle sessions in order to save myself from beatings. Finally, I told Uncle W about the attack on the soccer field two years earlier, and my feelings of shame, terror, confusion, abandonment, frustration, anger, and hopelessness.

Uncle W's eyes searched my face as I spoke, as if he were looking for clues to my true identity. He asked a few questions, but delicately, so that they never felt intrusive. He was the first one to tell me that I had been raped—and to explain what "broken shoe" really meant. He told me with a compassionate yet firm voice that it wasn't my fault.

I couldn't hold back my grief any longer. Tears spilled onto the floor like raindrops. When I paused to wipe the moisture from my eyes, Uncle W reached into his pants pocket and pulled out a handkerchief. He handed it to me and said, "You are precious, Ping-Ping. You must always believe that."

My heart swelled like a rising ocean tide under a full moon. So rarely in the past four years had I heard an encouraging word. Not once since I had left Shanghai had I been told that I mattered. "I am precious?" I repeated softly, my voice rising. I wanted to hear him say it again.

Uncle W patted my arm. "Yes, Ping-Ping, and you always will be. Please promise me that you will remember this. No matter what happens to you in life, you are precious. At some point, you might do something that you later realize was wrong and hate yourself for it. But even then, know that you are precious. You don't need to earn it; this is your birthright."

The Communists had taught me I had to be good so as not to be beaten. I was lucky to be allowed to survive. I was held responsible for my parents' wrongdoings. No matter what I did, I would never be able to change the fact that I had been born with black blood and that I was nobody.

In some ways, what my uncle had just told me seemed too good to be true. Yet I believed him. His words warmed my heart. I knew that I would hold on tightly to this notion and never let it go.

"You will be rewarded someday for your suffering and for your kindness to others," Uncle W added.

"When?" I asked.

"In little moments," he replied. "Your rewards will come in little moments of delight that will appear like shooting stars crossing the night sky."

When it came time for Uncle W to leave, my spirits sank. "Please don't go," I begged. But we both knew that he had no choice; he would be hunted down and severely punished if he did not return to his factory labor assignment in Tianjin.

"Will you at least leave your copy of *Gone with the Wind* with me?" I asked.

My uncle's brow furrowed as he considered my request. I knew how attached he was to the book; it was a prized possession for an intellectual like him during the Cultural Revolution. In addition, he was concerned for my safety; I risked reprisals, even death, should the Red Guard catch me with such contraband. But looking at my pleading expression, he caved in and handed the dog-eared novel to me, saying, "I suppose you're old enough to have it. Be careful, though. Don't let anyone see you reading this book."

Then Uncle W mumbled, his voice catching, "I'll write to you, if you like." When I nodded, he grabbed a pencil from his satchel, took the book, and scribbled his address on the inside front cover before handing it back to me. "I'll come to visit again, too. Next year, same time, I'll be here. And I'll bring more books."

Uncle W was true to his word. Two days after he left, I wrote him a letter about *Gone with the Wind*, which I had continued to read every night while hiding under the sheets, the book pressed up against my nose with a flashlight. I had to make up code names for Scarlett and Rhett so the authorities wouldn't know what I had been reading if they opened my letter, calling them by common Chinese names instead. I said they were survivors because they had adapted to the changes brought about by the Civil War and Reconstruction. I identified with their struggle.

Uncle W wrote back just a few days later, asking questions that made me think more deeply about what I had said. "If the book you're reading is about survival," he wrote, "then what makes some people come through catastrophes and others go under? What are the qualities of those who fight their way through difficult times triumphantly?" I wrote him back about the three friends of winter.

From then on, Uncle W and I corresponded regularly, swapping letters several times each month. I wrote to him about daily life, my factory job, and Hong when she got into trouble or amazed me by quickly picking up new skills. Uncle W always had something wise to say. Once, when I vented to him about a Red Guard bullying me, he quoted the renowned Chinese philosopher Lao Tzu: "He who conquers others is strong. He who conquers himself is mighty." He encouraged me to stay in a place of love toward other people, rather than sinking into resentment or fear. "Being deeply loved by some-one gives you strength, while loving someone deeply gives you cour-age," he wrote.

Thanks to his kindness, love, and sage advice, and by bearing witness to my suffering, Uncle W helped me reconstruct the sense of self that I had lost over the years. I was able to heal from some of the traumas of my young life. I remembered that once I had looked at the skies and dreamed of being the first woman to walk on the moon.

IN THE FLOW: 1988–1993

MOVING TO NAPERVILLE, Illinois, was easy compared with my move to San Diego. I rented a one-bedroom apartment in a com-plex near Bell Labs, next to the Fox Valley Mall. Miles of mono-chromatic suburban landscape surrounded me, so unlike the beaches of Southern California. But I didn't care—I was too excited about my job. Thankfully, Hong was independent, happy with her studies and her life in Albuquerque. I was able to focus exclusively on my career.

My job in the 5ESS digital switch division was to help transform the telephone, which our company's founder, Alexander Graham Bell, had invented just over a century earlier, from an analog to a digital device. A new technology called "integrated service digital network," or ISDN, was about to replace traditional circuits. Up until that time, the telephone system had been viewed only as a way to transport the human voice. The key feature of ISDN was that it integrated speech and data on a single fiber-optic line, making possible all sorts of bells and whistles that had not been available with the classic telephone system. Our team developed features that people take for granted today, like caller ID, call forwarding, and multiparty conferencing.

Bell Labs was a wonderful place for people who loved to learn. The company offered a wide variety of technical training classes as well as practical courses on time management, financial literacy, and human resources. I was like a kid in a candy store, signing up for as many as possible. These classes introduced me to, among other things, a new corporate vocabulary. Gender terms like "glass ceiling" and "affirmative action" puzzled me; in Communist China, women and men were treated equally in the workplace.

Still, on the whole I found myself bored by the work I was doing. There were too many long meetings, and people didn't seem to be bothered when nothing productive was accomplished. I missed the small company environment and realized that Lane had been right when he had cautioned me that I might not enjoy working at a large company as much as a start-up. At Lane's company, the dynamic atmosphere had challenged and stimulated me. I had taken pride in my contributions, and my coworkers were also good friends. I looked back fondly on the days when I had collaborated with the founder to solve sophisticated client problems. Lane and I would stay up late laughing, debating, and getting our work done. I had to admit that I also missed the beautiful environment in San Diego, with waves crashing outside our floor-to-ceiling windows. At Bell Labs, I worked inside a generic building and my office looked out over rows of identical offices, with the same layout on every floor.

I had accepted the Bell Labs position with a romantic notion of what it would be like to puzzle out masterful inventions alongside

Nobel Prize winners at a place known for generating a patent a day. Instead, it seemed that most "technical staff"—the title my colleagues and I were given—just clocked in and out of work, not unlike the busboys and cleaning staff at the Chinese restaurant where I'd once waitressed. More troubling, most people who worked there lacked a big-picture vision of what the company was trying to accomplish—and didn't seem to care.

After I'd settled in, a supervisor handed me a binder the size of an encyclopedia. Thumbing through it revealed a precise and mind-numbing list of our tasks. I could have boiled the entire manual down to this: "Here's the input. Here's the output. Here is the description of what the software module should do. Now go program." There was no explanation of why we should perform our tasks or what the end product would look like. I was stunned. My approach to work had always been precisely the opposite. I had sought to understand the *why* before *what* and *how*. It was as though we were masons constructing a magnificent cathedral, only without the vision being communicated or an architectural plan presented. How could we be inspired if we received nothing more than instructions about how to lay bricks?

The more I asked around, the more confused I became by the complexity of the system. We had five thousand people programming a single piece of software. It was madness, an unmanageable situation. Looking back, I see it was also a time when much of the modern software-building environment didn't yet exist—Bell Labs was just figuring the system out, as was every other company.

One of my guiding principles is to find joy in whatever I do. So after a few months, I discovered a way to get excited about a data-mining project. I noticed that the data stored in our database was highly redundant and wasted precious computer memory, which was expensive at the time. For example, the area code, zip code, and city name would be repeated three times for each phone number. By

designing intelligent relational database tables that reduced the rep-
etition, we could enact significant memory savings and performance
improvements. I proposed this project to my supervisor. He saw the
merit in the idea and formed a group of people to work on it. Our
team ended up saving $30 million for AT&T that year. The victory
won our supervisor a promotion to department head.

Most of my coworkers left the office around five p.m. They headed
home, went to the gym, or hit a few bars. I stayed at the office late
into the night working to complete my projects quickly, just as I
had done at Lane's company. Sometimes I went home early like
everyone else, but all I would do was stay in, cooking, reading, and
watching TV. I was almost thirty years old and had no personal life.
It had been more than five years since I'd landed in the United
States, yet I still wondered, What *was* an American life exactly? I
had much to learn and to experience if I wanted to make this country my home.

I noticed that the women in the office dressed up more than I did.
They styled their hair in fashionable updos and perms, and wore
makeup, skirts, and high-heeled shoes. In Mao's China, gender
equality was promoted and sexuality kept under wraps. Women
kept their hair short, dressed in uniforms much like the men's, and
wore no makeup. I still wore Chinese-style clothes—secondhand
gender-neutral suits that didn't fit me well. I didn't own a single
tube of mascara or lipstick. I had purchased my only pair of heels in
Shanghai before coming to America. They looked dull in comparison with the shoes I saw on display in the Fox Valley Mall. I needed
to get in touch with my "feminine side."

With a combination of curiosity and courage, I made an ap-
pointment at a nearby beauty salon. The next day, I walked into Bell

Labs with a great deal of trepidation, wearing acrylic nails gleaming red and matching lipstick. In China, red was the color of brides and celebration.

"Do you really expect to climb the corporate ladder looking like a hooker?" a female officemate joked. My face flushed until it matched the hue of my nail polish. The memory of being called "broken shoe" flitted across my mind. Noticing my reaction, my colleague quickly apologized, saying that she hadn't meant to insult me; I simply looked out of character. The awkward moment passed. I reminded myself that it was up to me to create the life I wanted here in the United States, regardless of whatever may have happened in the past.

I signed up at the Fred Astaire Dance Studio for lessons after work, but I was still painfully shy in social interactions. One South American teacher held me so close to him while demonstrating the moves that I felt uncomfortable and requested a female teacher instead. I failed to comprehend how much more there was to the tango than where you put your feet. Or perhaps I simply wasn't comfortable enough yet with my own sexuality to embrace the overt expression of it through dance.

What finally transformed my personal life was not a class I took or a book I read. It was something totally unplanned and unrelated to these well-intentioned, purposeful efforts to make myself "fit in": a romance.

Through Bell Labs' PhD assistance program, I began taking graduate classes at the University of Illinois at Urbana-Champaign (UIUC). The campus was a two-and-a-half-hour drive from Naperville, so Bell Labs brought some professors to our location to teach.

One course I signed up for was taught by Professor Herbert Edelsbrunner, a brilliant mathematician from Austria. Professor

Edelsbrunner was gifted in explaining complex concepts in a simple way. His style was exceptionally clear and illustrative, which made the advanced algorithm class an enjoyable learning experience.

It was late fall of 1988, almost the end of the semester. Professor Edelsbrunner told the class that he would be visiting China for the first time. When he said that he would be going to Nanjing, I mentioned to him that I had grown up there but hadn't been back since moving to the United States.

Upon his return from China, Professor Edelsbrunner told the class that he had taken some pictures and wanted to show them to us. We all went to lunch with him at Bell Labs' food court. But the other students, taller and more eloquent than I, surrounded him. I couldn't squeeze in closer or see anything from where I sat at the far side of the table.

When everyone had finished their lunches, I stood up to put my tray away along with the others, feeling disappointed. But Professor Edelsbrunner walked over to me and said, "Hang on a minute, Ping. I want to show the pictures to you."

Feeling strangely rattled, I lost my balance and spilled half a glass of unfinished orange juice when Professor Edelsbrunner placed a stack of pictures of Nanjing on my tray. He quickly gathered the photographs up as I rushed to find napkins to dry them. When we sat down a few moments later to look through the pictures, I saw one of a building on the NUAA campus.

"This is where I grew up," I said, my face lifting.

"Then you should have the photo," Professor Edelsbrunner replied, handing the picture to me. It was our first personal interaction.

After the course ended and I was no longer his student, Professor Edelsbrunner told me to call him Herbert and asked if I would like to go for a walk with him at a local park. We had a technical conversation about the way fluid flows through space and the formation of the sound of the wind. I found an underlying beauty in what he said that reminded me of Taoism. I gazed at the colorful maple leaves turning brilliant yellow and orange, stretching beyond the horizon like an endless canvas, and thought about the geometry of life.

—◦—

I didn't see Herbert for a year. He returned to the UIUC campus and I stayed in Naperville. In the fall of 1989, I went to Urbana-Champaign to sign papers for graduation and ran into Herbert at Espresso Royal. We went to his office, where he played Bob Dylan's album *Desire* for me. It included a song, "One More Cup of Coffee," that my favorite teacher had played many times in class during college—and it was the only English-language song that I had carried with me in my head from China to America. Its melody and the raw emotions conveyed by Dylan's voice had haunted me. I had tried to track down the music when I'd first come to America but failed. To hear Herbert play it, utterly by chance, seemed a confirmation of our connection. I intuitively knew in that instant that this was the man I wanted to spend my life with.

Nanjing Father's hesitant and socially awkward nature had always troubled me, and Nanjing Mother often had teased him about being a few inches shorter than she. I had made myself a promise in China: if I ever were to marry, my husband would be my birth father's opposite—tall, confident, and eloquent. True to my word, the only commonality Herbert and Nanjing Father shared was that they both were professors. For many months, as I continued to work at Bell Labs in Naperville and he taught at the UIUC campus, Herbert and I saw each other only on weekends, commuting through hundreds of miles of cornfields each time. It wasn't easy on either of us.

Herbert recently had gone through a divorce and told me that he couldn't imagine getting married again. Looking back, I understand that keeping distance was more familiar and comfortable to me than creating intimacy. I may have been thirty years old, but emotionally I was still a child.

Nevertheless, when, in the winter of 1990, a technical position at the National Center for Supercomputing Applications (NCSA) opened up in Champaign, near where Herbert worked, he encouraged me to apply. When I toured NCSA, I was instantly attracted to the Renaissance Experimental Lab, which contained cutting-edge computer graphics machines. Displayed on the wall were visualizations of five thousand years of global climate change, and a poster of *Tin Toy*, the first computer-animated short film to win an Oscar. I was interested in converging art and science through the use of technology, and that was clearly being done here. And unlike at Bell Labs, I could sense the extraordinary team spirit at NCSA, with experts from all fields of study coming together to work under the same roof.

My unconventional life trajectory—which had taken me from Chinese literature to software databases to computer networking—made me a perfect fit for this environment. I'd never felt so excited about a job. For the first time in my life, I felt a sense of belonging, that this place was my destiny. To my delight, NCSA extended an offer for me to join.

And yet from a personal standpoint, my decision to go was not so simple. I had grown up in cities and worried that life in a small town in the middle of nowhere would prove unfulfilling. I wondered whether it was a bad idea to move for a man who was not fully committed to me. At the same time, my job at Bell Labs continued to underwhelm me, and I was ready to quit. I also found myself gradually, if unsteadily, opening up to Herbert.

As I was questioning the move to Champaign, I realized that I wanted more: more of a challenge at work, more of a connection to Herbert, and a deeper sense of resolution in my life. Herbert proposed in the fall of 1991, the year I moved to Champaign. He didn't want a wedding, so I called Hong to fly out and witness our civil union at the courthouse. Secretly, I wished that I could have a traditional Chinese wedding and that my family could attend. But I was not welcome in my home country, and in the early 1990s obtaining a visa for travel to the United States was exceptionally difficult for Chinese nationals. So instead, I wrote to them—Shanghai Papa and Mama, Nanjing Father and Mother—about the good news. They blessed me from afar, wishing me a loving marriage with children soon to follow.

When we spoke on the phone to make the arrangements, Hong and I giggled with amusement at how our lives had taken such similar yet opposite turns. After graduating from UNM, she, too, had met a man and fallen in love, and was making plans to start a family. But we had swapped career paths. In China as an undergraduate, Hong had studied electrical engineering. She had then chosen to pursue a more artistic major, architecture, in America. Now she was working at her dream job, building magnificent homes, office buildings, and public school libraries in Santa Fe. I, a Chinese literature major, had switched to the far more technical field of computer science.

I informed my boss at Bell Labs of my decision to leave. He asked if there was anything he could do to make me reconsider. I told him no. He advised me to take an unpaid leave of absence rather than quitting outright. "Ping, you never know what might happen. I want the door to be open to you should you ever want to come back. You are the kind of person we want to keep around." His sincerity touched me.

I never did return to Bell Labs. My career at NCSA ended up exceeding my expectations. What's more, it led me down a totally unforeseen path—to starting a company with Herbert.

The National Center for Supercomputing Applications was on the vanguard of innovation. So it was not surprising that working there introduced me to not just one but many transformative technologies. When I joined at the beginning of 1991, the center had just come to the attention of the worldwide scientific community with the release of NCSA Telnet, an Internet connectivity tool that was made available to the public at no cost.

Taking on what were dubbed the "grand challenges of science," we worked on analyzing the folding of proteins, mapping the human genome, predicting earthquakes, and revealing the nuances of quantum mechanics. Every day I had fun, was challenged, and felt happy. Here in the middle of the endless cornfields, some of the computer industry's greatest and most creative minds had converged. We had few budget constraints and no limits set on our imaginations. We wrote history in scraps of software and tossed much of it into the public domain. We took the work of theoretical scientists and gave it dimension, color, and transparency. As I romped with my colleagues through the playground that was NCSA, much as I had gone freewheeling with other children across the NUAA campus during my youth, we made one noteworthy contribution after another to the field of computing: image processing, scientific visualization, massive storage, and user interface.

One of my early team projects was to create 3D digital objects for CAVE, a large virtual reality theater located in a conference room. The walls of the CAVE were made up of rear-projection screens, and the floor was made of a downward-projection screen. High-resolution images were displayed on the screens via mirrors, creating virtual surroundings that could be breathtakingly beautiful and serene. Users wore special 3D glasses while inside the CAVE, which made objects appear to float in midair. We could simulate downhill skiing, white-water rafting, or flying to the moon. But it wasn't all just fun and games. Engineering companies used CAVE to enhance product development. Caterpillar was able to test tractor movements, driver visibility, and bucket-loading capacity using a virtual prototype before a single penny had to be spent on physical parts.

There were always people who were skeptical about the virtual environment, complaining that it didn't look real enough. We had a game for these doubters. We would create an image of a virtual conference room and ask them to verify whether or not the conference tables were the same height. Inevitably, when they bent down to take a closer look, people would rest their hands on the virtual tabletops for stability, only to find themselves stumbling forward onto the carpet, faces alight with wonder. They had experienced "computer-augmented virtual reality" for the first time.

Other projects I worked on predicted galaxies colliding, replicated synthetic blood cells, and simulated the impact of global warming from accumulated climate change over the past five thousand years. Before we illustrated the data using images, the world knew only pages of numbers that, placed end to end, would have stretched from the earth to the moon and back multiple times. Our programs turned these numbers, which scientists had calculated using supercomputers, into relatable and powerful images. "A picture is worth a thousand words," the English expression goes. We changed it to: "A picture is worth a million numbers."

I took a class from Donna Cox, a professor in the School of Art and Design at UIUC, on computer animation. She said, "Offering a different perspective and challenging the dominant worldview—this is a role artists always have played in culture." Her words made me excited about the prospect of engaging people with technology in such a way that it changed their lives. Donna taught us that the most important ingredient for success in this line of work was storyboards. I had been a literature major in college, so that made perfect sense to me: the first step in luring anyone into your worldview was creating an engaging narrative.

We worked with Hollywood, whose studios used our supercomputers to render special effects for several major feature films. Donna's students and other employees at NCSA thrilled millions of people with their visualizations for the Oscar-nominated IMAX film *Cosmic Voyage*. In 1990 and 1991, Industrial Light and Magic (ILM), a digital special effects company founded by George Lucas, collaborated with us to create the first partially computer-generated main character: the T-1000 in *Terminator 2: Judgment Day*. We turned the robot villain into a puddle of mercury through a process called "morphing," which later became a household word. In 1996, my colleagues animated the scene for the movie *Twister*, in which cows flew through the air during a severe tornado.

As a child, I had always sought out beauty; it had been a critical part of my survival strategy. Now, creating beautiful objects from computer programs was an integral part of my everyday life. For the first time since I had been an undergraduate studying literature in China, I felt all sense of space and time evaporate as I lost myself deep within my work—the Taoist experience of being "in the flow."

By the early nineties, supercomputers—machines the size of blue whales that took up entire floors of buildings on the NCSA campus—were becoming passé; the new focus was on networking many desktop computers from different locations together. Scientists were replacing the old model of expensive, solitary monster brains by distributing their computing power among hundreds of smaller, less powerful, yet highly cost-efficient mini-brains. Now, experts across the globe were racing to figure out how to get these desktop computers to communicate more effectively. The Internet was still difficult to use and limited to a small audience of computer scientists, skilled academics, and government entities.

In 1992, I received a grant from the National Science Foundation (NSF) and was able to hire a few students to work with me at

NCSA. One of them was Marc Andreessen, a witty, upbeat, and extremely bright undergraduate who had done some user interface programming in Austin, Texas, as a summer intern at IBM. We talked about building a browser, which is a graphical user interface, to manage our public domain Web site at NCSA. We were bored with telling people to type cumbersome network addresses in order to access free software and research papers. We thought people ought to be able to click on a link to pull up words and images.

Our group began by studying the information wall created by Xerox PARC in Silicon Valley and discovered the hyperlink, a method for connecting information on different Web sites by underlining and highlighting the relevant text. But it was Marc who came up with the most ingenious improvements, which he shared during our weekly team meeting one gray autumn day.

"This 'view source' command would allow people to view, cut, and paste an existing page and customize the content without knowing HTML," Marc explained. "I also think that the browser ought to allow images to be viewed in-line, rather than having them appear as separate pop-up windows. For ease of use, the browser should include clickable navigation arrows to enable people to move from one topic to the next."

Building the browser wasn't rocket science, technologically speaking; many of the coding components already existed. Nevertheless, I was impressed when Andreessen and another colleague, Eric Bina, put it all together in just six weeks. They introduced Mosaic early in 1993, and NCSA offered free downloads of the software to the public. While the program was originally developed for Unix, our group released versions of Mosaic for PCs and Macs soon after the initial success became apparent.

One morning in February, I arrived at the office early to find several members of our team scrambling frantically at their computers. They seemed to be simultaneously cringing with embarrassment and laughing with delight. "What's going on?" I asked.

Eric glanced up from the computer where he was coding. Taking a large swig of coffee, he grinned like a child with a secret. "Downloads of Mosaic have exploded! We've crashed the university's servers because they can't handle such high-volume traffic."

"We're a hit. I knew it!" Marc added with a smirk.

In total, two million users downloaded versions of the software during its first year. While Mosaic wasn't the first Web browser, it was considered the first to make the Internet easily accessible to non-techies: available for every desktop, for free.

In 1993, both the White House and the United Nations came online, creating .gov and .org domain names. I wasn't able to go to the White House to install the NCSA Mosaic software because I did not have the security clearance required, but we sent a few programmers there at the behest of then vice president Al Gore.

Mosaic was a desktop application and fell outside the supercomputing mandate for which the federal government funded NCSA, so the university asked us to license it, to make a "technology transfer." But no one seemed interested—not Apple, Hewlett-Packard, Silicon Graphics (SGI), or IBM. Only Marc, now a senior in college, seemed to grasp the potential of the world's first multimedia browser.

Frustrated and excited, Marc talked to me about quitting college to start his own company. He was only a semester away from graduating. "Marc," I said, "you should finish your degree."

"Why? Bill Gates dropped out," Marc replied.

I laughed. "I know—he did that already. You should be the next Bill Gates, but with a bachelor's degree."

Marc graduated from the University of Illinois and moved to Mountain View, California, that summer. Three months later, he met Jim Clark, who had recently left Silicon Graphics and was looking to start something new. They teamed up with several of their former colleagues from SGI and NCSA early in 1994, secured financing from venture capital firm Kleiner Perkins Caufield and

Byers, and founded Mosaic Communications, Inc. The rest would go down in history.

But before the idea of starting a business ever crossed my mind, I had an important journey to make. I wanted to return to the country of my birth. The reunion with my family and memories it called to mind, the knowledge I gained about my ancestors, and my experiences of modern-day China would bring me newfound peace with and confidence in my life in America. Only then would I know for certain: I was precious.

FOUR

Blood
Is
Thicker
Than
Water

HOMECOMING: 1993

WHEN I LEFT China, I put my past out of my mind. A decade later, in 1993, I was well on my way to U.S. citizenship. Yet, strangely, the closer I came to becoming an American, the more Chinese I felt. I had grown so homesick that I had begun to dream of China. The past would blossom at night, fragrant and spiked with a sense of nostalgia and loss that I could not ease. When I awoke, I would feel my entire being crying out for me to return.

As soon as I had a U.S. passport, I booked my first trip back home. Right before I left, I found out that I was pregnant. I was thirty-five and excited to have a child. I liked the feeling of carrying my unborn baby to China, and imagined her tasting for the first time in my womb what had I missed all these years: authentic Chinese cuisine.

My chest felt heavy with pent-up feelings as I boarded the plane, recalling my lonely journey from China to the United States when I'd been exiled. What would it be like to see my Shanghai and Nanjing parents again, I wondered? We had exchanged letters on occasion, and I had heard updates about them from Hong upon her arrival in America, but I had no context for understanding their lives, given how fast China was changing now.

I nearly screamed in nervous excitement when, in a happy reversal of the farewell scene ten years earlier, I saw my entire family—both sets of parents, my five cousin-siblings, as well as various aunts and uncles—waiting in the crowd gathered behind the glass at Shanghai International Airport. I broke into a trot, pushing my luggage trolley in front of me like a bulldozer to move aside the tourists and returning locals who blocked my path.

As soon as I could make my way to them, Shanghai Papa took my hand. He examined my face carefully, and then broke into laughter. "Ping-Ping, you look exactly the same. You haven't changed at all," he said, patting my hand affectionately. I noticed that he looked quite distinguished. Dressed in a Western suit, he commanded an aura of elegance.

Shanghai Mama squeezed in. "Let me see my Little Apple," she said, touching my face with her palm. She was just as I had imagined, forever young and beautiful. True to character, my Nanjing parents were not as openly affectionate, standing outside the circle of people who had gathered around me. Still, I could feel how happy they were to see me.

I was so excited to share all my good news with my family that my words twisted like pretzels; I simply couldn't speak fast enough. I had a job that I absolutely loved, I told them, as well as an intelligent and handsome husband who was also a professor like Nanjing

Father. I let them know that soon I was going to be a mother. They nodded graciously but with eyes hazed over, as though they were confused. I realized that just as I had trouble imaging what their lives were like in the new China, my family didn't have any reference point for understanding my life in America or how I had made it there. More than anything, they simply were content that I had survived and that I looked healthy and happy.

I eagerly listened to their updates. My cousin-siblings were back home after having been exiled to the countryside; all had jobs and were now married with children. Shanghai Papa had survived years of forced labor, returning home halfway through the Cultural Revolution. When it ended, he started an accounting company, which brought Motorola and GM to China. At sixty-five, he was studying law at Jiao Tong University. "I must make up for lost time," he said excitedly. Shanghai Mama showed me that she had brought my favorite dish with her, into which she always put a heavy dose of love.

As for Nanjing Mother, we always had struggled to find our mother-daughter connection. On this trip, I found that the years had mellowed her. Although my time with her felt strained, I enjoyed her sharp mind. She seemed to grasp the essence of what I said about my life in the United States more than anyone else, and I could tell that she was proud of me.

China itself was changing at a rapid pace, and I didn't necessarily like what I saw. It was as though a Chinese version of the Berlin Wall had just come down, and the society was in chaos. The government maintained tight control over political freedoms, as witnessed by the world during the notorious Tiananmen Square student protests of 1989. Yet at the same time, China was liberalizing its economic policies and becoming more capitalistic, allowing for greater foreign investment and privately held businesses.

As much as I had suffered under the brutality of the Chinese Communist regime, the corruption of state officials, and the impunity of the Red Guard during the Cultural Revolution, the country had at least manifested a certain social purity at the time. People had talked about noble ideas such as the common good, equality, and health care for all. Now everyone seemed single-mindedly focused on making a buck as quickly as possible.

Shanghai Papa complained to me about our villa, where he and Mama continued to live. At the start of the Cultural Revolution, they had been forced into one room. The house had been co-occupied by a newspaper agency and several other families. Slowly, the government returned a few more rooms to them, but never the entire house. They now occupied the middle section of the house facing the scholar garden, including the old library. Nothing could prepare me for the emotional impact of seeing my happy childhood home destroyed. Its facade had crumbled like the wrinkled face of an old lady. Its overused rooms sagged like wilting roses given too little water to drink. I gasped when Papa walked me into the library, which had been turned into a shared storage area. In my favorite room, which had so enchanted me as a child, only one half-filled bookshelf remained.

Here among the remnants of our former life, Shanghai Papa encouraged me to continue his "legacy of entrepreneurship." He owned and operated his own business, he reasoned; so, too, should I.

I rejected the idea outright because I disliked what I saw happening in China. Everywhere I turned, people were asking me, the "wealthy American," to loan them money so that they could make more money, though they had no idea how to go about it. Money, it seemed, was an end in and of itself, which did not interest me.

"I'm sorry, Papa," I said, bowing my head and gazing steadily at my hands. "But I will never start a business. It is not my passion. Anyway, I love my current job."

He nodded sadly.

The longer I stayed, the more I felt out of place. The China of my memories, however horrific it had been in some ways, no longer existed. I traveled to Nanjing with my birth mother and father. The soccer field where I had eaten so many bitter meals had been converted into rows of undistinguishable condos. The canal that had run along the campus perimeter had been filled in to make more room for roads and buildings. The field where we had used old airplanes as our playground had vanished without a trace among the NUAA teaching facilities.

In the daily news, a heated debate had erupted around the construction of the Three Gorges Dam, the largest hydroelectric power station in the world. The question was whether the government should support economic development at the expense of destroying China's collective memories, historical relics, and cultural treasures. Should these be flooded intentionally or saved and moved to higher ground? As I took a boat ride from Chongqing down the Yangtze River, passing through the Three Gorges area, I became lost in a dense fog of memories. I realized that, like those opposing the dam, I was trying to hold on to the China of the past. As if by reconnecting with the China of my childhood, I might be better able to connect with myself.

FAMILY: 1970–1976

DURING MY FIRST few months at NUAA, I thought Hong had it easy because she was my younger sister. I managed the household, cooked meals for her, made up stories to tell her at night, washed her, soothed her when she cried—and generally yielded to her frequent demands for more food and play. But I realized over time that she had also suffered. At least I had benefited from eight years living with my Shanghai parents and siblings, who had showered me with love. Hong had been sent to a Chinese full-time day care when she was less than a year old. She had spent most of her childhood prior to the Cultural Revolution away from home, receiving limited attention and love from adults. She learned to fend for herself early on, and was unafraid of talking to strangers.

Hong was a carefree spirit who ate and played with gusto. Once, she eagerly dropped a glob of her saliva into a communal pot of soup so that everyone else would be too disgusted to eat it and she could have more for herself. When her tactic worked, she laughed and declared victory. She also had a limited attention span and could not sit still in study sessions. Unfortunately, these traits were frowned upon in China at the time, considered emblematic of someone lacking in virtue. People, even family members, made fun of her, calling her "the girl who loves to eat and play too much."

A tomboy, Hong loved to run around with the boys in our neighborhood. It seemed I couldn't leave her alone for a moment without her suffering some injury. Once, she broke her arm while sliding down an airplane wing at the abandoned NUAA airfield. Many days, she would come home from an impromptu soccer match covered in cuts and bruises, whining about how much her injuries hurt. I would sigh in exasperation and nurse her wounds with care.

In spite of her mischievous and accident-prone nature, I grew to know and love my little sister as a sweet, happy girl with many talents. Hong made our life at NUAA more colorful—sometimes literally.

One day when she was just five or six years old, I came home to discover that the formerly drab Room 202 had been transformed into a cheerful, cozy home. Our solitary wooden stool and single soiled mattress had been draped with brightly colored knit cloths, and curtains in spectacular kaleidoscopic patterns covered our windows. When Hong walked in the door a few minutes later, I was standing in the middle of the room, my jaw hanging.

"Hong-Hong, this looks amazing," I said, assuming that she had discovered the items near a trash bin, as I had done with most of our furniture. "Where did you find these beautiful decorations?"

Hong smiled smugly, clasping her hands behind her back as though hiding something. "I didn't find them. I made them."

I approached the stool and took the tablecloth between my fingers, admiring the knitting more closely. It looked perfectly made. "You *made* this?" I said, eyes wide.

Hong nodded, swaying from side to side with excitement.

"But how?" I asked.

"Ms. Yang showed me how to sew, knit, and crochet!" Hong burst out, her voice high and her speech rapid. She pulled a ball of yarn and two knitting sticks out from behind her back, displaying them to me with an immense grin.

Hong's outgoing personality amazed me. I kept to myself, rarely speaking to neighbors, and I had few friends. Hong, on the other hand, talked to everyone, serving as the eyes and ears of Room 202. She knew the names of all our neighbors as well as what they did on any given day, who their nearest relatives were, and what sorts of treats they might have to offer her. I didn't even know who Ms. Yang was, and here Hong had convinced the stranger to give her sewing lessons.

I asked Hong how long it had taken her to learn. She shrugged. "I don't know, a few days maybe. I just watched Ms. Yang and copied her. It's easy!"

"You are so talented, Hong-Hong," I told her, my voice cracking with pride.

Later, Hong knit hats, gloves, and scarves for us. Displaying an avant-garde sense of fashion that would make her famous in this day and age, she also mined the streets and garbage bins collecting the filthiest, most worn-out bits of clothing with the most outrageous colors and patterns. She would wash these, cut out the usable pieces of fabric, and stitch them together like quilts. Most Chinese at the time had few clothing items and were forced to sew discreet patches over holes in their shirts and pants. But our clothes, designed by Hong, proudly exhibited their patchwork. Sometimes, strangers on the street would point at us and laugh: "Look at those children, so poor their clothes are stitched together from rags!" But I loved our unique clothing and wore it proudly, feeling more like an artist than a street urchin.

In spite of her ability to learn quickly, Hong did not have the patience to stick with any one subject or task for long. I had more persistence and usually kept at whatever I was doing until I achieved perfection, so I gained the reputation of being the more intelligent child. But in my opinion, Hong was the smarter one. She was fearless in trying new things. She painted our walls in bright colors, using paint left on the street by Red Guards, who updated Communist propaganda daily. She made up dishes with limited ingredients, like a soup with chicken's blood that she called "red tofu." She built a playhouse with bamboo sticks. She thrived by cultivating her creative projects, which gave her a stable and enduring sense of identity and self-confidence.

A terrible typhoon hit Nanjing in the early spring of 1970, when I was eleven and Hong was seven. The skies emptied oceans of rain upon us, causing the streets to flood. The wind screeching past our windows sounded like goblins howling in the night. Massive, elegant sycamore trees, which dotted the city landscape, toppled like children's toys. We did not dare go outside to play.

I thought my little sister might lose her mind being cooped up in our tiny dormitory for days on end. But she and Su, a girl Hong's age who lived at the other end of the building, entertained themselves by running up and down our long hallways, giggling like crazy.

Su's father was a Russian engineer who had come to China in 1956 to help construct the Nanjing Yangtze River Bridge, a double-decker source of pride for our city and our country. He had fallen in love with and married Su's mother, a ballerina and classic Chinese beauty with fair skin and fine features. Su looked like a doll, with curly brown hair and big round eyes.

A "foreign devil," Su's father had committed suicide when the Cultural Revolution started, jumping out of a window. Su's grief-stricken mother adored her only daughter. But like all other black elements in those days, she would disappear for days on end with no explanation—summoned to the countryside or to military service or simply for interrogation. She was likely away on one of these assignments when the typhoon hit.

To this day, Hong has a piercing, infectious laugh that everyone who knows her can easily recognize. That evening, as the typhoon wailed, Hong and Su made their usual ruckus in the dorm hallway, playing their chasing games. I worried that a neighbor would complain.

Suddenly, cries of a different nature echoed down the hall—howls of agony from both Hong and Su. I sprinted out of Room 202, searching for my little sister. She and Su were flailing about at the far end of the hall, writhing in pain, their faces twisted like demon masks. They had knocked over a large pot of boiling water from one of the hallway stoves, where a neighbor had been preparing a late dinner or perhaps a bath. In typical Hong form, the spill had caused the maximum damage possible: all the water from the pot had poured directly onto the two girls, covering most of their bodies with burns.

I looked up and down the hall, but no neighbors came rushing to our rescue; people were still too frightened of being punished for overtly helping black elements. I had no choice but to manage the situation myself. I had to get the girls to the health clinic as quickly as possible. Trying not to touch their blisters, which only made them scream louder, I scooped up Su, who was smaller and lighter than Hong, and held her in front of me. Then I commanded my little sister to climb onto my back.

I stumbled down the stairs and out into the night. The rain had stopped, but knee-deep water ran through the streets and toppled trees were scattered everywhere. I had only about half a mile to travel, yet I feared that I would not make it. I moved slowly. When I reached the first downed tree, I left Hong on a patch of higher ground and climbed over carrying just Su. Then I placed her down and came back for Hong. I had to do this several times, making separate trips with each girl.

One tree I encountered was too high for me to scale. I would have to duck under it, I decided, swimming through the floodwater. Blessedly, the girls weighed less in the water. I thought they would moan even more, but instead, their cries lessened. "Get down in the water, please," they begged me. Apparently, the cool liquid soothed their burns.

As we came within sight of the health clinic at last, I found my legs giving out. We had reached a slight hill, so the road was no longer flooded. Dropping to my hands and knees, I piled both girls onto my back and crawled the last hundred meters, scraping my knees to a bloody pulp.

The moment I pushed the clinic doorway open and deposited Su and Hong onto the floor, I passed out. I came to a few moments later. The girls still howled with agony as a nurse peered into my face, attempting to revive me. "No, no. Not me," I murmured. "I am fine. Help them." The nurse left me lying on the floor, where I waited for the next hour while Hong and Su received medical care.

Fortunately, the doctors said, the girls had spilled water and not oil on themselves. Their wounds, though extensive, were not deep. If treated properly and with careful attention for the next several days, the skin would heal. Also, the trip to the clinic through the storm water, while risky in terms of infection, had actually helped to treat the burns and lessen their severity. As for me, I ought to get some rest. The nurses offered to help me carry the girls back home to our dorm room though the flooded streets.

For the next three days, with Su's mother still absent, I tended to my sister and her friend. Every few hours, I cleansed their burns with rubbing alcohol as the doctors had instructed, constantly soaking their bandages to keep them wet. Luckily, these supplies were cheap and readily available.

Hong and Su proved to be surprisingly gracious patients. Usually, Hong whined whenever I treated her injuries. But the girls said thank you when I applied fresh, cooling alcohol to their wounds. Though they both moaned in pain from time to time, I could tell each was trying to put on a braver face than the other. Whenever I asked how they were doing, they would quote a famous Russian movie, *Lenin in 1918*, which we had watched time and again during our study sessions: "We will have bread. Everything will be okay."

When Hong felt better, she said, "I don't know how you carried me and Su all that way—we weigh more than you. You scared us so much when you fell down. I thought you had died. I thought we killed you."

I flexed my arm, showing off my bicep, and smiled. "It's okay, Hong-Hong. I was so worried about you two, I somehow found the strength."

"We could have walked ourselves, but we were bad. We wanted you to carry us," Hong apologized.

I was touched by her gesture, but I shook my head. "No, you couldn't have walked, Hong-Hong. You were too badly hurt. Don't feel bad about that."

When Su's mother returned and found out what had happened, she raced over to Room 202. Falling to her knees before me, she clasped my hands in hers and thanked me for taking such good care of her daughter. Then she swept Su into her loving arms and carried her back to their room.

Su and her mother moved out of our dormitory a few months later. I never found out where to or why, but I had grown accustomed to living with such unsolved mysteries. They happened all the time.

I saw Shanghai Mama and Papa a few times during the Cultural Revolution. The first time was after receiving the letter from Shanghai Mama in 1967, about nine months after I had been sent to Nanjing. Homesickness had overwhelmed me. Trains and buses were free for anyone to ride, and some days there were no struggle or study sessions. I was too young to understand the danger, so I sneaked off to Shanghai one day.

Upon arrival, I hopped aboard Streetcar Number 24 and appeared without warning at my old house. I didn't know the villa had been confiscated by the government and divided up. But I found Shanghai Mama in the one room that had been left to her and Papa, on the second floor. We clung to each other for a few precious hours, crying and bemoaning the circumstances that had forced our separation. These were stolen moments. I had to return the next day to avoid being found out and severely punished.

The visit proved emotionally painful for me. As time went by, I also came to understand that I could bring trouble with these visits—not just to me, but also to my family. By the time I was ten, I had let go of the hope of ever visiting my Shanghai Mama again. I even stopped writing letters to her. I had to be strong and accept my situation: Hong and I were on our own now. I couldn't rely on anyone other than myself.

Then, in 1971, when I was thirteen, my birth mother came back to live with us. I never had dreamed about being reunited with Nanjing Mother and Father, since I had spent so little time with them as a child and never accepted them as my real parents. So when Nanjing Mother walked back into Hong's life and my own on a chilly autumn day, ours was not a typical reunion. When she appeared at the broken door to Room 202, she looked haggard and emaciated in her worn-out coveralls and shoes. She showed no love or excitement at seeing us—not even with Hong, whom she had raised. We circled each other warily.

"Would you like something to eat?" I asked. She nodded, so I walked over to my bag of rice and scooped some out into the cooking pot.

"What is this?" my mother's voice cried, rising suddenly. She was glancing over my shoulder. "This rice is moldy."

I remained silent as I added water and walked into the hallway to start the cooking fire. We were lucky to have rice at all, moldy or not. At times we had been on the verge of starving to death, surviving only thanks to the kindness of our neighbors. Surely my mother must know this? Anyway, after so many bitter meals, I didn't even notice how awful this old rice tasted. It seemed normal to me.

Nanjing Mother trailed me out into the hall, where her voice escalated. "You're feeding Hong-Hong moldy rice? Wash it! Wash it until it is clean!" She took the rice pot from me and started to rub the rice in her palm under the freezing cold running water. She rubbed and rubbed until her fingers turned red and I saw tears in her eyes.

My skin flushed purple with embarrassment as my neighbors peered their heads out of their doorways. I felt my resentment toward my mother harden into a stone in the pit of my stomach. But, faithful to being a good Chinese daughter who would never disrespect a parent, I retreated, bowing my head and silently starting the fire in the coal-burning stove. Nanjing Mother quit her scrubbing with a sigh of frustration, passed me the rice pot, and marched off down the hall.

"Welcome home," I muttered under my breath.

Over the following weeks, the stone of resentment in my stomach only grew. Nanjing Mother moved in with Hong and me. Cramped as our dorm room was, there was nowhere else for her to go. I wanted so much to be able to tell her about the bitter meals, the incident on the soccer field, and the suffering I had endured, as I would have if Shanghai Mama had arrived to live with us. But I couldn't share any of this with Nanjing Mother, because when I looked into her eyes, I didn't see love—only neutral consideration or anger. I didn't feel that I could cuddle up or open my heart to her, so instead I ignored her. Whenever she asked me a question or criticized me, I shot her a dirty look. I could tell how much my silent treatment bothered her, and it enhanced my sense of self.

I did break my silence to ask Nanjing Mother why she had given me away to Shanghai Mama to raise. Her answer made me sad. "I never wanted to have children," she said, gazing off into the distance, her voice soft as a whisper. She went on to explain that Hong and I were unwanted pregnancies, our existence due to China's "Hero Mother" policy, which was modeled after a similar agenda in Stalin's Soviet Union. At the time we were born, Mao was encouraging women to have more children. Birth control was unavailable and abortions illegal.

"I had no choice other than to give birth to you. But I needed to work—I had no time to care for you," Nanjing Mother explained. "I asked Shanghai Mama to come to Nanjing and help during labor, then take you to live with her when you were eleven days old."

I felt lucky to have grown up in the comforting embrace of my Shanghai family, but Nanjing Mother's story closed my heart to her even further.

One day, Hong and I went to pick mushrooms from the forest not far from the NUAA campus. Not knowing the edible from the poisonous ones, we picked and ate many beautiful-looking specimens. The next day, we both fell ill. Hong lay in bed helplessly crying and begging for water in a sweet voice, while I stubbornly and silently stayed out of bed, cleaning up our room whenever she or I made a mess throwing up.

Nanjing Mother could not stop Hong from whining or me from moving about rather than lying down to rest. Frustrated, she said, "Why can't you add yourselves together and divide by two? That way you both would be more balanced people. You are driving me crazy!"

My mother quickly learned to stay away from my affairs. She had been home for a few weeks, earning a small salary from working at a factory, when she came back one afternoon with presents for Hong and me. We opened them enthusiastically; it had been years since either one of us had expected to receive a gift from our parents. She had bought both of us skirts with her first month's wages, she told us proudly.

"Mother," I chastised her, "you don't know anything! Hong and I would get in trouble for wearing these skirts. We must wear clothes or uniforms like the other children. Anyway, how much money did you spend on these? We need the money you earn to pay for food. How could you waste it on frivolous clothing?"

After that, Nanjing Mother turned over her paycheck each month and all the household management—including budgeting, cleaning, clothing purchases, and meal preparation—to me. I had been taking care of it successfully prior to her return, after all. At least my skills in this arena earned me some praise from her. "I don't know how you do it. You are never stingy with money, but you know how to spend it wisely. You are very sensible, Ping," Nanjing Mother said.

⁓

Even though Nanjing Mother and I did not show each other much affection, she was my birth mother and I longed for her approval. The first Chinese New Year after she returned, she invited a few of her colleagues from the factory over for a New Year's Eve dinner, announcing that I would be the chef since she didn't know how to cook. The pressure was on. The most important holiday in China traditionally is celebrated with a banquet, a never-ending parade of elegant dishes. In addition, one of our guests would be the lead Communist Party member for the factory, the person Nanjing Mother certainly would be most eager to impress. Preparing this meal would prove extra challenging because food was scarce and we received rations for everything.

I had saved enough money to buy extra fresh vegetables, which were relatively cheap. I also had been raising a hen and a rooster for the past year, so I had extra eggs. Chickens were the only pets residents of NUAA were permitted to have, and almost every family had received at least one by 1970. I had been raising mine since they were chicks in a cardboard box in my dorm room, feeding them scraps of rice along with mealworms that I dug up from the earth. The chickens' beaks would tickle me as I held the food for them in my cupped hands. I named my hen Lemon, after her bright yellow feathers. I called my rooster Prince because he loved to flourish his white tail when we walked.

Once Lemon and Prince were fully grown, I had to keep them outside. Learning from my neighbors, I constructed a cage from bamboo in the courtyard against the brick wall next to our apartment building. Others told me that hens were picky about laying eggs—their nests had to be just so. I added an extra-thick layer of hay at the bottom of my cage to keep my chickens soft and warm.

One steamy summer day while I was outside caring for my chickens, Lemon approached the nest in a hesitant way, clucking and scratching her feet, and then finally entered. She sat quietly on the hay for half an hour, maybe longer, with eyes closed. Suddenly, Lemon stood up with her feet wide apart, tail raised, rear feathers upright—and a moist egg popped out. She inspected the egg with her beak and then rushed out of the nest clucking loudly. Moments later, she appeared to have forgotten about it entirely. I gathered the egg, still warm with a trace of blood on the shell, and squealed with delight. From that day onward, Lemon produced an egg a day, rarely missing one. Each time, I rewarded her with a mealworm.

For our New Year's Eve feast that year, Nanjing Mother asked me to make chicken soup.

"I can't make chicken soup. We don't have a hen," I argued.

"What about Lemon?" she asked.

"Lemon is not for soup; she is my pet," I said. "Besides, she lays an egg every day, which we always eat." I considered telling Nanjing Mother about Uncle W's Soup of Chicken Soup, concocted of nothing more than wild greens and MSG, but then thought better of it. I knew his dish would not be fine enough for my mother's special guests.

"I'll get more chicks for you next year. Lemon is for dinner," Nanjing Mother said in a voice that left no room for an argument.

Guests started to arrive in the early afternoon, as it was customary at the Chinese New Year for people to socialize for hours before dinner was served. Nanjing Mother brought them into our tightly packed dorm room. We had pushed our mattress against the wall in order to accommodate an additional table and several chairs that we had borrowed from our neighbors. Hong had decorated with her bright cloths. I counted five coworkers from my mother's factory, plus the three of us. One chicken could make enough soup to feed us all. I wanted Nanjing Mother to help me with the meal preparations, but she seemed busy entertaining her guests. I had to save face for her and make her life easier. I had no choice but to kill Lemon myself.

When I walked outside to Lemon's nest, she ran up to me eagerly, anticipating a mealworm treat. I picked her up, burrowed my face in her soft down, and gave her a kiss. She made delightful chirping sounds.

"Lemon, please forgive me," I whispered as I carried her across the yard to a rope, which I used to tie her legs together. This made Lemon cluck and flap her wings frantically, her eyes filled with terror. When I put my face close to hers in an attempt to calm her, she pulled her head back away from me. I felt worse than a Red Guard betraying her own family; I was a murderer, a monster.

My hands shook but I would not cry. It was New Year's Eve. I would not embarrass my mother or myself. My heart grew heavy and solid, as though it were filled with lead. I bent Lemon's neck backward toward her body, then used a pair of scissors to cut her throat.

I had no appetite that evening, in spite of the guests' profuse compliments for my cooking. I winced whenever they told me how delicious the chicken soup was. Nanjing Mother's coworkers praised her as well, saying that she was lucky to have a daughter like me, so capable already at such a young age. Mother beamed. I had never seen her gaze upon me with such pride. But later that night, I had a nightmare. Lemon came back to take her revenge, pecking out my eyes.

I never forgave Nanjing Mother for making me kill my pet chicken, but I did gain a fresh perspective on our relationship. I should not expect to receive affection from her; it was simply not in her nature or life experience to offer me a hug or say, "I love you." But I could earn her respect for my accomplishments. If I excelled in my work assignments, study sessions, and the household management, she would offer me generous praise.

Looking back, I am certain that my birth mother did the best she could. Unlike Shanghai Mama, Nanjing Mother's intellectual nature had always made her more practical and efficient, rather than warm and nurturing. Even her reaction to the moldy rice was, in all likelihood, her way of showing love, an expression of her frustration at not having been able to prevent the trauma that Hong and I had suffered at the hands of the Red Guard. During those early years of the Cultural Revolution, she, too, had endured brutal living conditions and psychological abuse due to Mao's purging of intellectuals. I learned later that she had always had a reputation for a bad temper.

I can see now how I played a part in our lack of mother-daughter bonding as well. By the time Nanjing Mother returned, I was a teenager who had spent the past five years living completely without adult supervision. I had my own ideas of how to take care of myself. Adolescence, rebellion, and independence did not add up to make me the most loving daughter.

Ironically, I realize now that I had the best of both worlds with my two mothers. Shanghai Mama's unconditional adoration and tender nurturing from when I was a baby until I was eight years old gave me a foundation of love, compassion, and appreciation for beauty that helped me to survive the harsh years of the Cultural Revolution. But if she had raised me until I was an adult, I don't think I would have been as strong or capable as I am today. Nanjing Mother's more analytical, rational way of thinking and her tough, unemotional style pushed me to accomplish more. She also afforded me tremendous independence and encouragement, which led me to gain self-confidence and develop new skills.

Mao's favorite philosopher was Friedrich Hegel, who maintained that life manifests itself in a set of contradictions: spiritual soul versus rational mind, matter versus the void, and so on. This duality ultimately must be integrated, without eliminating either pole or reducing one to the other. Later in life, I would study both art and science, embrace both a Chinese and an American identity, and develop as both a mother and an entrepreneur. Had I not grown up under the influence of two such different women, it may have proven far more difficult to reconcile these dichotomies in my own life and evolve a unified sense of self.

Precisely one year after his first visit, and six months after my mother's return to live with us, Uncle W reappeared at the door to Room 202. With him he brought three American novels, which he said he had selected just for me: *Uncle Tom's Cabin*, *The Scarlet Letter*, and *The Old Man and the Sea*. I was ecstatic to have fresh reading material. I had devoured *Gone with the Wind* so many times by then that I could recite long passages of it from memory. I didn't sleep and polished off all three new books in a matter of days, discussing the themes with Uncle W as I read. I identified with the slaves in the first book, the shamed woman in the second, and the lonely old man in the third.

Uncle W had brought a sleeping bag with him. At night, he camped out in the hallway next to our cooking stove. Nanjing Mother called him "the gypsy." She didn't mind that Uncle W had brought me these forbidden books. She was well educated and had read them herself as a young woman when they had been permissible in China. In fact, Nanjing Mother encouraged my friendship with Uncle W. She felt that I would benefit from the education he was giving me beyond studying Mao's writings. However, she did not approve when, after reading *The Scarlet Letter*, I yanked the red star off my moss green military cap and replaced it with a red A that I had fashioned from a piece of Hong's cloth.

"Why would you want to declare such shame?" Mother asked, grabbing the cap from my head and ripping the red A off the front. She knew that the letter stood for sexual promiscuity in the novel, but I doubted that was why she was so horrified by my behavior. In all likelihood, she was more concerned about the punishment I would receive for tampering with the Communist red star. Nanjing Mother had never asked and I never did tell her about the rape, though I suspect at some point she guessed what had really happened. I took comfort in not having to face the issue with her head-on. In China, people do not talk about rape because it brings shame to the family and no one wants to marry a woman who is openly known not to be a virgin.

"You might have been killed for this!" Nanjing Mother yelled after me as I stormed out of the room without arguing about the scarlet letter. I had to admit that my mother was right to save me from certain punishment. But it had felt good to act out. The way I saw it, people already called me "broken shoe." Wearing the red A on my cap would have helped me reclaim my identity in a subtle, secretive way, proving that I could be proud of myself in spite of the brutal events in my past.

Every year after that until I was eighteen, Uncle W came to visit me with books in hand. I looked forward to his appearances with the eagerness that American children display for the arrival of Santa Claus. He brought me *Jane Eyre*, *Pride and Prejudice*, *The Sun Also Rises*, and other great works of Western literature. These forbidden books became my oasis. Reading them transported me to a different world, allowing me to escape from the smelly hallways of the NUAA dorm and the noisy monotony of the factory floor.

I was old enough to have begun noticing incongruities between Mao's teachings and the reality of the society in which I lived. It was obvious to me that our Communist system was no utopia. I longed for a proper education, with the opportunity to study a variety of subjects and not just Mao's teachings. I saw how some people did not share their resources equally, in accordance with Communist ideals, but rather hoarded what little they had for themselves. Many Communist leaders had servants and drivers. People would bribe them with fresh fruits and the choicest cuts of meat to get better jobs or favorable notes in their personal files. At my factory job, I heard that a woman was sexually abused by her boss and then shamed for the resulting pregnancy, while her boss suffered no punishment. I began to doubt whether it was really "better to grow Communist weeds than eat Capitalist rice," as Mao had famously said.

I couldn't write to Uncle W about my thoughts on such matters, as we still had to assume that the authorities were randomly checking our letters. Instead, I looked forward to discussing them with him during his annual visits. On long ambles around Nanjing, we would delve into every topic imaginable. We would lose track of time and distance as our thoughts drifted with the clouds.

"I am not mad," Uncle W told me once, though I later learned that he had been tortured to the point where many people thought he was. "This country is mad." On and on he went, about the restrictions placed on our freedom as individual thinkers, the lack of choice in where we lived, what we did, or who we were supposed to be.

I found myself responding viscerally to Uncle W's words. Long ago, Shanghai Papa had told me that people could take away your wealth and health, but your mind—the way you think—would always be yours. No one could take that away from you. I always had remembered his advice and guided my mind carefully to maintain autonomous thinking, in spite of being surrounded on all sides by Communist propaganda. Now, it seemed, I had an ally.

After 1972, when I was fourteen, Mao's iron-fisted grip on China loosened; he was getting older and his health was deteriorating. Following several months of "Ping-Pong diplomacy," President Nixon came to visit that year and in time reestablished normal relations between the two countries. I still had no life outside of caring for my family and working at factories, but political pressure against black elements lessened. Reading Western novels was no longer a crime deemed worthy of severe punishment. For a short period when Deng Xiaoping was brought into power, school even resumed. I was ecstatic to be given old poems from the Tang and Song dynasties to memorize rather than Mao's Little Red Book.

Nevertheless, my frustration with the political system and my living conditions continued to grow. No matter how hard I worked to clear my name, I always would be held accountable for the multiple generations of black blood in my family. I never would be permitted to join the Communist Youth League of China or, after age twenty-five, the Communist Party. I would not be able to get a decent job, pursue my interests, or influence our society. In Uncle W's Western books, people could choose what to do for a living and succeed through a combination of effort, intelligence, and luck. Everyone had an equal right to study the subjects that most interested them, work at jobs that paid well, and love the people they desired.

"Why can't we say what we really think in China?" I asked Uncle W on one of our walks. "People who live in other countries can say whatever they want! Here, our true opinions stay hidden beneath the surface. I can only say things that won't get me in trouble or recite what we learn in study sessions, even if it's not what I believe. We can't even talk about our real feelings, and no one talks about love. Isn't love a natural human emotion? Do people in China fall in love before they get married?"

Uncle W sighed. "These are good questions." He paused. Looking back, I'm not sure whether he believed what he said next or whether he was just worried about filling my young mind with dangerous ideas. "Ping-Ping, you should follow Mao's teachings, knowing that some Communist concepts are good. Eventually, you may choose either to reject or accept the existing system. What matters most is that you can think independently." I took comfort in his wise words, which reminded me of Shanghai Papa's so many years before.

THE RELUCTANT ENTREPRENEUR: 1993–1996

REVISITING MY CHILDHOOD memories led me to recall just how confused I had been about Communist Chinese society and my place in it as a teenager. My recent visit had further shaken my identity. When I settled back into life in Illinois and my job at NCSA a few weeks later, I found that something had changed inside me. I no longer questioned whether I was Chinese or American. I was an American, an immigrant just like everyone else. My life here was an embodiment of the American dream. I felt lucky and at peace. As for my life in China, I resolved, once again, not to think about it anymore or talk about it to anyone. Looking back now, I can see this was healing and healthy for me in some ways. It allowed me to forget old wounds and open my heart to fully embrace the woman I had become.

Early in December 1993, I gave birth to a precious girl, Xixi. I was expecting her on Christmas Eve, but she came three weeks earlier. The birth was easy. Nurses said that in all their years of midwifing, they had never seen a delivery like mine: I didn't push my baby out with cries of pain, but with hysterical laughter. We were so in love with her, Herbert and I, that our eyes caressed each other with tenderness we had not found before.

"Indigo comes from blue, but it is a deeper shade of blue," I told Xixi in Chinese as she snuggled into my bosom. This is a colloquial expression meaning "Children are a better version of their parents." I vowed to make Xixi feel loved and cherished, as Shanghai Mama had made me feel. She was the one who had shown me what love was meant to be, something that welled up endlessly from inside. I wrapped my arms around Xixi, trying my best to be soft and strong at the same time.

"I love you," I whispered, choking on the words. The last time I had told someone I loved them I was eight years old. I had found it challenging to say those three words ever since. Then little Xixi appeared. She reached inside me and pulled on something: my heartstrings. With one tiny breath, she rescued me.

Not long after Xixi's birth, I began to wonder what it would be like to raise a child in America. I also worried, What sort of mother would I be, disconnected as I was from my family and country of birth? Perhaps I had been wrong to dismiss my heritage so abruptly. Wouldn't Xixi want to connect with her Chinese roots when she got older, as well as her Austrian ones?

When a temporary position opened up in 1994 at the Hong Kong University of Science and Technology (HKUST) to help them build a "mini-NCSA," I took it. Herbert came along and was offered a visiting professorship at the same university. Being based in Hong Kong, I reasoned, would give me an opportunity to further explore my Chinese American identity. A British colony for a few years longer, Hong Kong offered a convenient cultural and political distance, while remaining physically close enough to make it easy for me to travel to Mainland China.

I loved being a working mom. I took Xixi everywhere with me, nursing her in my office and carrying her into meetings. The year in Hong Kong was a blessing; I was able to spend much more time with Xixi than I would have otherwise. The close bond we formed then remained strong, even through darker days ahead.

In Hong Kong, a Chinese publisher asked me to write a book in Chinese about my first ten years in America. I was reluctant, but I wanted to have an opportunity to sharpen and renew my Chinese language skills, which I had neglected while living in America. Ah Cheng, a Chinese writer famous for his book *Chess King*, was conducting a fiction writing class at HKUST. I enrolled and scribbled down notes in my spare time, breastfeeding Xixi with one arm and writing with the other. By 1994, I had accumulated enough notes to turn in a manuscript, and my first book was published in China.

I ranted in that book against becoming a businessperson. My Communist education still influenced my thinking back then. I thought of making money as a crime, an exploitation of the laboring class, soulless and completely unappealing. "I will never be an entrepreneur," I wrote naively, "because businesspeople hate their jobs and love money. I love my job and hate money."

Before Herbert and I completed our year at HKUST, Shanghai Papa asked me to travel back to China to meet with him in private. There was heaviness in his voice, and I wondered what he had in mind. I arrived at our old Shanghai home and found Papa quietly staring out his second-story window.

"Here, this is for you," he said, his face expressing a mixture of sorrow and pride. He handed me two hand-bound, silk-covered scrapbooks filled with pages of handwritten calligraphy, aged photographs, and yellowed news clippings. "Your grandfather assembled these at his sixtieth birthday and gave them to me before he died."

I had seen my grandfather bury some of our family heirlooms under a tree in our garden at the start of the Cultural Revolution. Had he hidden these photographs and documents there as well? How else could they have survived? And why, I wondered, was my Shanghai Papa giving them to me, when I was not his child by birth? He had four sons and one daughter of his own. Did they even know these books existed? I had so many questions, but Papa stopped me from speaking by placing his hand lightly on my leg. All he would say was, "I want you to have them. I know you will treasure them and keep them safe."

On our long plane ride home to the United States, I pored over the journals while Xixi and Herbert slept. Here was the key to my past. I recalled an evening, just before I had been taken away from my family in Shanghai, when my grandfather had gazed out over the city and pointed to darkness where once whole neighborhoods of light had appeared. My grandfather had grown up in that light, I learned now, as I read and reread the newspaper clippings and traced his delicate handwriting across the timeworn pages. He had founded one of Shanghai's first banks.

I witnessed the enormous commitment my family had made to education. I learned from an old newspaper report that my paternal and maternal grandfathers, both entrepreneurs, had asked guests to bring only cash as gifts to their children's wedding, the marriage of my Shanghai Papa and Mama. They doubled the donations themselves and put all the money toward building neighborhood schools in the wake of the Japanese occupation. Their efforts had enabled hundreds of poor children to receive an education.

The Chinese have a proverb, which is also common in English-speaking countries: "Blood is thicker than water." The expression has two meanings. The first one is: Family bonds are more powerful than any other ties. I felt the strength of my connection to my ancestors for the first time in many years as I absorbed my grandfather's journals on that flight. We were family; my heart pumped to keep their blood flowing through my veins. I had a legacy to carry forward on their behalf.

The second meaning of the saying is: You can't pollute blood with dirty water. I saw no sins in my grandfather's story. I had understood years ago that it was Mao himself who had caused millions of people to starve to death during the Cultural Revolution and years preceding it, not my family. But that had been an intellectual reckoning. Reading my grandfather's journal, I realized that the little girl I used to be, Ping-Ping, Little Apple, had never come to terms with the trauma of being held responsible for her family's "black blood." Now I knew, once and for all: red or black, it didn't matter—the blood that flowed in my veins was good.

When I returned from HKUST to NCSA in the summer of 1995, Mosaic had changed its name to Netscape due to a dispute over intellectual property with the University of Illinois. The company went public on August 9 of that year. The stock was set to be offered at $14 per share, but a last-minute decision doubled the price to $28. On the first day of trading, the stock's value soared to $75, nearly setting a record for first-day gains. It closed at $58.25 per share, a market value of $2.9 billion for a company that had almost no revenue.

Clearly the Mosaic browser our group had created at NCSA had been a success—millions of people had downloaded it within the first two years. Nevertheless, none of us at NCSA had anticipated how Mosaic would spark the Internet boom, shaping the era of the "dot-com bubble" and its characteristic "irrational exuberance." None of us—other than Marc, I supposed—was a visionary. Even Marc said that he hadn't seen it coming; he was just obsessed with making the Web accessible to everyone. We were computer geeks who wanted to create cool software applications that other people might find useful, and we gave them away for free.

By 1996, University of Illinois administrators had been stung repeatedly by media criticism: how had they let so much money slip through their fingers? At the same time, NCSA's federal funding was coming to an end. Suddenly, entrepreneurship was the next big thing. The Internet was red hot and everyone wanted a piece of the dot-com boom. At NCSA, we participated in many presentations to venture capitalists with investment funds and commercial companies with an interest in licensing promising technology.

Nothing seemed to stick and no one started a new company. We were scientists and tenured professors with good pay and interesting work; we knew it would be highly risky to start a company, and completely out of our comfort zones. In addition, most of us felt that Netscape's runaway success was an aberration.

Then, during an ordinary staff meeting one day, my boss, Joe

Hardin of the software development group, became impatient with the situation. "We're all talk and no action around here," he moaned. "Who has the guts to start a business?"

I found myself raising my hand and saying, "I'll start one." The move shocked everyone, including me. To this day, I don't know what came over me. Perhaps I still felt like a nobody who secretly wanted to be somebody. NCSA's future was unclear, and my husband, a professor, was making enough to support the family even if I didn't draw an income. It didn't occur to me to consult with Herbert first; I knew he would back me up. Not only that, he would cofound Geomagic with me and be a pillar of strength throughout the turbulent start-up years.

Yet here I had written a book just a few years prior saying that I would never start a business. I was unqualified for the task at hand. I was shy, an introverted scientist and artist by nature. I had no MBA, and I lacked completely what people call "the profit motive": I had been hardwired to think that money was evil, and traumatized as a child because of my family's success. On a personal level, starting a business now didn't make sense in many ways: I had a small child at home, loved my current job, and enjoyed the freedom of being able to travel with Herbert on his breaks and live overseas during his sabbatical.

But facing the unknown did not scare me. I saw the promise of the blank canvas in front of me—unlimited space in which I could create something new. I could feel ideas swirling inside my head. It felt exciting: another challenge to conquer, another mountain to climb. I thought about the social impact of transferring some of the NCSA technology to the commercial world, making useful products that people would love and solving problems to ease their pain. In some ways, I felt that my life, so full of trials and change, my studies ranging from literature to computer programming, and my experiences as a factory worker had prepared me to take this next step.

The university administrators had offered support with fund-raising to all start-ups. Most of us at NCSA didn't realize that this was a goodwill gesture and not a promise. I was naive enough to go forward without understanding the complexity of a large public university and the primitive start-up support infrastructure in our area. Even though they couldn't ultimately help with funding, the university administrators did grant me a sabbatical. I thought that I would return to the academic life once I had developed a market-able product and executed the technology transfer to a commercial company—a year, I figured, maybe two.

In the blink of an eye, there I was: a reluctant and unlikely entre-preneur without a business plan.

FIVE

Everybody
Is
Somebody

FACTORY WORKER: 1968–1976

WHEN I WAS ten, several months after the attack on the soccer field and two years prior to the appearance of Uncle W and Nanjing Mother, I received my first factory assignment. A local Communist organization, in accordance with Mao's teachings, made arrangements for all the children of black elements in our area to be reeducated by workers. I was assigned to a site about an hour's walk away from the NUAA dormitory. I would work there six days a week for six hours a day, with a two-hour break each day for a study session of Mao's teachings with other children.

I awoke before dawn on my first morning of work, head explod-
ing with questions. What would I be doing? How would I learn to
do it? While I felt nervous, my mind also hummed with excitement.
After two years of an almost completely unstructured existence, I
was ready for an assignment. I needed a reason to get up in the
morning, something meaningful to do with my time. During the
long walk to the site, I felt as though I were embarking on a grand
adventure.

The factory building stretched like a reclining concrete giant
across a quarter mile of open land. Eyes wide, I approached the door
and stepped inside. At once, my senses were assaulted. Massive machines resembling an alien species come to take over the earth made
explosive hammering and whirring sounds. Conveyor belts whisked
metallic parts furiously from one station to the next. Dust-filtered
sunlight pierced through the open doorway, revealing chunks of
metal and pools of oil littering the floor. Hundreds of androgynous
adults, dressed identically in one-piece denim coverall suits with
hair tucked up into caps and greasy soot covering their faces, skit-
tered across the floor like ants constructing a nest. I found the whole
scene petrifying and thrilling at the same time.

A manager spied me gazing awestruck at my surroundings and
asked if I was there to work. When I nodded and told her my name,
she led me through a maze of crashing machinery to the far side of
the factory. Occasionally, I spied what looked like another child
scrambling to and fro like a chicken lost in a pigsty. My ears were
ringing by the time the manager introduced me to the worker who
would be my supervisor. Then she disappeared into the controlled
chaos of the factory floor.

Wang towered intimidatingly over me. His lean muscular body,
large rough-skinned hands, round golden brown eyes, and high
cheekbones made him look like the star of a Communist propaganda film: the idealized Chinese worker, a hero of the Cultural

Revolution and master of our developing modern economy. I instantly felt respect for him, as I did for all workers. Yet I was also fearful, not knowing how he would treat me.

Crouching down until his face came level with mine, Wang said, "They sent you here, huh?"

I nodded.

"Where are your parents?" he asked.

"I don't know," I whispered.

Wang's brow furrowed. He looked me up and down as though sizing up a fish he'd just caught. "You're going to build radios with me. Do you know how to build radios?"

I shook my head, silently wishing I did. I worried that Wang would be angry with me. But he just shrugged casually. "Then I'll show you."

Wang led me to a long metal table covered in boxes, cylinders, and tiny parts. He pulled up two chairs and we both took a seat. Then he picked up a radio from the stack of those he had already made. When he removed the four screws on the back of the box, I was surprised to discover that the inside was mostly empty. I could see only a large cone-shaped object, a dozen or so metal bits that looked like tiny beads and candies wrapped up in rice paper, and a few wires.

"This can talk?" I asked.

Wang started to laugh, a big, comfortable laugh like a wide-open cloudless sky. "Don't you know what a radio is?"

I frowned. "Of course! I listen to it every day."

"Well, yes, you use one, but that doesn't mean you know how it works," he said.

"How does it work?" I asked eagerly, crouching over the open box to take a closer look at the pieces inside.

Wang spoke deliberately, pointing to the parts as he talked. He reminded me of my first elementary school teacher before the Cultural Revolution started. "A radio is a tool for picking up broadcasts of sound. This box is the container—it's like your head. The cone here is the speaker. That's where the sound comes out, just like your mouth. These little pieces are the electrical components. Don't worry about how they work—you're too young to understand. Just think of them as magic. These wires are like your brain—they help the different parts of the radio communicate with one another."

"Where are the ears?" I asked.

"Good question," Wang answered, pulling up two thick, straight wires from the top of the box. "The antennae are the ears. They are what pick up the sound waves that are broadcast through the air."

For the next half hour, Wang showed me how to assemble a radio. He took an empty box and slid one of the speaker cones inside. Next, he taught me to solder the parts together using a special tool. "Think of it as a pen, only much hotter and far more dangerous," Wang said. He dipped the red-hot tip of the tool into a round metal box that contained a brownish block of solder, and then touched it delicately to the components until they stuck. The beads and wires were color coded, so I quickly memorized which ones went where. Finally, he attached the back with four screws.

"That's all there is to it," Wang said. He then gave me a drawing with all the pieces numbered, which mapped out how to put the radios together, in case I had forgotten anything.

I went to work, my mind keenly focused on proving my worth and not letting my factory hero down. By the end of the day, I had made maybe thirty radios. But would they talk?

I walked up to Wang's table. "Would you help me check my radios?" I asked. He picked one up and spun the knob to the right. No sound came out, not even a sputter of static. My stomach dropped. Wang picked up another radio. It didn't work, either. I swallowed, my mouth gone dry. One by one, he went through my pile. Not a single one of my radios made a sound.

I gazed at Wang with terror in my eyes, certain he would punish me. Instead, he just looked perplexed. He unscrewed the back of a radio and traced the wires with his fingers. "Aha!" he cried. "Here is the problem—you didn't attach the circuitry for the volume control knob."

I gulped and stared at the filthy factory floor. It wasn't my fault. Wang hadn't shown me this step, and it was not indicated on the instructional map he had given me, either. But two years of living under Red Guard rule had taught me to keep my mouth shut. What sort of punishment and ridicule would wasting thirty radios earn me?

To my surprise, Wang didn't reach out to strike me or march angrily away to report me to our manager. He just smiled gently. "You look like you're about to pass out. Don't worry—it's an easy fix." He then showed me how to take the missing step, soldering one end of a wire to the volume terminal and the other end of the wire to the ground loop. When he turned the knob this time, the sound of a Communist worker's song floated into the dusty air, and my mind danced with it. "Just be sure to check that the radio is working before you screw the back on," Wang said, handing me the now functioning device.

I couldn't believe my good fortune. It didn't trouble me one bit that I had to go back and repair each of the thirty radios I had already built. I wasn't being punished, and I hadn't wasted any materials. How lucky was I to have been given such a gentle and patient supervisor?

My heart filled with pride. I could build something—and not just anything, but something that hundreds of millions of Chinese used every day. In fact, Wang told me that our factory had manufactured cars and trucks prior to the Cultural Revolution. The government had converted it because many of the poorest peasants living in the countryside still didn't have radios. This work was important, he said. Thanks to us, tens of thousands of Chinese families would be able to tune in to hear Chairman Mao's voice each morning.

It was motivating to have been given such an opportunity to re-deem myself. My factory work gave me a sense of self-worth. Rather than drifting aimlessly without school or parental supervision, I had a purpose: I was doing good things for our great leader, Chair-man Mao, by helping to spread his teachings. I was one of the peo-ple, at last.

⌒

I built radios for almost a year, completing on average forty to fifty a day. The work was repetitive: I sat at my workstation, my head bent over, soldering the same parts together day in and day out. But I glowed with satisfaction. It gave me a sense of relevance to be making useful products and helping my country.

The following year, Wang was transferred to another department of the factory, where he would be making speedometers for cars. I went with him; it seemed we had become a team. Though the work proved less challenging than building radios, I nevertheless felt lucky: at least I had Wang on my side. I always made tea for him in the morning, pouring boiling water into a glass jar with green tea leaves. He looked after me as he would a younger sister, defending me from any criticisms made by other factory workers.

On the whole, I quickly realized that workers were good people, far kinder and calmer than the Red Guards. For one thing, they were adults, not rude, crazy teenagers. I could tell that they genu-inely cared about one another. Like members of a big family, they asked how things were going and offered assistance—a kind word, a bit of extra food, an excuse made to a manager—when someone in their work group needed help. When my face got dirty, my co-workers would tease me without ever making me feel threatened, bullied, or belittled. In general, they were amazed that this petite girl could do their jobs as well as they could.

After just six months making speedometers, I was sent on rotation to the countryside outside of Nanjing for half a year. I found a similar situation there—the farmers were decent people. We black elements had to work hard and do our share without complaining about our aching bodies or the bloodsucking leeches that attached themselves to our legs in the rice fields. But if we did, the farmers allowed us to take breaks and sometimes would even help us out. In the best circumstances, the farmers' wives cooked aromatic meals for us. Everything tasted better in the countryside because it was so fresh—rice, vegetables, and meats.

All in all, working in factories and on farms proved far better for me than my first two years of existence under the tyranny of the Red Guard. I wasn't being abused anymore, and I had a tribe to belong to.

I went back to factory work in 1971 at age thirteen, after having spent some time completing mandatory military service. I was elated to discover that I would be rejoining Wang, this time as an electrical engineer. Later, I found out that he had requested me because I was a quick learner and reliable; he never worried about the quality of my work. He also enjoyed having a little assistant who was eager to bring him tea or fetch him lunch.

At first, we would get orders to change lightbulbs or repair blown electrical circuits. Wang taught me how to find a circuit breaker and change a fuse, and gave me lessons about electrical currents, voltage, and the safety importance of grounding. He also showed me how to read engineering diagrams. Studying maps of electrical wiring systems fascinated me. Like radios, here was something we used every day, and yet most of us didn't understand how electricity worked. Now I not only understood what happened when I flipped a switch and made a light come on, but also I could set it up myself. I can do this at home for our dormitory, I thought. When the lights go out, we don't have to wait for weeks for the government to send us an electrician anymore.

Over time, Wang taught me how to wire entire buildings. He showed me how to set up light circuits in serial, so that all the lights would turn on at once, or in parallel, so that each line of lights operated from a different switch.

One day, the manager told us that a factory that would manufacture motorcycles was being constructed from the ground up in the outskirts of Nanjing. It required a complete, brand-new electrical system, and Wang and I had been tasked with the installation. We enthusiastically took the assignment, high-fiving each other right there in the manager's office. We felt so excited to be given the opportunity to create something entirely new. This job would prove a true test of our abilities.

But my excitement turned to anxiety the moment we stepped inside the factory. The ceilings stretched over twenty feet high. Most of our work would have to be done at the top of tall ladders— and I was afraid of heights.

Vertigo gripped me as I climbed slowly upward to do my first bit of wiring. Wang stood at the base, holding the ladder steady, but it didn't matter. My stomach churned with each step I took. My palms began to sweat, and I worried that my grip on the rungs would slip. The farther I climbed, the more I felt as though I were going to pee in my pants. When I reached the top of the ladder, I froze.

"Don't look down—look straight ahead or up," Wang called from the factory floor, sensing my panic. I did as he said, but my dizziness persisted. There was no way I would be able to release my hold on the top rung and raise one arm, much less two, toward the ceiling to get my work done.

"I'm coming down," I mumbled as tears threatened to leak out of my eyes. My face flushed deep purple with shame.

When I reached the bottom, Wang sat down on the bare concrete floor with me. "I could tell you were scared to death up there," he said, staring intensely into my eyes. His voice held steady, but I detected a note of concern. "Ping, you need to learn how to do this. You must overcome your fear."

"How?" I asked. "How do I do it?"

"I don't know how, but you must," he replied. A few minutes passed as we sat in silence, our minds racing. Then Wang's face lit up like one of the bulbs we so often replaced. "I have an idea. If I put a rope around your waist and tied it to a crane, and I used that crane to raise you up to the ceiling, would you feel safer?"

"I'm not sure, but I'll give it a try," I replied, determined not to let him down.

The next day, Wang found a mechanical lift with a small basket that I could sit inside while performing our high-altitude electrical work. He took a cloth he had brought from home, which resembled a roughly woven bedsheet, and spun it around to form a thick rope. Then he tied one end around my waist. The other end he secured to the railing of the lift basket. He yanked at the rope, causing me to stumble a few feet forward. "See?" he said. "It's strong. You're not going to fall."

I climbed into the basket and took a few deep breaths as Wang began to raise me up toward the ceiling. Sure enough, with the rope tied around my waist, I felt more secure. My stomach still churned and my palms grew damp with perspiration again, but I did not freeze. Once he had me in position, I raised my arms up to the ceiling and did the wiring as Wang cheered me on from below. Looking back now, I see what a creative solution he dreamed up for my problem. The experience made me realize that sometimes there are very simple steps we can take to overcome our fears, or just minimize them enough so that we can function.

As we were nearing completion of our work on the motorcycle

factory, Wang suggested that I take over the wiring of one of the main rooms. "I know you can do it by yourself," he said, handing me an electrical map.

I hesitated for a moment. "Are you sure?"

He smiled his broad, easy grin. "It's like learning to ride a bicycle, Ping. Someone runs along beside you holding the back of your seat until you are able to pedal off on your own. You're ready to do this without me."

I felt inspired that Wang would entrust me with such a task. Yet anxiety also clawed at the corners of my mind as I worked; I had better not mess up. I paid close attention to the diagram, double- and triple-checking each wire and every connection. When I finished a week later, I showed Wang my handiwork. Every light turned on as it should and every outlet worked properly. Wang gazed at me with the same pride that Shanghai Papa had years ago when I recited one of his Taoist sayings in front of our dinner guests.

The next day, I was surprised when a group of several dozen workers, some of whom I recognized from my prior assignments, arrived at our building around lunchtime. The factory was not ready for them to use yet. Wang gathered them into the room that I had just finished wiring.

"I want you to see what this little girl did all by herself," he announced to the crowd. Then he turned to me. "Ping, flip the switch."

I took a deep breath, fervently hoping that nothing had gone wrong overnight. But when I did as Wang had commanded, the factory flooded with bright light. The assembled workers began to clap their hands, whistle, and cheer my name. I thought I might float off the ground from sheer elation. I had earned the respect of the workers, the people I revered most. I could imagine no greater honor. I was a somebody at last.

From age fifteen to eighteen, I worked on and off at a factory that made car parts. Wang no longer worked with me, but we remained friends throughout those years. My first assignment was to manually operate a milling machine that made screws and fasteners. That experience taught me how to read mechanical engineering drawings—side, top, and front views. I had to measure the hexagonal screw heads precisely so that the fasteners would thread properly. It was my most dangerous job yet: hair caught in the turning belt would get yanked out in giant chunks; fingers could be sliced off completely if we weren't careful. I wore safety goggles to keep bits of metal from flying into my eyes.

Next, I was tasked with making gears with teeth. I discovered that the size of the teeth and the diameter of the gears were of utmost importance. They had to fit together precisely with the other gears in order to turn the machinery properly. This work required me to interpret even more sophisticated mechanical engineering drawings. I learned a great deal about size, speed, velocity, and torque—mechanical engineering concepts that I had never encountered in study sessions of Mao's teachings.

Later in life, I realized that many students learn the theory behind engineering and mathematical principles without ever applying their education through hands-on experience. I did just the opposite: I learned by doing, and slowly filled in the theory behind my work through intuition and by asking questions of others. Eventually, I studied some of the principles in books and college courses—but that would be years down the road.

My final factory task was stamping and sanding large pieces of rough, flat metal until it was mirror smooth. I would work on the same piece of metal for months on end. Today I can't imagine enjoying this tedious task that I spent two years of my life doing, yet I embraced it in the moment.

Several of us worked together on one sheet of rough metal at a time. We each held a long chisel with both hands, resting the flat end against our stomachs for leverage as we used the sharp end to take out small bumps in the metal. Next, we placed a sheet of blue ink paper, like carbon paper, on top of the rough metal surface. Using a machine, we lowered an equal-sized piece of smooth, flat metal until it touched the rough metal's surface. The machine moved back and forth, causing the blue ink from the carbon paper to be transferred to the bumps on the rough metal sheet. When the machine lifted the smooth metal piece away, we could see from these blue ink spots where we needed to do more sanding. We went back to work with our chisels, removing all the remaining bumps marked by the blue ink.

It was a mind-numbingly slow and repetitive process. I became bruised, with thick skin and calluses covering my hands and my stomach where I rested the flat end of the chisel. Fortunately, we did the work together as a team. The other workers were older than me, but they, too, treated me kindly and respected me for my work discipline. Being able to share stories, crack jokes, and laugh with them throughout the day made time pass more quickly.

When my colleagues and I had finished making our first piece of metal mirror smooth, I caught sight in it of a perfect reflection of my face. We didn't have mirrors at home or around the dormitory— Mao's Communism discouraged concern with one's physical appearance. This was the first reflection of myself that I had seen in a mirror in years. I was surprised that I looked all grown up. I recalled the well in the courtyard of my Shanghai family's home where I had gazed at myself before I was taken away.

Suddenly, sense memories flooded me. I longed to taste Shanghai Mama's elaborate dishes, to feel the soft touch of her hand on my cheek, to smell the sweet jasmine she always wore in her hair, to see the dragonflies buzzing around the scholar garden. I missed the tender warmth of Shanghai Papa, the rambunctious energy of my cousin-siblings, the quiet wisdom of my grandfather. Tears came to my eyes unbidden. I frantically tried to wipe them from my face

ABOVE: My family's home in Shanghai was a grand three-story villa. I have many wonderful memories from my time in this house.

LEFT: My family has always been invested in education. When Shanghai Mama and Papa got married (here, on their wedding day), in lieu of gifts, they asked guests to donate money toward rebuilding neighborhood schools destroyed during the Sino-Japanese war.

RIGHT: My Shanghai family was loving and nurturing. I enjoyed being the youngest of six children, with older brothers, seen here, who always tried to protect me.

BELOW: Shanghai Mama (right) was a welcoming and caring woman, while her sister, Nanjing Mother (left), was more serious and focused on her work.

BELOW: Although I did not know that Nanjing Mother and Father were my biological parents until the beginning of the Cultural Revolution, I did visit them and my sister Hong (bottom left) many times as a young child.

My grandfather, Shanghai Papa's father (right), sold all his valuable possessions for mere pennies in order to feed his family.

LEFT: Hong (right) and I (left) lived together in Room 202 at the NUAA dormitories. This picture was taken by my third brother during his brief visit to Nanjing in 1972.

BELOW: When I lived in the dormitories, I spent much of my time with students my age. During our mandatory study sessions, we recited slogans from Mao's Little Red Book. I am second from the right in the bottom row.

ABOVE: My first best friend, Li (center) was more than just a friend; she was also my protector. Here we are standing outside of Li's house. I'm on the right and Li's older sister is on the left.

BELOW LEFT: Nanjing Mother (left) came to stay with me (right) and Hong in Room 202 when she returned to Nanjing. I had just turned thirteen.

BELOW RIGHT: After Mao's death, the government reopened universities. Competition for admission was intense, but I was accepted to Suzhou University to study literature.

LEFT: At Suzhou University, my friends and I founded a club called the Red Maple Society. We published a literary magazine composed of poems, essays, and articles about campus news. We were accused of being an illegal underground society that published anticommunist propaganda, and the club was shut down.

ABOVE RIGHT: The night before my departure from China, our family gathered for a banquet. I'm in the middle; to the right is Nanjing Father, and to the left is Nanjing Mother. The woman on the far left is Shanghai Mama.

BELOW LEFT: Hong (left) joined me (right) in New Mexico eighteen months after I arrived in 1984. She adapted quickly to the American way of life and grew to love the United States.

BELOW RIGHT: To pay for my tuition at the University of New Mexico, I waited tables at a Chinese restaurant in Santa Fe.

The day my daughter, Xixi, was born my life changed for the better forever. I loved playing on the playground with her. She made me feel like a kid again.

In 2010 I had the great honor of meeting the president and his wife at the White House and sitting in the first lady's box at the State of the Union address.

LEFT: Here, I'm doing fieldwork with the Long Now foundation. We scanned the 10,000 Year Clock site in West Texas and used Geomagic software to process data and visualize the geological information.

BELOW LEFT: In September 2010 I visited Jay Leno at his "Big Dog Garage" in Southern California. We fixed his Duesenberg 1920 vintage car using Faro Scanner, Geomagic software, and Autodesk software.

BELOW: Designed by Janne Kyttanen of 3D Systems, these shoes incorporate a pocket that holds an iPhone. Just one example of the wonders of 3D modeling and printing.

LEFT: Geomagic software was used by Scott Summit of Bespoke Innovation to create this custom prosthetic leg. Not only is the leg functional, but it looks and feels real, which inspired the soccer player to play as if he had his own leg back.

TOP: The Geomagic technology lab in North Carolina is where we test-drive the latest technologies. It's also a place for community service and education outreach.

BOTTOM: The Geomagic team at our campus in North Carolina.

with my shirtsleeve before the others noticed, but one of my co-workers had already caught sight of me.

"What's wrong?" the middle-aged woman asked.

"Nothing," I replied, excusing myself to take a bathroom break so I could clean myself up. What was there to say? I had kept myself sane for a decade by pushing away thoughts of the life that had been stolen away from me. But now I wanted my family to witness me. I had started with a rusty, bumpy piece of metal and turned it into a beautiful shining work of art. I hoped they would feel the same way about me—an unfinished child who had transformed into a proud and capable worker as an adult.

THE PERSONAL FACTORY: 1996–1999

THE YEAR 1996 was nearing its end and I was determined to get a company started. Xixi was three, sweet and chatty, and I truly enjoyed being a mother. Ironically, it took me a little over nine months to bring Geomagic to life as well.

I spent the first few months gathering information and researching potential business ideas before plunging into anything. I interviewed, and mostly just listened to, dozens of people: experts, scientists, and business founders—anyone with an opinion or an idea. I also attended conferences and learning sessions. This was the height of the Internet era, and everywhere people were chattering about starting dot-com companies. At a panel at NCSA with representatives from Kodak, Sun Microsystems, GE, Morgan Stanley, and IBM, each one proudly pronounced, "We are a dot-com company."

That doesn't make sense, I thought. Why would they call themselves dot-com companies? I had learned that whenever there were breakthroughs in transportation and communication, big things happened. The invention of the railroad, highway, and aerospace industries had helped transport people and goods to new places with unprecedented speed. The radio, telephone, and now Internet enabled us to access information and connect virtually. Those innovations in transportation and communication had fundamentally altered our perception of space and time. Nevertheless, when the telephone came into being, businesses didn't rush to call themselves "phone companies" simply because they used the new device. Why should they redefine themselves as "dot-com companies" just because they now had a .com in their domain name?

"I don't want to create another dot-com company," I told Herbert one evening.

He nodded. "Well, at least you know now what it is that you *don't* want to do."

"I want to create something of value," I said. This was my New Year's resolution in 1997.

I asked three questions:

1. Why should I start a company?
2. What will it have to offer?
3. How can I build it?

One day, I saw a demo of a 3D printing machine called a stereolithography apparatus, or SLA. I was mesmerized by it. From my factory work in China, I knew the subtractive (milling) and formative (casting) process. But this was different—it was additive. Just as a regular printer lays down colored ink on a blank page in order to form two-dimensional words and pictures, this machine laid down printable materials—plastic, metal, or ceramic—a layer at a time. The SLA machine was capable of re-creating complex three-dimensional shapes that couldn't be milled or casted.

Three-dimensional printers were not yet advanced enough to make complex consumer products like cars or cameras. But they could produce specialized parts for the space shuttle or one of Frank Gehry's buildings. Engineers could print the parts in solid form as a prototype before sending their designs off to a factory for expensive manufacturing.

These printers depended on 3D computer models, which I wrote software to create at NCSA. Herbert was a leading research figure in the field of computational geometry. It was alpha shapes, a theory developed by Herbert and his PhD students, that had enabled us at NCSA to help scientists create and visualize 3D shapes on their computer screens that were either too small for our eyes to see or too large for our minds to comprehend—from the 3D structure of molecules to the shape composition of galaxies. I already knew that people were downloading alpha shapes software from the public domain site where we gave the software away for free, but I had not checked into what anyone other than the scientists at NCSA were using it for.

I discovered that many people were using the alpha shapes software to process data captured by 3D scanners—not medical CT and MRI scanners, but industrial ones made from digital cameras. With the aid of either a laser or light patterns, they would produce 3D point clouds. Imagine dots floating in space, arranged to cover the surface of an object to form an impression of its shape. In 2D digital pictures, those dots lie directly on the paper or flat screen; we call them pixels. In 3D, the dots are not projected onto a flat surface, but rather retain the depth of an object's true shape in space.

This was my aha moment. State-of-the-art 3D appliances, such as 3D scanners and 3D printers, already existed. If we offered software that could take the data from 3D scanners, process it, and output it on 3D printers, our new company could do in three dimensions for desktop fabrication what Adobe had done for desktop publishing in two dimensions. My head spun with possibilities.

After graduating from UNM and starting a family, Hong had founded a specialty retail store in Scottsdale, Arizona. She told me that shoes were one of the most challenging merchandise items to carry because the store needed to stock so many different sizes and styles, yet the one the customer wanted always seemed to be missing. In the nineteenth century, cobblers measured people's feet and made shoes to fit them precisely. But their skills were not scalable, and the shoes they custom made were costly. In the twentieth century, such personalized products gave way to factory assembly lines. Scale was achieved and costs plummeted, but the products became standardized. Stores carried racks full of shoes that nobody wanted because so many didn't fit quite right—in size, shape, or style.

Ask a factory today to make you a single pair of shoes of your own design and you will be presented with a bill for thousands of dollars. If you produce thousands of shoes, each one of them will be much cheaper thanks to economies of scale. For a 3D printer, though, economies of scale matter far less. Its software can be endlessly tweaked so that it can make just about anything. The cost of setting up the machine is the same whether it prints one object or many. It will keep going, at about the same cost per item, until it runs out of materials, just like your home printer will keep going until it runs out of paper and ink.

I wondered, Could we develop technology and software to enable a digital form-fitting and manufacturing system that made shoes and thousands of other items that were *both* one of a kind *and* produced with the efficiency of mass production? "Mass customization": I had heard people talk about it before, but so far it had come to mean little more than nonfat-soy extra-foam lattes and made-to-order jeans that still didn't fit well.

I started to get excited. The more I thought about it, the more it made sense.

"We'll call it the Personal Factory," I told Mike Facello, a bright PhD student of Herbert's who would become one of our first employees. "It's intuitive. People already know the PC. Now we'll have the PF."

"Cute, Ping," he observed. "You've managed to name an industry after your own initials."

I was possessed by the idea of revolutionizing the manufacturing process, just as Henry Ford once had with his invention of the assembly line. That night when I fell asleep, I had a dream about the years I'd spent in factories in China. I awoke the next morning with visions of spinning parts and shining metal floating through my head. I found that I could recall details about those years that I hadn't been able to for decades. I thought to myself, No wonder I came up with the "personal factory" idea for my business. Working in factories had ingrained not just the knowledge but also the visceral experience of manufacturing into my brain and body.

That day, I felt even more convinced that I should build a technology company to enable the "personal factory." This was my destiny, I realized, my calling as an entrepreneur. I could see where it came from—the depths of my subconscious. For the first time since volunteering to create a business, I felt confident that I could actually do it because I had found my reason why.

The Chinese have a saying: "Puppies don't know yet to be afraid of tigers." In English we say, "You aren't afraid of what you don't know." I moved forward with the founding of Geomagic in a manner that may have seemed courageous to some. In truth, I was more like an innocent pup stumbling around a tiger's den in the dark: I had little sense of the risks I was taking.

As soon as I left NCSA, I realized how much I had been taking for granted. All at once, I had nothing: no office, no phone, no computer, no lawyers, no accountant, and no money. Herbert and I put in some of our own savings to get things started.

Our first order of business was to find a suitable name before we incorporated. I went to the library and checked out a book about naming and trademarking. It said that either you could make up a word—such as Xerox, Kodak, or Kinko's—or you could name your company by two common words that had nothing to do with each other. Apple Computer was a prime example of the latter: apples have zero connection to computers.

It was a rainy evening in Champaign, and the wind smashed against our windows as Herbert and I lay in bed dreaming up names. On the wall across from our bed hung a painting of colorful raindrops by Austrian artist Friedensreich Hundertwasser.

"How about Raindrop Geometrics," Herbert suggested.

"I love it," I responded with excitement. "Raindrops are points in space, and they form interesting shapes when they meet. This is a poetic version of what we want to do."

The corporate attorney who helped us to register the company didn't like "Geometrics"; he thought it sounded too technical. We settled on Raindrop Geomagic, and incorporated the company under that name. Years later, we dropped "Raindrop" because it was too long a name and people would end up using the abbreviation RGI, which I disliked. We couldn't get "raindrop" as the domain name, but we had secured geomagic.com. It proved confusing for trade shows and company listings because people were not sure whether to look us up under R or G. Naming a company well is tricky, I learned, but not nearly so complicated as running one.

At the start, it seemed that Herbert and I were the perfect partners to found the company together. He had depth and I had breadth. He was the mastermind behind the technology and I focused on developing the applications and markets. He could stay in academia and bring home a regular paycheck while I risked everything to start the company.

Although we used Herbert's mathematical insights and elegant algorithms to build our software at the beginning, it soon became clear that he wasn't interested in the business issues. Solving real-world problems was too messy for his academic research. He was a theoretician who preferred spending his time contemplating elegant proofs of unsolved problems while his head floated above the clouds. He declined working for the company, but remained involved with Geomagic as an adviser. He never questioned my judgment or attempted to alter my decisions. When things got tough, he always offered his wisdom and support with an air of detached collectedness.

With our own savings as the initial cash investment, I hired two MBA students and naively asked them for a business plan in two weeks. They looked at me as though I had four heads. "Two weeks?" they gasped. It took three months and stock options for them to deliver. I enrolled in an entrepreneurship class—clearly, I needed to learn business management skills on my own.

Next, I hired two technical students for software development— Mike Facello and Dmitry Nekhayev, who remain at Geomagic today—and rented an affordable office space. It was an incubator in a manure field the agriculture department was using to experiment with human fertilizer. Every time I walked in the door, the putrid smell reminded me of the open latrines from my childhood in the dorms at NUAA. I laughed to myself: I had come so far, yet here I was again, literally in a pile of shit.

I marvel sometimes at the magic of the software our talented team created. The process started with digitally capturing a real-world object using a 3D scanner. The dots—also called a "point cloud"—gathered from the scanner were not projected onto a flat plane, but rather floated in virtual space. Geomagic software then magically linked the dots together into a coherent 3D digital model representing the shape of the object. Our algorithms allowed us to reach inside every nook and cranny of any object, no matter its size or complexity.

It is difficult to convey the mathematical power behind the software. Imagine making a model of a car from beads. The software's job was to figure out how to string the beads—of a point cloud—

together with a single thread, without ever crossing back over. The resulting model not only retained the overall shape of the object, but also recognized its functional components, such as doors, wheels, and body. All this could be computed in a matter of minutes. For many customers, we had reduced the process of scanning a physical object and creating a digital model from weeks to minutes.

⌒

We didn't know how much money was needed to run the company, but bills kept arriving more quickly than Herbert's University of Illinois paychecks. Our first employees courageously offered to chip in some of their savings, but it wasn't enough. I applied for a bank loan. The loan officer took one step into our stinky incubator office, gave a sniff, and walked out with her nose held high.

Hong and her husband, Anselm Bischoff, had a popular and successful specialty retail store, Bischoff's Shades of the West in old-town Scottsdale. Hong was excited about my new venture. She and Anselm offered me a great deal of practical advice and, when we needed it, cash. They were Geomagic's first investors. My younger sister's support meant the world to me—and it did to her as well. For the first time in our lives, I was following in Hong's footsteps and she was able to help me, instead of the other way around.

Development costs came in higher than we'd expected. I learned that it took far more people and time to develop a commercial software product than an academic prototype. We hired more developers: Tobi Gloth came to us from Germany; Yates Fletcher, a brilliant mathematician, joined us from the Sun Microsystems graphics group; Thomas Jensen had valuable experience in medical imaging; and Steve Perkins became the technical support director with the ability to make every customer fall in love with Geomagic. I am indebted to these early employees for their passion, brilliance, and loyalty. In addition, there were lawyers' fees for patents and trademarks, incorporating, taxes, liability, and all the other business terminology I was just beginning to learn about in my entrepreneurship class. We needed to raise money fast, this time from seasoned angel investors.

I had no idea that it would be so easy.

"Imagine your mother's face as she receives a 3D print of her grandson's first sculpture project," I told a room full of angel investors and a panel of venture capitalists at the start of my ten-minute pitch at a Chicago investment conference in 1997.

"Now imagine viewing a 3D animation of your daughter's teeth as they move into a perfect smile—on the day of her first visit to the orthodontist . . .

"Imagine walking into a shoe store, getting your foot scanned, and returning the next day to pick up your custom-fitted hiking boots . . .

"Now imagine your orthopedic surgeon printing a 3D model of your prosthetic knee, a perfect fit, a week before your surgery . . .

"While these examples may seem like dreams, Geomagic will transform them into reality."

After my presentation, people bounced around me like chattering balls of energy. Each one had a story to share: "My left foot is bigger than my right, so shoes never fit me"; "I hate going to the dentist, but this technology would change that"; "Have you ever thought about using your 3D processors for . . . ?" Ideas tumbled into the room. It seemed that we had tapped into an unmet market need.

Donald Kurasch, an attorney and private investor from Chicago, handed me a check on the spot to make sure he got in on the first round. Peter Fuss, a venture capitalist and the former president of Tellabs, followed me out the door and engaged me in a long conversation about our technology and its opportunities. He later became an investor and board member. Within a month, we had closed a $1 million round of private placement funding.

I felt happy. There was a deep current of humanity in our vision that resonated with people. I couldn't believe strangers would give us money so easily. At the same time, I felt an enormous sense of responsibility and a little bit of uneasiness. Although I knew why I had started the company and what we could offer—mass customization software for the benefit of humanity—I had little clue as to how we were going to deliver on our promises or pay back the money and trust given to us by our earliest investors.

But never mind—our employees and I felt much more excitement than fear. Geomagic was a real company now.

My daughter was four years old when Geomagic got off the ground in 1997. I may have had my hands full running a tech start-up, but no one could get my attention better than Xixi. She was at an age where she wanted engagement, and she knew how to get it. Her smile started my day, and her hugs melted my worries away.

"I love having Xixi," Herbert teased me. "I get to enjoy fantastic home-cooked dinners because she loves your cooking." I laughed at his indirect encouragement. The fact of the matter is, if Xixi hadn't demanded my full awareness, our family life and health would have suffered. It was truly a blessing to have a child so young when I started Geomagic: she was my priority, and Herbert and I both benefited from that. Without her, I would have worked every minute of my waking hours, including weekends. Being a mother also gave me deep respect for and understanding of other employees who already had families or wanted to start one.

Taking Xixi to the playground was a pleasure for me. While other moms sat on the park benches chatting with one another, I climbed onto the equipment with Xixi and played alongside her. One day, when it was raining, I took Xixi to an indoor playground. As usual, I tried all the activities: I bounced with Xixi in the padded jumping room, pulled out toys and tested each one, and scrambled like a monkey onto the climbing gym. Then, when I went down the covered spiral slide, I got stuck. The turn was too small for me. I called for help. A few kids came sliding down behind me and pushed at my back with their legs, but it wasn't enough to dislodge me. Finally, two of the mothers came over. They reached inside to grab hold of my feet and yanked me out onto the cushioned floor. We all collapsed into hysterical laughter.

"You're like a kid yourself," one of the women observed once we had caught our breaths. It struck me just how true her statement was. Half of my childhood had been stolen away from me. Now I was getting to re-create it with my own daughter. I knew Xixi loved my involvement, but all at once I realized that my behavior was doing just as much for my well-being as it was for hers.

I made many mistakes in the early years of Geomagic, some of which were quite funny. Running a start-up is not for the faint of heart. I love how Reid Hoffman, the founder of LinkedIn, describes it: "You jump off a cliff and assemble an airplane on the way down."

In 1998, a year after we got Geomagic started, we demonstrated our technology at SIGGRAPH, a premier computer graphics conference. At our booth, I met Mark Keenan, an Intel executive who invited me to present at headquarters. He said that he was intrigued by our technology because it pushed the limits of the central processing unit, or CPU.

"Should I bring my computer?" I asked. I wanted to feel confident that the software would perform smoothly when I demonstrated it. Also, I knew of Intel as a chip manufacturer; perhaps they didn't have computers everywhere in their office, I thought. Mark said yes.

As I was preparing to leave, I realized that I had not thought about how on earth I was going to get my heavy desktop computer and monitor from Illinois to California. We didn't have laptops to demo our software in those days; they weren't powerful enough machines.

I bought a padded suitcase, put my desktop computer and a small monitor inside, and hauled it with me to the airport, where I checked it along with the rest of my luggage to San Jose. By the time I arrived, the suitcase wheels had broken off. Luckily, the computer and monitor had not been damaged.

I was staying with my friend David Knapp, the founder of a microchip design company in San Jose. He was surprised when I showed up with a large broken suitcase and a forlorn look on my face.

"What are you doing?" he asked.

"I'm going to Intel to give a demo, and they said I needed to bring a computer," I said.

David laughed. "I kind of doubt it," he said under his breath. But he was such a good friend that he figured out a solution. True to his maker's nature, David had a wood and metal workshop in his garage. Stealing the plastic wheels off his large garbage bin, he fashioned me a rudimentary wooden trolley. The next morning we loaded the trolley, computer, and monitor into the trunk of my rental car, and off I drove to Intel.

I pulled up in front of the high-tech giant's sparkling headquarters a half hour later. As soon as I stepped into the lobby, I wanted to run away. Here I was at one of the most advanced computer companies in the world, pulling behind me a squeaky homemade trolley. As I made my way from the front door to the reception desk, I could see people's jaws dropping.

The receptionist called my contact, Mark, down to the front

desk. Just as David had, he tried his best not to laugh out loud when he saw me.

"What happened?" Mark asked.

"My suitcase broke, so my friend made me this trolley to carry the computer."

"Why did you bring it?"

"You told me to." I started to giggle.

He winked. "I thought you were going to bring your laptop."

Several people stopped and looked at my trolley in amazement.

"Well, did you bring the software?" Mark continued.

"Yes."

"Does it work on a PC?"

"Of course," I replied.

"Then I've got you covered," Mark said. He had the receptionist store the trolley and suitcase with my computer in the closet behind the desk. We went upstairs carrying only a CD.

The software installed perfectly on the state-of-the-art desktop in Intel's conference room, although I think my trolley left more of an impression than did Geomagic's technology. Today, I wish I had kept the trolley as a memento, but David disposed of it after I returned to his house. He needed the wheels back for his garbage bin.

In 1999, we identified two potential launch partners with different manufacturing challenges: Boeing and Mattel. Boeing's airplane parts were large, technically demanding, and difficult to replace. Mattel's toys included an enormous variety of shapes, from Hot Wheels to jungle animals. Both could benefit from 3D imaging and printing technology.

As soon as the beta version of our software was ready, I made trips to both Boeing and Mattel to do demos. This time I knew better than to bring a computer along; we made sure the software had been preinstalled on the companies' machines prior to my arrival.

I traveled to Mattel first. My knees shook as my contact introduced me to the twenty men gathered in the room: VP of manufacturing, VP of information technology, VP of products, and so on. I hadn't expected such a high-powered group; I'd thought I was meeting a handful of engineers. A Mattel engineer loaded the data for one of their toy horses, which he had scanned. Within five minutes, Geomagic software had threaded the numbers together to create a complete 3D digital model of the horse on their computer. A designer could rotate it to view every angle, zoom in to see small details, and modify the design before sending it to production. I could tell they were excited because they all began speaking at once, talking about how useful this technology would be. A feeling of pride washed over me as it had when I'd turned on the lights for the workers at the Chinese factory decades before. It was a magical moment to have these people, whom I respected greatly, marvel at Geomagic technology, which our team had created.

I set off for Boeing with some degree of confidence. Their facility was located outside of Seattle. When I stepped into the meeting room, the audience appeared far less intimidating than the one at Mattel. There were only four engineers present, all with PhDs in mathematics. They wore jeans and gentle expressions on their faces.

"What do you have to show us?" one of them asked. I told them about Geomagic software. One of the scientists gave me a disc with the data from a 3D scan of a damaged door that had come off a Boeing 747 jet. I popped it into their computer and, just as it had with the toy horse data, our software worked its magic. I showed the engineers the 3D replica of the door from every different angle. Unlike at Mattel, I also attempted to explain some of the computational geometry algorithms behind the software, which I had learned from Herbert. I figured that, as mathematicians themselves, they would appreciate the insider knowledge.

A silver-haired man in a crisp collared shirt interrupted me. "I'd like to try something," he said, showing me on his laptop the image of a cube with a cylinder inside of it. The cube had only corner points and edges like an outline, no walls. The cylinder was composed of just a few simple lines as well. "Let's try to wrap this," he said, loading the data onto the computer with Geomagic's software installed on it.

It seemed like it ought to have been an easy enough task, far simpler than replicating a toy horse or an airplane door. But the Geomagic software failed to reproduce the cube and cylinder correctly. When I saw the messy lines that appeared on the screen, I felt like melting into the floor from embarrassment. All my childhood insecurities flashed in front of my eyes: I was onstage, declaring that I was a nobody. I'd taught myself math only a few years ago. How had I dared to think that I could make software to withstand the test of an advanced math group at an iconic American company?

Steadying myself against the conference room table, I apologized and asked the group for a quick break so I could consult with our technical people. I ran outside with my cell phone and called an engineer back home in Illinois.

"Dmitry!" I exclaimed with relief when he picked up his office phone. "I need your help." I explained what had happened just moments before.

Dmitry answered with an almost cheerful voice. "Oh, Ping. That's kind of evil. Of course you failed! We developed the software for dense point clouds representing complex shapes. With scan data, an object is covered entirely with data points. That guy knew the software would fail if he gave you a wire frame with only a few corner points. Just the outline of the cube and cylinder isn't enough data; the software is not designed to handle this.

"Think of a printed picture of a person's face," Dmitry continued. "The colored pixels have to completely cover the paper. If they don't—if you have only a few pixels—then you won't be able to make out the image of the person's face at all."

"Thank you, Dmitry," I said. "You're a lifesaver."

I understood immediately what was going on. I was married to a mathematician, after all. This is what mathematicians do: they are trained to falsify assumptions. A good mathematician often focuses on finding the one case that fails rather than all cases that work. The silver-haired Boeing man wasn't being mean; it was just the way his mind worked.

I walked back into the conference room feeling more comfortable and confident. I said to the man who had given me the cube and cylinder test, "You're so sharp that you could identify right away the case in which our software wouldn't work. Only a mathematician would do that."

"You're right. You are in the Boeing Math group, after all," the man said, handing me a coffee mug with their logo on it. He laughed loudly, without a hint of derision, and I joined in along with the others. By the time I was ready to leave, they had come up with a dozen ideas for how our software could be useful at Boeing. They also offered suggestions for how we could improve the software so that it could handle special cases.

After those visits, both Boeing and Mattel placed purchase orders for Geomagic software prior to its official release. They were invaluable in helping us understand market needs.

The experience taught me the importance of working with customers who will use the new technology. I realized that we are not, nor should we be, the smartest people in the room. Customers appreciate creativity, authenticity, and honesty. They buy from us not because we impress them but because we have something of value to offer and we are willing to listen to their feedback to improve our products continuously. It is far more important to be interested in the customers' needs than to be interesting.

Our software was first put to use for 3D scanning and manufacturing of Winnie the Pooh and Barbie, and the door of a United commercial jet that just happened to be of the same vintage as the one that had first brought me to America. In the process of working with Boeing, I learned that, on an airplane, even mass-produced items are not identical. As soon as planes fly, variations begin to emerge, as each aircraft is subjected to different stresses and environmental forces. Over time, each develops, in essence, a form or "personality" of its own. Geomagic software could scan the entire aircraft body in order to create a digital replica of it. The replica was used to replace damaged parts, such as doors. Thanks to Geomagic technology, the replacement parts would fit the timeworn aircraft's body precisely, keeping the plane flying—which was the only way the airlines could make money off it. The speed Geomagic software provided was critical to making airplane maintenance and repair more cost-effective.

Mattel had launched a "Build Your Own Barbie" Web site. Xixi was five years old and spent hours creating her very own doll: selecting face shape, eye color, hair color, clothes, shoes, and accessories. Once she had finished, she clicked the big pink button that read "PRINT." Our home printer hammered away, cheerfully spitting out a colorful picture of Xixi's Barbie just moments later.

"Oh, no!" Xixi cried. "I want my Barbie doll, not a picture of her."

"Xixi," I said, "this is why Mommy is working so hard. We are creating technology so that you can print your actual Barbie doll, not just a picture."

Mattel sent me many toys during our initial collaboration, some of which had yet to be officially released, others of which were test concepts that never made it to market. I became very popular with

Xixi's friends. They came to know me as "the mom who makes and gives away cool toys."

⁓

I have heard some people say that they want to start a company because they don't want to work for anyone else. This is one of the myths of entrepreneurship. The truth is, an entrepreneur works for everyone but himself or herself.

When I was an employee at Bell Labs, I worked for myself: I strove for knowledge, career development, and personal fulfillment, and was pleased when a paycheck showed up in return. But when I started running Geomagic, I found myself working for many others: employees, investors, and customers. It reminded me of motherhood; both are serious, long-term commitments. People often say that a woman fully matures when she becomes a mother, and I believe there is some truth to that statement. The first time I heard my baby crying in the night, I woke up and realized that, from now on, I would always put this little creature's well-being before my own. Being an entrepreneur pushed me even further in terms of what I thought I could do and how much I could care.

In many ways, I stumbled into becoming founder and CEO of Geomagic as I had stumbled into becoming a mother to Hong at age eight. In both instances, I had very little preparation for the role I'd been given. And in both situations, I felt heavy with the weight of my responsibility for those who now depended on me. Having to make payroll for Geomagic employees and cover any and all expenses every month, I developed a fresh perspective on accountability.

The upside was that I was making personal progress by leaps and bounds, gaining confidence with every milestone Geomagic achieved. During the Cultural Revolution, it was beaten into my brain that I was a nobody who didn't even deserve to be loved. Now a wife and mother at the helm of her own company, I finally felt as though I were somebody. Even more important, I came to see that *everybody* is somebody. But no one will hand this belief to us; it must come from within our own hearts.

SIX

Who
Can Say
What
Is Good
or Bad?

GOOD PEOPLE CAN MAKE BAD
CHOICES: 2000–2001

I FELT OUT of place as soon as I entered the air-conditioned splendor of the Phoenician hotel lobby in Scottsdale, Arizona—an expanse of glass and waterfalls that overlooked a shimmering emerald golf course. It was January 2000, and I had never been a guest at a five-star hotel before. It would have been easier for me to stay with Hong and her husband, who happened to live nearby, but my colleagues had advised me to stay here. I was attending a prestigious technology conference put on by Morgan Stanley, which had done over $100 billion in deals with some of the biggest names in the high-tech industry in the past year alone. This was my chance to "rub shoulders" with CEOs I had only read about in magazines, one of my investors had counseled when he'd secured me an invite.

In the spring of 1999, after establishing Boeing and Mattel as launch partners, Geomagic had raised $6.5 million in venture capital funding from Franklin Street Partners' Paul Rizzo, the legendary CFO and vice chairman of IBM. At that time, we already had an additional private placement of $1 million from a friends-and-families round in 1997, the year Herbert and I had founded the company. My primary objectives were to craft the vision of Geomagic, set it up with the right culture, and put the company on the road to explosive growth with adequate capital in place.

When I checked into the hotel, a bellman took all my bags, even my laptop, because I didn't know that I was allowed to keep any. I then found my way to the conference reception desk. The woman working there handed me a preprinted name tag that read: "Mr. Ping Fu."

"Excuse me," I said, clearing my throat. "My badge should read 'Ms.'"

"Only the CEO of Geomagic is registered for the conference," she replied politely, glancing up from her paperwork. "Spouses are not invited to the meeting, though you are welcome for the social hour, of course."

"I am the CEO," I corrected her. "I am Ms. Ping Fu."

As soon as she had processed my remark, the receptionist flushed a deep magenta hue. She stood up from her chair, apologized profusely, and disappeared behind a nearby curtain. A few minutes later, she reappeared with a freshly minted and accurate name tag in hand.

I understood her confusion better the moment I walked into the hall where the opening reception was being held. Arrayed before me was a tapestry of a thousand men, all dressed in black: hip young entrepreneurs in Steve Jobs–style black turtlenecks and ponytails;

tall men with blue eyes and desert sunburns who moved about with the ease of athletes in their black slacks and collared shirts; gray-haired men in black sports jackets who called one another by their first names, as if they were lifelong friends. Everyone seemed to know exactly who mattered and why—except for me. The sound of ice tinkling in glasses and cards being drawn out of wallets overwhelmed me. Voices overlapped, knowing just when to break into one another's sentences and when to laugh.

My breathing grew shallow and my mind froze. I felt small, shy, insignificant, and irrelevant. I wasn't big enough to "rub shoulders" with anyone—literally or metaphorically speaking. For many long moments, I stood against a wall, utterly invisible to the men who networked their way around me. One fellow across the room seemed equally out of sorts, hands tucked nervously into his suit pockets. We made eye contact, but neither of us summoned the courage to approach the other.

Eventually, two men talked to me. The first stood out from the crowd because he looked like a teenager and wore a red tie with his black shirt. I was forty-one, old enough to be his mother. He fumbled awkwardly as he reached out to shake my hand while attempting to balance his wineglass on a plate filled with cheese.

"Are you Chinese?" he asked after we had exchanged names. The question was far more complicated than he realized.

"I'm an American citizen," I answered. He lost interest and moved on.

The second man was a waiter carrying a tray decked with wineglasses. "White or red, madame?" he asked.

Wine gave me migraines, so I declined, asking for a glass of water instead. When I overheard a group of guys talking about "tee times" a short while later, I went in search of tea that I never did find, only coffee. I didn't even drink the same beverages as these men.

My orphaned upbringing at NUAA had taught me to be comfortable with silence and feeling like an outsider, but this was different. An alarming loneliness rose up inside me, a pang as sharp as when I was a lost little girl who had just arrived in Nanjing. You don't even know how to "break the ice," a nasty voice in my head whispered. How do you expect to run a company?

The next day, we were invited to pitch our ideas before an audience of fellow entrepreneurs and venture capitalists. The high-tech industry and the country as a whole were still on a dot-com high—the bubble wouldn't burst until a few months later. I believed strongly in my vision for Geomagic, but it was nothing like Netscape's or that of the other Internet start-ups at the conference. We were developing software for manufacturing companies, which people here tended to dismiss as the "old economy."

Nevertheless, I spoke passionately and confidently—at least the public confessions of my youth had taught me to conquer stage fright. I painted the audience a picture of hand-designed products coming down factory assembly lines, each one unique, each one a perfect fit for a specific person.

"Someday, thanks to Geomagic technology, a patient will go into open-heart surgery knowing that he will receive a heart valve shaped exactly like his own, not one that has been manufactured on a mass scale and has to be ordered in sizes. Someday, we will help make products that don't wind up crossing the globe only to get buried in landfills," I said. "With Geomagic technology, companies can focus on making products that people want, not junk that none of us need."

I received a warm response from the crowd, which fueled my confidence in Geomagic. Yet, oddly, I felt more uncertain than ever about my ability to lead. The mechanics of running a fast-growing company seemed daunting, given my limited entrepreneurial experience, and there is really no class you can take on how to become a CEO. Furthermore, I was a newcomer to the business world and an immigrant—I didn't know how to fit in. These insecurities were only reinforced when I walked into the closing cocktail gathering that evening: I had chosen an elegant, long black dress, while everyone else wore jeans.

Clearly, I was the wrong person to run a company. I needed a tall, smart, charming white guy to take charge of Geomagic. Leaving the conference with that realization early the next day, I felt proud for recognizing my own limitations. I would not let my ego get in the way of building a great company that created value for the world.

Jon Field was charismatic, incredibly intelligent, and came highly recommended by Peter Fuss, an independent board member whom I respected a great deal. Jon had degrees in math, philosophy, and business. He had held an executive position at IBM, where he had managed business divisions with revenues exceeding $600 million. Recently, he had successfully sold a start-up company.

Impressed with his qualifications and personality, the board and I hired Jon to serve as president and CEO of Geomagic in the spring of 2000. With a sigh of relief, I stepped down to assume the role of chief technology officer while still serving as chairman of the board. I felt confident that my plan of combining a capable executive with significant venture capital funding and innovative technology was a sure bet. Geomagic was on its way to becoming the next big thing.

Within months, with Jon Field at the helm, Geomagic had an office in the Research Triangle Park (RTP) in North Carolina. All of our Illinois people except the receptionist, twelve in total, had come with us. We moved the company from Champaign to RTP because it was a business-friendly place for a start-up for several reasons. Here, we had better access to a highly educated population, thanks to the three universities located nearby. The area was consistently rated one of the best places to live in the United States—hence recruiting talent from other states was easier. Investors and capital were more readily available. Finally, neither rent nor employment costs were nearly as high as they were in red-hot Silicon Valley.

On a personal level, the move made sense for my family. Herbert had landed an art and science chair at Duke University, which made him happy. While I preferred to live in a big city, Herbert preferred small towns, so this area presented a good compromise. Anyway, after living in rural Champaign, Raleigh-Durham felt like a city in comparison. Xixi enrolled in Carolina Friends School, which fostered curiosity and an intimate community. She loved it. We bought a house on a quiet cul-de-sac surrounded by pine trees in Chapel Hill.

I was ready for the next chapter of Geomagic's story to unfold in a new city, with a new CEO. I experienced a sense of relief, feeling as though I could relax just a little for the first time in years.

⌒

I read somewhere that men learn from studying theories, whereas women learn by observing others. Whatever the truth of that assertion, I took full advantage during the next year to watch Jon Field in action. I had run a low-key operation in Illinois with one salesperson. Jon set up sales incentives and brought in teams of confident salespeople with impressive track records. Colorful charts appeared on our office walls listing the *Fortune* 500 companies that were reviewing our technology. Within a year, our office was filled with spanking-new equipment and over fifty employees. With all the laughter and chatter, the air felt hotter and the sound levels several decibels higher.

I was filled with hope that Geomagic would grow fast. This hope was backed up not by data but by blind trust. Many years later, Bo Burlingham articulated the different ways of running a company in his book *Small Giants*. In it he talks about "command and control" versus "trust and track," and encourages the leaders of small businesses to practice the latter. I realized that back when I'd handed over the reins of Geomagic to Jon Field, I had practiced trust without the track.

My naïveté in hiring and knowing what it takes to run a start-up business almost killed the company. While Jon indeed had a top-notch education and a solid track record in terms of building a network division at IBM and the sale of a successful start-up, he had almost no prior experience *growing* a start-up—one that had no brand awareness and no steady revenue stream. We both soon discovered that his job at Geomagic demanded a skill set far different from the ones he had developed in his career so far.

Six months after Jon had assumed leadership of Geomagic, we had few paying customers and a dozen highly paid, heavily traveled direct salespeople. We were rapidly depleting our cash with no revenues and no visible sales pipeline. Didn't that matter? I asked in my role as chairman of the board.

The truth of the matter was we were all caught up in the dot-com bubble mentality; traditional business acumen was being challenged. Jack Welch, the famed CEO of GM, was poking fun at it by raving about "DestroyYourself.com." The new economy was all about market share, so Geomagic's executives focused on building value by creating market awareness. Our CFO assured me that I needn't be alarmed; this is exactly what our investors wanted us to do.

I nodded in agreement, but a skeptical voice had awakened inside my head, and it wasn't totally appeased by these responses. I began to worry that perhaps Geomagic had taken a wrong turn. Still, I wanted to be conscientious in supporting the CEO and the team we had hired. So I kept silent.

Another six months flew by. At that point, we had blown through nearly $6 million in investment capital, had borrowed $1 million in equipment leasing, and yet still had negligible sales to show for it.

The board members asked about the reasons for this predicament at the next board meeting.

"Well, the salespeople have proven track records," Jon explained. "The problem is that the product is premature. It's hard to sell a product when people aren't clear about how to use it."

He didn't say it to put me down, but it felt as if Jon had just punched me in the gut. Could it really be the case that our inventions were so undesirable? That certainly had not seemed to be the case early on when I was testing the concepts. At conferences where I presented or spoke, it seemed that audiences responded positively to our technology.

Looking back, I can see there was much truth to what Jon said. What I didn't understand was the difference between technology and product, and product versus market. I was still a technical founder who thought that superior technology was all that a company needed in order to succeed. Still, I took Jon's feedback seriously. As CTO, I buried myself in improving the product, asking the sales team for feedback about what customers liked and disliked, and making the recommended changes.

Our biggest problem, however, was not an inadequate product. It was the market. We were operating on the cutting edge of technology within a small market segment that had no visibility. We learned later that it always takes a long time to create a new market in such cases. Our software depended on 3D scanning hardware to collect data, and yet there were not many units sold each year. Three-dimensional scanners were difficult to buy, hard to get support for, and overpriced. It would have been like Microsoft trying to sell its software packages before many PCs had been sold. For the time being, we were stuck without many potential buyers. I continued to watch from the sidelines as the company plowed forward with what I considered to be wasteful spending, garnering only limited results.

In December 2000, Jon asked me to meet him at a coffee shop in Durham, close to the Duke University campus. It was a gray day, chilly and windy.

"Ping, I have bad news for you," Jon said, clearing his throat. "We have only six months of cash left."

"What do you mean? We raised $6.5 million eighteen months ago and took out a $1 million equipment loan. Is all that money gone?" My head spun. I should have known our situation was so bleak. I would have, if only I had read the quarterly financial statement.

Jon continued with a calm, matter-of-fact tone to his voice, watching me carefully for my reaction. "It gets worse, Ping. We also have to lay off half of Geomagic's employees. The cash will support us for six months only if we operate at 50 percent of our current expenses."

I was speechless. Our eyes locked.

"I will help you with the layoffs. But there is only one thing I can do now to help you with the cash situation. I suggest that I accept a job offer at Align Technology, which will save you my severance pay. Do you agree with this approach?" Jon asked carefully.

"You are leaving us? You are leaving me now, with no money and only half our staff?" I asked in disbelief.

Jon stared into his coffee mug. "Yes, I think it is the right thing to do. You should speak to the board about this. I will resign as CEO and from the board of directors as soon as you do. I am sorry, Ping."

Why don't you talk to the board yourself? I wanted to say. Then I remembered that I was the chairman of the board. I slowly nodded.

I sat for several minutes in silence, sipping my tea with vacant eyes. I was so shocked by Jon's words that I couldn't think straight.

I wanted to hate him, to shout at him, but I knew that ultimately I was responsible for what had happened. I had made the choice to step down, I had hired Jon, and I was part of the executive team who had agreed to his business decisions. I felt ill. Geomagic was about to go under, and many of the people who had trusted me enough to uproot their lives and move to North Carolina were going to lose their jobs.

As I considered Jon's remarks, my mind could find no other way out of the current situation than what he had just proposed. Jon had been working closely with Align to form a business partnership. The company was interested in using Geomagic technology to manufacture clear custom orthodontics devices—just as I had envisioned in my very first investment pitch. It made sense for him to accept their job offer. I told him to let go of the people he absolutely had to cut and then leave. I left the coffee shop in a daze.

That night I didn't sleep a wink. Anxious thoughts raced through my head: What about all the employees who were about to lose the careers they loved? What would they tell their families? How would the investors respond? What about my sister and her husband, who had provided the initial seed money to found Geomagic? How would I ever repay them? I ran the numbers and realized that I couldn't make enough money in my whole lifetime to pay everyone back. I had a panic attack, soaking my bedsheets with cold sweat.

One potential female investor, Sonya Wang, had warned me before I hired Jon that while he had experience selling a start-up, he had no experience building one. She had predicted that this could be a major risk for Geomagic. She had insisted that I remain CEO or else she would not invest. Why hadn't I listened to her? Why had I stepped down when no one had forced me to?

At some point during the early daylight hours, I had an epiphany: I had given the leadership of Geomagic away because I had been scared of taking responsibility for the $6.5 million we had raised. I simply hadn't had enough confidence in myself. On the surface, I had been proud of myself for putting my ego aside to step down as CEO, but what really had been guiding me was fear. Borrowing that kind of money and realizing that you might not ever be able to pay it back can be terrifying for anyone, but this was especially true for me. I had grown up in Communist China with mere pennies to spend and in a culture that taught me about how having money was wrong. It dawned on me that my fear of managing such a large amount of investment capital was rooted deep inside me because of my past. Instead of confronting my fear, I had let it win, subconsciously. Everyone has blind spots—this was one of mine.

Feeling nauseated and disappointed in myself, I walked into Xixi's room and watched her as she slept. I had given birth to her. My responsibility to her was unconditional and I was fully committed. Yet, while I had given birth to Geomagic as well, I had abandoned it in a moment of insecurity. I felt that my integrity was being tested. I was not a quitter. Now I must take responsibility for Geomagic as I would for my daughter.

When I wandered downstairs the next morning with deep dark circles under my eyes, Herbert tried to comfort me. "You can always go back to a university job," he said.

"No, I can't," I said. "I already backed down as CEO. I can't retreat twice."

Hong and Anselm, as well as our other financial backers—those who had believed in us from the start—hadn't just invested in a *company*, I realized. They had invested in *me*. Our employees who had followed me from Illinois to North Carolina were like family. I would not let them down.

When I was eleven, I had fainted rather than drop out of a marathon race forced upon us by the Red Guard. At its core, this situation was no different. I felt grateful for the traits I had been forced to cultivate as a child: fierce determination, curiosity, and kindness had served me well in the past. I hoped they would come to my rescue once more.

The first action I took was to call a meeting of the board as chairman. I had to inform them at once that Jon was leaving and that the company was in dire straits financially. The board members knew about our cash flow problem, so they were not terribly surprised. But they were shocked to hear of Jon's decision to leave for a job at Align Technology.

I took responsibility for being part of Geomagic's failure and their disappointment. Once I had answered their initial questions, I asked the board to give me a chance at saving the company. "Let me return to run Geomagic," I said.

One board member put a question on the table. "You've had a very experienced management team and capable CEO at the helm of this company for the past year and a half," he said. "What makes you think you can succeed where they failed?"

For a moment, the phrase I was made to repeat as a child in China so many years before flashed through my mind: *I'm a nobody.* My instinct was to back down. But I pushed that thought away by reminding myself of my more recent mantra. No, I'm not a nobody, I said to myself. I am somebody.

I took a deep breath and said calmly to my board, "I'm not asking for your complete faith in me. But I am asking you to give me a fair shot at this. Anyway, I'm the best bet you have. Jon is gone, but I am here."

I requested three months to get Geomagic back on track. With little to lose and some respect for my tenacity, the board agreed. I was CEO once more.

Next, I gathered all of Geomagic's remaining employees into the large conference room in our office. Standing there before a staff half the size of what it had been a few days earlier, I knew they were all wondering whether our company was a sinking ship. I was also aware that my facial expressions were like a weather report, and that everyone was watching closely for signs of a hurricane. When I was a waitress, I learned to calm impatient customers with open communication and a caring attitude. So while I was nervous and uncertain inside, I kept my demeanor steady and relaxed. I told my employees the truth: yes, the company was in trouble. My first loyalty during this time of crisis was to them, I explained, and my second to our investors.

Then I said, "I need your help."

Without sharing the details of my life story, I told them that I had lived under conditions of torture, poverty, and abuse during my childhood in China. "I can handle pressure," I said. "In fact, I thrive under challenging circumstances." I also let them know that I was willing to make the necessary personal sacrifices—including putting up my house as collateral and working without a salary—in order to save the company.

With determination, I said, "We can execute a survival plan. We have enough cash to pay everyone a salary for three more months. It will take the next month to go after three potential deals. We should aim to get two to three million in cash in the door. If we can get just one of those three deals closed, with Align Technology, then we'll have sufficient cash for at least six months. If we can secure all three deals, then we can survive for at least a year." I paused.

The employees sat in tense silence.

I continued: "I'm asking you to give us one month. If we are 90 percent there, I'll ask you to stay on for another month. If we're nowhere close to any deals, then I'll pay you one month of severance and let you go. I don't want to get down to the wire and not be able to pay you at all."

In conclusion, I stated an important fact. "Without you, there is no Geomagic."

One of the employees raised his hand. I nodded for him to speak. "That sounds like it will take a miracle," he said.

"Yes, and you are all part of that miracle," I replied. "Cash is king. We need two million to stay alive."

Silence.

My heart pounded. Would the Geomagic family abandon me? I wouldn't fault them if they did—they had families to support, and in a sense I had already abandoned them when I had stepped down as CEO.

"I can't do it without you," I said. "Who will stay?"

Every hand went up.

The financial situation at Geomagic in early 2001 was worse than I'd thought. We had offered employees who had been let go three months of severance pay, which came out of my personal savings account. The bank was calling in a $1 million equipment loan and demanding our patents as collateral. If we gave the bank what they asked for, it would not only force us to close Geomagic's doors, but also render the company valueless in the eyes of potential acquirers. To add insult to injury, the Internet bubble had burst and investors everywhere were losing money. The markets were turning sour on start-ups.

I told Herbert that I wanted to use our house for collateral rather than the company's patents. I also said that I needed almost everything we had saved in our bank account—$250,000 at the time. Herbert didn't bat an eyelash. He agreed to whatever I wanted throughout the crisis.

The challenge wasn't just money. The fallout atmosphere at Geomagic was heavy with anger and resentment. People were mistrustful and pointing fingers. The managers who had joined the company at its inception were capable, passionate, and had great track records in large corporations. Most of them were failing for the first time in their lives and having difficulty handling the stress and strain. My job, in part, was to limit collateral damage, avoid lawsuits, and show compassion for those employees who were bitter about being forced out of the company.

In addition to three months of severance pay, Geomagic guaranteed all the laid-off salespeople commissions for a full year on product sales for customers that they had entered into our sales database. That deal seemed more than fair to me, and I assumed that they would be appreciative. They certainly appeared to be, walking out the door with heavy hearts but also amicable best wishes for our company's success.

There was one employee in particular, Karl, whom I considered a friend. He was one of the first two salespeople we'd hired after moving to North Carolina. One time many months prior, as I was walking into the office, I had fainted due to a terrible migraine and nearly cracked my skull open on the sidewalk. Karl, a former marine, had raced to my aid, carrying me into the office, bringing me back to consciousness, and dressing my wounds. I dreaded letting him go. But Karl, like the newer sales folks, seemed to take the news relatively well. He told me that he'd always enjoyed working for Geomagic—it was the best job he'd ever had.

A few months later, Karl asked me to meet him for lunch at a restaurant near our office. I leapt at the chance to see him and find out how he had been doing. As we ate, Karl shared news with me that he had a lead on a new sales position. Relief washed over me—one less burden to carry on my shoulders. I told Karl about three deals that we were pursuing, which I hoped would save the company.

I received a letter from an attorney a week later demanding that I deliver Karl's unpaid commission or face a lawsuit. Karl had informed the attorney that one of the deals Geomagic was pursuing was with his client, a contact that he had entered into the database. Karl was wrong. He had not delivered this contact, and so we would not owe him any commission on the deal, even if it were to go through.

I felt as though Karl had stomped all over our friendship. First of all, he hadn't asked me over lunch, when the subject had first come up, to clarify who the client was. Why hadn't he just spoken up then? I could have eased his mind within minutes. Second, if he felt he was being wronged, why wouldn't he approach me about it face-to-face? Finally, why would he try to destroy me with a lawsuit when he knew how hard I was struggling to keep the company running?

Saddened by Karl's betrayal, I was about to respond with an equally harsh letter from my attorney. Then I caught myself: If I didn't like what he did to me, why would I behave in the same way? Why wouldn't I ask him about the situation directly? I recalled the time when I had passed out at Geomagic and Karl had cleaned up my bloody face and knees. I had observed him acting with the utmost integrity in sales negotiations. Decent people sometimes could do terrible things when undergoing great stress. Karl is a good guy, I reminded myself. It is simply not his true nature to hurt me so. For as long as I had known him, he was a man of principle.

I picked up the phone and called Karl at once. "What's going on here, Karl?" I asked. "If you had asked me, I would have been happy to let you audit the deal so that you could see for yourself this isn't your client. I am really hurt by your actions."

"Ping, I'm so sorry," Karl replied. "I went out for drinks with an old buddy from the Geomagic sales team and told him about the deals you had mentioned over lunch.

"He said, 'Geomagic owes you a commission!'

"I thought he might be right, but I was too embarrassed to ask you about it. So he offered to have his neighbor, who is a lawyer, write a letter. I agreed to it, but— Ping, I didn't even get to see the letter before it was sent to you. You've always been so good to me. I feel terrible about this whole situation. I'm really sorry."

I accepted Karl's apology and he withdrew the attorney's letter immediately. If I'd had a lawyer contact his attorney, I never would have found out the real story behind his actions. I would have continued to feel betrayed. In that case, I wouldn't have trusted other employees as much going forward. And of course, I would have wasted time and money on a lawsuit. Instead, Karl and I remain friends to this day. I even wrote a letter of support to a Chinese orphanage where he and his wife were adopting a baby girl.

As I dealt with various employee issues during those dark hours, I kept reminding myself: it's all about love. Blaming others, being fearful and angry, acting vengefully, building resentment, destroying trust—these negative responses to trying situations suck us into a downward spiral and sap our energy, like water spinning down a drain. The only way to triumph in business and in life is to love what we do, and love our customers, our colleagues, our investors, and our community. Love even the people who drive us crazy, those who undermine us, and those who fail us, offering them compassion and forgiveness.

I have never been good with spreadsheets. All those rows of numbers make me dizzy. Maybe it's because I didn't go through normal schooling, and so I never did memorize the multiplication tables or properly learn long division. However, I knew that Geomagic needed $2 million to survive. My top priority was securing that cash as quickly as possible.

There were three companies I could approach, all of whom had prior relationships with us: Align Technology, 3D Systems, and Parametric Technology Corporation (PTC). Align seemed the most promising. It had plans to take the company, which manufactured Invisalign clear custom orthodontics devices, public in the near future. Align's problem was that its technology relied heavily on skilled labor. In order to generate a complete set of customized aligners, lab technicians used animation software on computers to manually move each person's teeth, in two-week increments, into a perfect smile. Each client would get approximately forty-eight aligners total: twenty-four for the top arc of teeth and twenty-four for the bottom. In order to meet the needs of its thirty thousand customers, Align had to rely on nine hundred computer operators in Pakistan working between four and eight hours per case to manually create the digital models of each person's teeth. In other words, the company couldn't scale. The manual process was too time consuming and cost prohibitive.

Geomagic's technology would enable Align to automate the process of straightening each customer's teeth. We could reduce the time it took an operator to generate a complete set of aligners for one person from over four hours to just fifteen minutes. Align wanted our technology. By implementing it, Align could scale its business successfully after going public.

I went into negotiations with Align Technology in the spring of 2001. Jon Field had already been talking to them about Geomagic software for several months prior to going to work for them, but he removed himself from the negotiations process because of a conflict of interest. It was time for me to close the deal.

I started out trying to negotiate a contract whereby Align Technology paid Geomagic two dollars for every aligner manufactured. But Align didn't want to pay a per unit royalty. Knowing full well our desperate financial situation, they refused to cave. Instead, they offered a onetime flat-rate payment of $2 million for our technology.

I asked Align to pay us in cash within thirty days. They agreed to do so if we dropped the total fee to $1.8 million. I said yes on the spot and got their signatures before leaving the room.

It was a fantastic deal for Align and they knew it.

I was keenly aware that I had signed a bad contract, from a business perspective, due to the lack of recurring revenue. I could see clearly that we ought to have insisted upon a per unit royalty from Align, or some sort of licensing agreement on an annual basis.

However, my sole focus at that time was getting $2 million in cash into our bank accounts as quickly as possible. We didn't have the luxury of a year or even three months to spend in business negotiations when we were running out of money by the second. I could not hold out until Geomagic and Align had come to the perfect agreement. The bottom line was that if we didn't have the money by the end of the month, Geomagic would have to let go of its remaining employees and shut its doors forever. I was not going to take the risk of not closing this deal—for any reason.

My rational mind was telling me that I should discuss this decision with the sales team and consult with our board members and attorneys. But I chose to ignore the normal process and the fears I had about not doing the right thing. I was more concerned at that moment with the employees who might lose their jobs and the investors who might lose their money if we didn't secure a deal than with my own credibility. My mothering instinct and determination to survive took over. I was willing to take sole responsibility for my actions and face whatever consequences my decision might bring.

PRECIOUS TREASURES: 1966

EVERY NIGHT AS I lay in bed trying to fall asleep during that stressful period when Geomagic was falling to pieces, I would be haunted by images of my grandfather hovering above me. I would see him in my eight-year-old mind's eye as an elegant aging man at the start of the Cultural Revolution. Spring 1966.

My grandfather had a collection of traditional Chinese "scholar arts": inkwells from dynasties past, fans hand painted by famous artists, *zitan* wooden brush holders, chicken-blood stamp stones, and rare books of calligraphy. For two months before I was taken away from our Shanghai home, every night before he went to sleep, my grandfather would pull these objects carefully out of their wrapping papers and examine them. He would touch them delicately, as though they were dear old friends. Then he would select one object to keep on the nightstand next to his bed. The following day, a mask of sorrow covering his usually serene face, he would go out into the streets of Shanghai and sell it for a pittance.

Mao's Red Guard had shut down the farmers' markets and taken control of the city's food supply. Each family was given limited rations of rice, cooking oil, sugar, vegetables, and meat. Sometimes it wasn't enough to feed everyone in my household. A few farmers were selling produce on the black market because they didn't have enough money to support their families. As a merchant-class family, we had always had enough money to eat. But in those days food was increasingly hard to come by. My grandfather knew that if he wasn't willing to part with his precious heirlooms, his family might go hungry. It was a sacrifice he was willing to make.

Each night when my grandfather took out the valuable pieces that he planned to sell the next day, he would describe to me why he loved them. One night, he showed me a fan that had been painted by a famous Chinese opera singer, Mei Lanfang. As he told me the story of how he'd gotten the fan—it had been a gift from his beloved wife, who had gone to extraordinary lengths to purchase it for his sixtieth birthday—he touched his fingers to it gently. Then he held it up to the light and fanned it out, revealing a picture of plum flowers that sparkled like fairy dust.

Another evening, my grandfather drew a small gold nugget out of his pocket and massaged it between his fingers as he spoke. Although it was a simple, rough chunk of metal, he had rubbed it so often that it had developed a fine, smooth finish.

"Once, many years ago," my grandfather explained, "I was walking down the street when I caught notice of a blind man playing the *erhu*"—a traditional Chinese musical instrument. "About three hundred children were gathered around to listen, so I stopped as well. The blind man's music was enchanting. After he finished his song, I left him a few coins, expecting to continue on my way. But the man began tugging at my robe.

"'I want to sell you this gold nugget,' the blind man said. 'Won't you buy it from me? I need the money to feed my children.'

"'No, I don't collect gold nuggets,' I replied, refusing to buy this one from the blind man. I said good-bye and walked away.

"The next day, I saw the same man playing. Once again, I was enchanted by his music and stopped to listen. Once again, the blind man pulled at my robe and asked me to buy his gold nugget, but I refused.

"It went on like this day after day. Finally, on the fifth day, when the blind man begged me to buy the nugget so that he could feed his children, I caved. I probably paid far more than it was worth because I emptied out my pockets and gave the blind man all my cash. But it wasn't about the value of the gold. I simply felt moved to help this gentle soul who made such beautiful music. I wanted him to be able to care for his family."

My grandfather sighed heavily. "Tomorrow, I'll sell this nugget to a pawnshop for maybe seventy yuan—about one one-thousandth what I paid for it. What makes me most sorrowful is not the money. It's the fact that I'll be selling my lucky charm. You see, ever since that day when I bought this gold nugget, I've carried it with me in my pocket and rubbed it to bring our family good luck. That's why it has been polished to this glossy sheen."

At that moment, my grandfather's lips turned up into a heart-breaking smile. "Then again, it seems right, somehow. Buying this nugget was how I once helped a man save his children. Now, in selling it, I'll be saving my own children. I guess this gold nugget has done what it was supposed to do."

A BAD CONTRACT
CAN BE A GOOD DECISION: 2001–2003

THESE MEMORIES OF my grandfather in the final days that I would spend with him before being separated from him forever strengthened my resolve to move forward with the Align deal. A bad contract can be a good decision, I thought. For my grandfather, it was worth selling his prized collector's items for pennies in order to feed his family. Similarly, for me, this contract was about something far more precious than money. It was about the survival of the company and the dream we all shared.

Exactly three months after resuming the CEO role at Geomagic, I called the board of directors together again. I told them that we had landed all three contracts and now had almost $3 million in the bank. Of this, $1.8 million in cash had come from Align Technology. They'd gotten the technology they needed at an attractive price, and we'd gotten the cash we needed to survive.

Paul Rizzo, of Franklin Street Partners and also a Geomagic board member, asked if I had heard of a strategy called "DROOM." It sounded good, so I listened attentively.

"It stands for Don't Run Out Of Money," he said with a chuckle, and the rest of us joined in.

Later that day, we celebrated in the company kitchen with all our employees, knowing that we were safe for at least a year. The room was filled with beer, jokes, and laughter.

"Hey, Ping," our Russian mad scientist Dmitry called out. "We actually didn't believe a word you said about saving the company. But we were not going to let you die alone."

"Yes, let's toast to 'Till death do us part!'" Mike Facello, our director of R&D added, raising his glass. This remark was met by even more laughter.

I was deeply touched. "Wow, our bond at Geomagic is as strong as marriage vows," I said, joining Mike and the others in the toast.

〜

At the end of 2002, I stood at Align Technology's factory in Santa Clara, California, and watched my original vision for Geomagic come to life as thousands of invisible aligners sped down the assembly line. It was a true milestone of the modern era—arguably the first real-world example of mass customization, a revolutionary model for manufacturing in the new millennium. No two aligners were identical. Not only were they fully customized for each person, but also every person had a new set of top and bottom aligners for every two weeks of treatment. These custom devices would be morphing people's teeth in a far less labor-intensive, more elegant, and less painful way than braces ever had.

I was thrilled. I couldn't believe that the concept I had laid out during my fund-raising pitch in 1997 was in full automatic production five years later. My dream had come true! This was the personal factory in action.

Years later, when our executive team has looked back on the decisions we made in earlier years and how those influenced the path we are on today, constructive criticism has arisen about the contract I signed. Venture capitalists, in particular, will point out how much better a per unit royalty would have been for Geomagic. I feel no regret, nor do I become defensive. The general business analysis was logical, but taken out of context it can seem just the opposite. Under normal circumstances, I might have followed a more strategic approach to drive a better contract with Align Technology. But these were extraordinary circumstances. Had I focused on negotiating a good contract, Geomagic might very well not be here today.

I learned from the Align deal that decisions and contracts are not the same thing. Contracts usually follow a standard set of rules. We can plug in the numbers and terms to make a rational business case. But we can't do that with a decision. Context always matters. We have to take into consideration not just the short-term impact, but also the long-term repercussions of our choices.

Over time, I have truly come to value the importance of quality decision making—not just for me, but for the entire organization. Jack Stack, author of the bestselling book *The Great Game of Business*, once said, "What separates a great company from a failed one is whether or not they have a culture that encourages and enables people to make good decisions."

Making good decisions means being clear about what really matters—in the case of the Align contract, getting cash in the door to save the company. It also requires giving people the authority and freedom to fail. We rarely know in advance whether a decision is correct. Fortunately, decisions often are reversible; such is rarely the case with a signed contract.

On occasion, hindsight may suggest that I could have taken a different path with Align. But I have learned not to second-guess myself. Once I made the decision, I let the chips fall where they may. Mission accomplished: Geomagic had the money it needed to move forward.

⌒

The years 2001 and 2002 were terrible for many technology companies. NASDAQ crashed. Terrorists attacked the World Trade Center. Netscape was sold to AOL and faded out of consumers' short-lived cultural memories. Mosaic, our NCSA creation that had started the dot-com boom, would resurface only as a credit on the "About" pull-down menu of an Internet Explorer browser.

And yet I woke up with an enormous sense of relief on New Year's Day 2003. Geomagic had turned a profit for the first time. I no longer had to worry about making payroll and I finally had the luxury of thinking strategically. In the process of working around the clock to save the company, I had also learned new skills and gained more confidence. I could now comprehend the monthly financial statements—not as an accountant, but as an executive. The numbers no longer made me feel dizzy, because I had found relevance in and connection to them: they provided a record of our company's operating history.

We started to teach our employees about financial literacy and how their actions could affect the company's performance. I was amazed at the way in which knowledge empowers people. Our receptionist noticed how much paper our employees wasted because they often just hit the "Print" button without thinking, printing an entire seventy-page document instead of just the one page they needed in hard copy. She calculated how much money we spent on printer cartridges each month and published the results. People's behavior changed immediately: everyone became more conscious of their printing habits.

I was still shy and felt in many situations that I didn't fit in, but I made up work-arounds so that people wouldn't notice quite as much. "What do you think of that wine?" I learned to ask the men in black suits at conferences, one of my icebreakers. I began to enjoy working in the male-dominated tech industry. Most professional men are raised to respect and to help women, and I found that they would try their best to treat me as an equal or better.

As Geomagic became more successful, I noticed other women looking up to me as a role model female executive, woman in technology, and mother. After I spoke at conferences, many of them asked, "How can I break through the glass ceiling?"

The question gave me pause. On the one hand, I care a great deal about women's equality in the workplace. On the other hand, I don't believe in limits and ceilings. "If you don't believe in the glass ceiling, it does not exist," I would say. I looked to nature for inspiration. Nature does not operate according to principles of constant growth, because infinite growth is not possible in a finite world. One tree trying to grow high enough to touch the sky does not make a forest. Rather, nature excels at constant movement. It is infinitely creative and adaptive. "Think about moving forward to make personal or social progress, rather than moving higher to gain a superior position," I advised.

It wasn't until I matured as an executive within these past couple of years that I realized how many valuable lessons I had absorbed from Jon Field's tenure as CEO: how to think big about Geomagic's possibilities, how to hire people with the appropriate skills and experience for the job, and how to take more risks. I also gained confidence that I could do what he had done with Geomagic and more. There were no mysterious qualities a suave American businessman possessed that I didn't—other than being taller.

At times, I had allowed people within the company to cast blame on Jon, making him our scapegoat. After a while, I couldn't feel good about that. How could I let someone else take the blame for what had happened? I was one of the founders of Geomagic and a member of the executive team. If the company didn't perform well, I was equally if not more responsible.

We often forgive people for making mistakes such as burning a dinner, say, or even causing a car accident. But how much room do we allow for our own limitations, blind spots, and human selfishness? It was Jon's first run at being a start-up CEO, and he might have acted in his self-interest when he left Geomagic. Who said when we were born that being good and selfless was the only way we were supposed to behave? Haven't we all made choices in life that we wished we hadn't, especially during times of extreme danger and scarcity, when faced with the tension of self-preservation versus promoting the well-being of others?

I called Jon and asked him to lunch one day. I wanted to apologize—not just for his sake, but also for my own. I didn't want to profit from gamesmanship, and I needed to accept responsibility for my own mistakes. He seemed surprised but accepted my invitation.

Over lunch, I told Jon, "At the time you left, I was really disappointed and scared. I and the other members of the board of directors couldn't believe that you'd abandon our sinking ship. I felt trapped because we had $6.5 million in cash and no debt when I handed you the company, and you returned it to me with $4 million in losses, no new revenue, and little cash to survive on. I blamed you for wasting the money and not helping me to build a viable company. I understand now that was not a fair point of view. You were just as inexperienced as I was, and I was just as responsible as you were. I admired you then, and I continue to admire you today. Also, it has always been clear to me that fundamentally you're a good person. I wanted you to know."

"Thanks," Jon said in a low voice.

I continued: "We probably both said some ugly things to and about each other back then. But the truth is, I learned a lot from you. Without observing you and your team in action, I wouldn't ever have dreamed as big or imagined what might be possible for Geomagic. I really wanted to thank you for that."

By this time, Jon had become a little emotional. He said, "I'm so glad that you reached out to me and we had this talk, Ping."

Jon and I remain friends to this day. Whenever reporters try to make him out to be a villain, I leap to his defense. He has thoroughly impressed me by never saying one bad word against me in public or to the press. When asked about his time at our company, Jon always says, "I admire what Ping Fu did with Geomagic." Jon even advised my team on Russia when we first started working there, and we found his insights invaluable.

❧

The Buddha famously asked, "Who can say what is good or bad?" That question has proven itself a source of great comfort in my life. Good people can make poor choices; and bad contracts can turn out to be excellent decisions. Good and bad is not a matter of black and white; in life, we are regularly confronted by shades of gray.

When I was young, Shanghai Papa made me memorize many classical Chinese stories. Here is one of them:

Among the people who lived close to the border, there was an old wise man who led a kind and peaceful life. Without reason, his horse escaped one day and fled into barbarian territory. Everyone in the village pitied him. But the old man said: "What makes you think this is not a good thing?"

Several months later, the old man's horse returned, and a superb barbarian stallion accompanied him. His neighbors congratulated the old man. But he said: "What makes you think this cannot be a bad thing?"

The old man's grandson enjoyed riding the new horse. But one day, he fell while riding and broke his hip. Everyone pitied the old man once again. But he said: "What makes you think this is not a good thing?"

One year later, a large party of barbarians invaded the border region. All the men from the village drew their bows and went to battle, where nine out of ten of them died. But because he was lame, the old man's grandson did not have to go to war. His life was spared.

"Who can say what is good or bad?" is a widely known Buddhist teaching about radical acceptance and nonjudgment. My life journey has taught me not to count on a better outcome before life

presents you with it, which is quite different from the Western desire to "think big." Perhaps—like my arrival in America at age
twenty-five with no language or relevant career skills, or my stepping down as CEO of Geomagic only to watch it stumble—an un-
pleasant event will open new doors and teach even greater lessons.
It often does. I know that I am a wiser, more compassionate person
with a deeper understanding of myself and the world as a direct
result of looking at "hardship" and "success" through a different
lens. Our choice is how to interpret what happens to us on our journeys and how to treat the people we meet along the way. Our choice,
always, is to love and to understand.

SEVEN

The
Number One
Strategy
Is
Retreat

NEGOTIATIONS AND
EXPANSION: 2002–2005

THE CHINESE HAVE a proverb: "The number one strategy is retreat." I have often called it to mind during times of personal crisis. Mao Zedong famously used this tactic in battling for control of China in 1945. When it became clear that he would not be able to conquer Chiang Kai-shek's Nationalist army—which was backed by Western nations—by fighting in the cities, Mao retreated to the countryside in what came to be known as the Long March. He built up his peasant army and starved the cities of their food supply.

Eventually, Mao won the Chinese Civil War and claimed the role of China's leader, driving General Chiang and his troops to Taiwan.

Time and again, we witness the harm done by people's unwillingness to compromise, no matter what the cost—in war, divorce, or politics. We underestimate the value of stepping back because we are trained to perceive a willingness to make concessions as a weakness, or looking for alternatives as being inconsistent. Yet my childhood taught me that retreat is not about being weak or allowing others to manipulate you. It is about finding an alternative solution. "The number one strategy is retreat" holds true in the business world as it does in other realms of human relations.

Not long after I resumed the CEO role at Geomagic in 2002, I realized that I didn't know how to negotiate. Business would suffer if I did not quickly develop this critical skill. Whether arranging contracts with customers, setting priorities with employees, creating quotas and commissions for the sales team, or establishing target delivery dates and feature sets with engineers, I needed to grow my ability to listen with respect, communicate with clarity, and influence with authenticity in order to reach agreements.

As I so often do, I wound up wandering into a bookstore in search of answers. In the business section, I found the bestseller *Getting to Yes* by William Ury, Roger Fisher, and Bruce Patton. I loved the book, which lays out a concise yet compassionate method for achieving desired outcomes in negotiations. The book's principles align to an uncanny extent with my Chinese philosophy of being open to seeing the opposing view in life. I felt validated, able to look back with pride on how I had handled challenging situations as a child and teenager. It was as though I had a personal connection to the authors. (Years later, I had the good fortune of meeting Bill Ury face-to-face. I thanked him profusely for the positive impact he has had on my life.)

Getting to Yes talks about "going to the balcony" during the negotiation process—giving yourself and the other party space to think clearly and gain a big-picture view. It calls to mind another of my favorite Chinese proverbs: "Take a step back: the ocean is wider and the sky higher." Overall, the book emphasizes how important it is to approach the negotiating table with respect for the other people involved and a global sense of our interconnectedness as human beings. You must do this, the book instructs its readers, even if you don't agree with what the other party has to say. You will be most likely to attain positive results if you come from a place of believing in people's inherent goodness.

Negotiating is not about winning a battle, or even positioning yourself to win. It is about not getting into a fight in the first place. By resolving conflicts before they escalate, respecting mutual interests, and engaging others with compassion, you can achieve something far greater than victory: peace.

An opportunity to put the lessons from *Getting to Yes* into practice arrived quickly. In 2002, when Geomagic was still teetering at the brink of bankruptcy and I was not drawing a salary in order to keep us afloat, two large multinational technology companies served us with a lawsuit. The sheriff walked right into my office to deliver the subpoena. My heart pounding, I tore open the envelope. Two customers, both large global companies, claimed that Geomagic had violated the non-disclosure agreement (NDA) while negotiating business contracts with them.

I immediately called a meeting with our board members. We all cried foul. "We need to fight this! We have done nothing wrong. This is a typical tactic deployed by large companies in order to threaten a small company into giving them a better deal."

Our corporate attorney, on other hand, expressed reluctance at diving into a lawsuit. "I have two big concerns," Fred Hutchison explained. "First, these are massive multinational corporations who have millions to spend on lawsuits, whereas we have almost no funds at our disposal. Second, one of the companies is based in New Jersey. The courts in that state are notorious for their protectionism. They undoubtedly are going to side with one of their largest employers."

Fred is a highly respected attorney specializing in high-tech start-ups, so we all valued his opinion. I asked him what we should do. "You need to find a litigation attorney who is licensed in the state of New Jersey," Fred advised.

That afternoon, I went on the Internet and began searching for a firm in New Jersey to represent us. It proved to be quite a challenge. The first attorney I called said, "Ping, you sound like a nice person. I'd like to help, but I can't."

The second attorney asked, "How much money do you have to defend yourself?"

"Geomagic is a struggling start-up," I replied.

"I'll get back to you," he said, and hung up the phone.

The third attorney I contacted gave me another polite no, but at least she explained why. "Ping," she said, "I know this is not what you want to hear, but you are the defendant. Even if you win, we can't collect any money from the corporations who are suing you—there is no contingency fee. We would have to collect our payments from you, and your company is cash-poor right now. I'm sorry, but this case just doesn't make sense for us to take on."

I refused to believe that there were no attorneys willing to represent us. I changed tactics and started searching for the best intellectual property (IP) firms in the country who had offices in New Jersey. My rationale was that a larger firm might be willing to take more of a risk on a small client like us. What's more, a great defense attorney ought to hold dear the value that everyone, regardless of money, is entitled to representation. My instincts and trust in the American legal system paid off.

My search landed me on the Web site of Hale and Dorr, LLP, one of the nation's top IP firms. I checked with Fred, who confirmed that they had a great reputation. As I looked up the profiles of their various attorneys, my eyes were drawn to a picture of a junior partner, Victor Souto. I picked up the phone and dialed his number. Miraculously, his assistant patched me through. I spent a few moments introducing myself and explaining Geomagic's situation.

"Why are you talking to me?" Vic asked. "Did anyone refer you?"

I had little hope, given the rejections I had received thus far, but I had nothing to lose, either. "No references," I said without editing my thinking. "I need the meanest defense attorney possible to take on our case. Your picture on the firm's Web site called to me. It told me that you are fearless—scary actually."

Vic started laughing. "That's some criteria."

We spoke for a while longer. It turned out that Vic knew of and respected Fred.

"So," I said, taking a deep breath, "will you represent us?"

"I'll book a flight down to Raleigh-Durham tomorrow," Vic replied. He did not even ask for a retainer.

⌒

Vic and his assistant arrived from New York City the next day. He proved to be a compassionate and intelligent litigation attorney.

I told Vic that I didn't understand why these two large companies would sue us. I had met with the executives from each organization separately many times in the past, and we had always enjoyed a friendly, collaborative relationship.

After we had reviewed the case in detail together, he said to me, "Ping, winning is losing in this case. Geomagic will run out of money before you even get to court, not to mention the time and energy you will waste if the case drags on for years. If you want me to fight, I will fight for you. But to what end? You'll just wind up stuffing my pockets and those of the other attorneys on the case."

I learned from Vic that in New Jersey's local courts, if we won the case as a defendant, we would walk away without penalties. This was the best-case scenario. If we were found to be even a little at fault, we could end up paying all the legal fees for the companies who were suing us along with whatever settlement resulted from the case.

"Do you think that such powerful companies will ever admit that this problem is their fault?" Vic argued. "They have money to throw at this lawsuit. They will fight you until the bitter end."

I felt powerless to protect our company and our people. "Are there any alternatives?" I asked.

Vic nodded slowly, his eyes narrowing. "There is one, but I don't know if you will be willing to consider it."

"Go on," I said.

"You could back out and settle out of court," Vic offered.

"What do you mean?"

"Well, you said earlier that you know the decision makers at these companies and have enjoyed a friendly relationship with them in the past. Do you believe they're good people?" Vic asked.

I nodded. "Oh, yes. I know them and have the highest respect for them."

"That's good," Vic said. "I suggest you call a meeting with them and tell them not to bring lawyers. I will not come with you."

"What would I do in that meeting?" I was puzzled.

Vic said something that surprised me. "If you believe they are good people, you can rely on some common sense. I'm telling you— there is no way two white males would gang up against a woman. We are not raised that way. If you genuinely want to resolve the is- sue, one if not both of them will be fair and help you."

It seemed as though Vic's suggestion was my best option. I im- mediately thought about how taking this approach would utilize the retreat strategy. It fit so well with my own experience and what I had just read about in *Getting to Yes*. I called my contacts at the companies behind the lawsuit at once and suggested that we meet without our attorneys. Both graciously accepted my invitation. We set a date for two weeks out, and one of them booked us a conference room at the Marriott airport hotel in Newark, New Jersey.

In the meantime, I had homework to do. I needed to find out exactly why the companies were suing Geomagic for violating the NDAs, something that I couldn't imagine our employees doing. I also didn't understand why the two companies were collaborating on the lawsuit, when previously Geomagic had been dealing with each of them separately.

The events had occurred when Jon Field had been CEO. I discovered that salespeople who were no longer with Geomagic had handled the two accounts. When I investigated the details, it turned out that we had made an innocent mistake, but a mistake nonetheless. These two companies had been competing to sign exclusive contracts with Geomagic; they were competitors. We had signed an NDA with each company, which specified that Geomagic would not reveal their corporate identities. A Chinese firewall had been established within Geomagic to prohibit one team from talking to the other.

One fateful day, a salesperson from each client team had approached the same engineer and asked him to send a beta version of our software to their prospective customers. They forgot to caution him about the firewall. The engineer, who did not know about the contract negotiations, sent the beta software to both companies in the same e-mail. As a result, the companies had learned about each other—they knew who else was bidding on exclusivity with Geomagic. This action had indeed violated our NDAs with them.

I wondered why, rather than revealing the seemingly small, harmless error to us, the two companies had decided to team up and file a lawsuit against us. I speculated that perhaps they believed they would get a better deal on our software.

"Maybe when they saw each other's names on that e-mail, they realized that they would have more collective bargaining power with Geomagic as a team than as separate entities bidding each other up," Vic agreed. "Legally, it doesn't matter what their reason is in the end. They can find fault, and therefore you can't win the case."

In addition to investigating the facts, I also prepared for my meeting by picking up *Getting to Yes* again. I studied it closely, then practiced several of the techniques. With my senior management team, I established my floor, the lowest deal I would accept in the negotiation. I also had coworkers role-play the parts of the two corporate executives with whom I would meet, asking them to act as devil's advocates and disagree with every option I put forward. Could I leave a back door open so that they wouldn't feel stuck? Could I actively show my respect for their opinions, even if they attacked my company or argued with every point I made? How could I seek out and identify what mattered most to them?

By the time the meeting date arrived, I felt ready for anything.

I flew into Newark that morning and met with the two executives— let me call them Adam and Bob for the moment—at the Marriott hotel conference room. Looking official in their formal black suits, they were friendly with each other and polite to me. I began by thanking them both for their willingness to meet me without their attorneys present. Then I took responsibility for our being there. "Please accept my sincere apology for our mistake. We never should have sent that e-mail revealing both of your identities to each other. The error showed that we didn't have adequate firewall processes in place. I feel really bad about what happened."

The two gentlemen paid close attention as I spoke. Bob responded, "Well, Ping, there really isn't much harm done here. You shouldn't feel too bad." Adam nodded in agreement.

I continued. "Geomagic almost went bankrupt this past year.

The truth is we have no money to fight this case. I called this meeting because I believe it is not your intention to put Geomagic out of business. There must be something else you want that is not expressed in this lawsuit. Can we talk about it and see if we can settle out of court?"

The two executives hadn't expected this. They were accustomed to people positioning themselves to win an argument, not asking for help. Their demeanors shifted as they leaned back in their chairs, staring thoughtfully at the ceiling. Bob once again led the way in responding to me. "You're right—we certainly have no intention of destroying your company."

Adam nodded and then got to the point. "Ping, the trouble is that Geomagic filed patents in our field. We consider that unacceptable because you used the knowledge we had given you during our negotiations with Geomagic to develop these patents."

I caught myself reacting to what Adam had said, thinking, If you were after our patents, why didn't you fight us in patent court? This is not fair. But I had practiced enough in the office before the meeting to keep myself from saying anything aloud. Retreat is the best strategy, I reminded myself.

"So, your true interest is in our patents?" I asked for clarification, biting my tongue so as not to say anything that might start a fight.

"Yes." Adam continued, "We want those patents."

"I'd be happy to license the patents to you," I offered at once.

Adam looked agitated. I wasn't sure whether it was because he didn't like playing hardball or whether he really felt that we had wronged his company. "We want you to hand the patents over to us, free of charge," he said. "We want to own these patents outright. You shouldn't have filed them in the first place without our approval."

I was stunned. What? *Give* you the patents? I nearly asked, outraged at the request. I knew full well that we had every right to have filed these patents. I felt quite certain that I'd be able to prove in a court of law that Geomagic had not relied on any of these two companies' proprietary information. But I stepped back to gain a larger view. At first glance, it didn't seem fair to me for these companies to take ownership of our patents. At the same time, I had no other choice: agreeing to their terms was the only way out of Geomagic's current predicament.

I recalled William Ury's advice to focus on the desired outcome rather than short-term consequences. It was more important for me to be able to run a financially viable company than it was for us to own these two particular patents, which comprised a relatively small market anyway. Handing over the patents in their field would be the "golden bridge," as Ury calls it, that these executives needed to cross over and drop their lawsuit. All Geomagic required was the ability to use the patents going forward, and assurance that the customers who bought or licensed our software and technology would be protected.

I said to Adam, "I hear you. You want the two patents we filed in your field." Then I looked straight at Bob and asked, "Can you tell me whether that is also most important to you?"

Bob cleared his throat. "Ping, you don't have to be so agreeable. We are not going to exploit you because you are vulnerable. Would you give us five minutes alone?"

"Of course," I replied, and stepped out of the room.

When I came back, Adam and Bob had a reasonable settlement ready for me. It released Geomagic and our customers and partners from further legal action and provided a financial payout for our two patents and legal fees. It took us a total of twenty minutes to agree on everything. We typed up the terms on Bob's computer, and he e-mailed a copy to each of us. I thanked Adam and Bob again for agreeing to meet with me. I complimented their open-minded, straightforward, and cordial style and told them to call on me if they ever needed my help. They thanked me in return for reaching out to them, saying that they never could have initiated a meeting like this. We shook hands and bid farewell. I glanced at my watch on the way out the door. The entire meeting had taken less than an hour.

Stepping outside the hotel, I called Vic. I could not contain my excitement: Geomagic was saved once again. "Vic, we did it!" I exclaimed. "They agreed to drop the case."

"Congratulations! Tell me what happened and what they agreed to," he said. When I finished, Vic said, "Wow, Ping, you did even better than I expected. And you even managed to get them to cover your legal expenses."

I thanked Vic for having guided me through this harrowing experience with such levelheaded advice. Then I added, "Let me know when they pay your legal fees. If they don't, I will definitely cover your expenses."

"Oh, don't worry, Ping," Vic replied with a robust chuckle. "Hale and Dorr is a big law firm. We know how to collect our own payments."

I laughed. "You'll be my litigation attorney forever, Vic." Although we have been fortunate enough not to have any other major lawsuits filed against Geomagic, Vic earned my enduring gratitude and respect. I also had learned valuable lessons about how, in negotiation, vulnerability can be a strength.

～

My 2003 New Year's resolution for Geomagic, which had achieved profitability, was to focus on growth. In January, *Fast Company* named me one of its "Fast 50," strengthening this desire. I didn't know it yet, but growth is not a goal; much like losing weight, it is an ongoing commitment to progress.

Geomagic's vision to make mass production personal was audacious, especially given that there was no defined market for our products at the time we launched. We came out with our first software tools before there was much awareness of 3D printing and imaging, and found that we had to build it, slowly, ourselves. Our early customers, such as Mattel, Boeing, and Align Technology, were enthusiastic but could not offer us enough recurring business based on our existing software offerings. Developing custom products for them was too expensive and time consuming; it didn't provide sufficient cash flow.

Requests from potential new customers, on the other hand, pulled us in many different directions. If Geomagic's software could help make aligners, could it assist with the manufacturing of custom-made hearing aids? What about fully customized knee replacements and, ultimately, valves made to precisely fit every individual's heart? If we could create 3D models of the parts on commercial jets, what about military aircraft? What about repairing and maintaining turbine blades used in jet engines and power plants, an industrial sector in which the United States retained a global lead? Could we enable owners of Harley-Davidson motorcycles to custom design their own gas tanks? Make Olympic bobsleds go faster? Keep blimps in the air? We didn't have enough people on staff to adequately explore, much less implement, every request.

The most obvious way to expand was geographically, by selling our existing products to new customers in international markets. Our first choice was western Europe, where we already had a few sales, thanks to some 3D scanner manufacturers. A business contact referred us to a German national, Gerd Schwaderer, who had the skills to sell our product and understood our target customers. Gerd had worked for ImageWare, one of the early software companies in the 3D scanning space.

I flew Gerd to Raleigh-Durham for an interview, forgetting that Herbert's mother was scheduled to arrive from Austria the same day. Herbert was out of town. I didn't want to leave my mother-in-law and ten-year-old daughter home alone without dinner, so I decided to bring them both along with me. I naively imagined that since my mother-in-law spoke German, this would be fun for Gerd. It never occurred to me how odd it might appear to a businessperson to have a CEO show up for an interview with two of her family members in tow. Gerd looked surprised when the three of us arrived at the restaurant, but handled the situation with grace. We had an enjoyable dinner and Geomagic hired him.

To set up our European expansion in Germany, we had three choices. One, we could ask Gerd to set up his own business and act as Geomagic's master distributor. Two, Gerd could set up a German sales office for Geomagic. Three, we could create a German subsidiary of Geomagic, which Gerd would join.

The first option required Gerd to be an entrepreneur, a role he was not prepared to take on; that choice was out. Setting up a sales office would have been simpler than establishing a subsidiary. To create a wholly owned subsidiary that was an independent business entity, we needed to register our company in Germany and set up legal, HR, and accounting systems. The advantage of a subsidiary was that it would signal our commitment to the European market, a move that would be favorably received by our customers and resellers. I reasoned that if we wanted to be a global company, we needed to show the world we were serious. We went with option three.

Geomagic GmbH was established in November 2003, and we recruited an exceptional team. Our European division grew quickly from zero dollars in 2003 to more than 30 percent of our business by 2008. Gerd remains a sales manager who, to this day, enjoys teasing me about "joining the family business."

Around the same time we were opening our German subsidiary, I made my first acquisition. It was unplanned and ultimately not as successful. In December 2002, I attended EuroMold, one of the largest industrial trade shows in the world, held in Frankfurt each year. There, I met BMW and Volkswagen engineers who were using Geomagic software to design cars at their manufacturing facilities. They both independently mentioned a Hungarian research and development company, Cadmus Consulting, whose technology they loved.

"We are big fans of your software and their technology," the automobile engineers said. "If you could put the two together, you'd have a killer product that every car company would want." They explained that while Geomagic's software enabled the engineers to scan and create 3D digital models of their cars, Cadmus's technology allowed them to functionally break down the data into meaningful pieces by separating the car's various components. The Cadmus software could split apart metal, glass, and rubber from the car door data with ease.

My curiosity piqued, I spoke with Herbert about Cadmus after returning home. He had heard of the company and its founder, Dr. Tamás Várady. Hungary, he explained, is famous for having great mathematicians. This group hailed from the prestigious Hungarian Academy of Sciences.

During the summer of 2003, while I was working in Europe to establish Geomagic GmbH, I hopped on a plane to Budapest to meet Dr. Várady in person. As we talked, Dr. Várady showed me around the old city, whose ethereal beauty delighted me. I loved his passion and noticed that he was a complex and logical thinker.

After a few hours of wandering through Budapest, I asked Dr. Várady, "Would Cadmus consider becoming part of Geomagic? You might come on board as our chief technology officer."

"That's an interesting proposition," Dr. Várady replied, raising his eyebrows. "I'll think it over. By the way, Ping, you can call me Tamás."

When Tamás accepted my offer a couple of months later, I traveled to Budapest as soon as I could. We sat down at a café and sketched out the deal on the back of a paper napkin. Tamás agreed to a stock buy, which was helpful because Geomagic didn't have much cash.

The acquisition closed smoothly, but the road got bumpier after that. Both Tamás and I were inexperienced; neither of us had done an M&A before. We had different expectations of the outcome and very different personalities.

I made several mistakes and naive assumptions. For one, Hungary itself had no markets and brought in zero revenue. The cost of supporting fifteen people in our Budapest subsidiary was substantially higher than I had anticipated. Prior to the merger, Cadmus employees had taken reduced salaries and worked on the side at various university jobs; now we paid them at full salaries at market rate. Inflation in Hungary was high, and within a couple of years their salaries were only moderately lower than the going rate in the United States. We also had to cover the costs of extra office space, administrative support, and travel. We weren't a large enough company to afford such an expense increase.

Language was another challenge. It turned out that most of our Hungarian employees did not speak English well, although their skills were sufficient enough to read and write software. This made communication between their office and headquarters difficult. It also meant that we could not fully utilize our employees in Budapest as a technical support team for our European customers, which would have benefitted sales and marketing.

The biggest contention was a misalignment in our mentality and attitude—a lack of what is known in business terms as "culture fit." Though technically brilliant mathematicians, our Hungarian employees came from an academic background in the former Soviet bloc, where funds were not tied to results. They had no practical experience of what it takes to build a product for end users.

Tensions between Hungary and headquarters quickly emerged. We asked a small team in Budapest to build a dental product for a client in Germany. True to their scientific nature, the Hungarian mathematicians developed complex algorithms to solve several challenging problems. However, they came in behind schedule and over budget. The product didn't work well in the dental lab environment, where average users had no technical training. The team developed the software until it was 80 percent complete, but we couldn't get them to finish the last 20 percent—the user interface features. Without good user interface and workflow design, the smartest software does not show or function well. Our Hungarian technical team didn't seem to grasp the importance of usability. I had to move the project back to the United States for completion.

We simultaneously began working on the project that had originally brought us together: integrating Cadmus's technology into Geomagic Studio software. Studio was our market leader at the time. It enabled industrial designers and engineers to transform 3D scan data into highly accurate models for product design, rapid prototyping, and analysis. We wanted to expand Studio's functionality to allow designers to shape more stylized products that are free-form and beautiful, such as the exterior of a car. We named the product Geomagic Fashion, and assigned Tamás and his team to develop it.

Thirteen months later than we'd expected, we sent the beta version to some expert users for field-testing and feedback. Our beta testers liked the software's new capabilities, but found it only half usable—they could not finish their designs for some parts. It is known that the first release of any software rarely works perfectly, so I wasn't too disappointed. I also knew that we had given the Hungarian team a difficult problem to solve. I trusted that Tamás and his team would make it work better.

The next phase of improvements again came in several months behind their release schedule, and yet again we didn't have a finished product. At this rate, it was clear that it would be another two years at least until Fashion was mature enough to be a groundbreaking product.

My patience ran thin. I didn't recognize at the time that we were part of the problem for having unrealistic expectations. I started questioning whether Tamás had sold me a company that didn't have the capabilities he said it had.

Tamás seemed surprised. "But we're thrilled with our progress. We've solved several complex theoretical problems that no one has ever been able to tackle before. That takes a long time." I could hear his excitement, like a child about to ride his first roller coaster.

Tamás's goals were noble, but he was not accustomed to operating a commercial company. Inventing theoretical solutions was a task that belonged to a university or research institute and was rarely a priority in business. Tamás was passionate about being the best researcher he could be. Making money and meeting deadlines did not motivate Tamás and his team. Making scientific discoveries did.

I took a deep breath. "Tamás, your team has worked on just a few data sets so far. We need to test two hundred varieties of data sets to make sure the software works. We've got to make sure Fashion is a product, not a prototype."

"I know, Ping, but that is the job of Geomagic's engineers. You guys know better how to build a product," he replied. "I think we should change the organizational structure so that Hungary only builds prototypes and Geomagic builds the products."

I wanted to reach through the phone and shake Tamás by the shoulders. "Your job is not just invention; it's mostly engineering. You need to deliver a product that works."

When Tamás began arguing again, I cut him off. "I'm sorry, Tamás. You're just going to have to adapt."

The discussion did not end there. During every one of our scheduled weekly calls, Tamás would argue with me about something. He would criticize my business decisions or question why I thought product usability and company growth should come ahead of solving the most difficult theoretical problems.

"Just put Geomagic into steady state mode and let's solve all these unsolved problems," Tamás would say.

"You're not working for the Academy of Sciences anymore, Tamás," I'd reply. "If the company doesn't grow, it shrinks. The world is not waiting for us."

It seemed to me that Tamás had a lot of time and energy to talk, which I did not. He loved to debate with me for hours. Often, I'd hang up the phone feeling as though I'd just hauled a twenty-pound stone up a hill, only to watch it go tumbling back down again.

Eventually, I had to give up. I was genuinely fond of Tamás and deeply respected his intellect and imagination, yet we were always at odds. An inveterate tinkerer, he could not shift to a more commercial mind-set. When we talked, I said, "Tamás, I'm sorry, but I can't do this anymore. We need a more productive way of channeling your talent and energy." I suggested that he step down as CTO and accept a position as chief technology adviser.

I thought Tamás would be hurt and disappointed, possibly even angry. Instead, he let out a huge sigh. "Thank you, Ping. I really didn't enjoy being CTO. I felt that I had to debate those issues with you because it was my duty as a corporate officer. I'd rather help out by solving technical problems and leave the business decisions to you."

True to his word, Tamás stopped debating me. Our two-hour weekly calls ceased. He went about his new advisory role with gusto, engaging our engineers enthusiastically on any complex issues they faced. I couldn't believe it—simply by changing his title, I had altered his perception of his responsibilities and reduced stress for both of us.

Nevertheless, Geomagic never did manage to integrate the Hungary team effectively, mostly due to our own inexperience. We didn't give them full accountability or autonomy. Six years after the acquisition, we spun the Budapest subsidiary off, offering a job at headquarters to anyone who wanted to stay with Geomagic and relocate to U.S. headquarters. Tamás remains as an adviser.

The Hungary acquisition was not a total failure. The team contributed critical pieces to the Geomagic Studio software, enabling it to remain a world leader in its category for many years. I learned a great deal about the importance of culture fit, market synergy, and postmerger integration.

Finally, I set my sights on China. By 2005, the country of my birth had firmly established its position as a leading manufacturing hub of the world. We bought a company that Geomagic had contracted with in the past for software testing. Initially, we had them do only quality assurance work, testing our code during their daytime hours while it was night in North Carolina and our engineers were sleeping. Our Chinese employees proved productive and reliable, and we soon added a sales and marketing team.

The biggest challenge in China was software piracy, a business condition over which we had very little control. Rather than fighting it, we chose to view it as a way to enter the market and establish ourselves in China. We knew that only the large multinational companies operating there would pay full price for our software. If the local companies, many of them too small to afford our products, wanted to poach it for free, we would go along with that. We would rather have our software used than not known at all. It could help local companies to produce better products faster and enable them to grow. Once they made enough money a few years down the road, we had faith that they would purchase our software legally— and we were right. Today, China is Geomagic's fastest-growing region and comprises 15 percent of our total business.

When I visited China in early 2005, I was amazed by the massive changes my native country had undergone. All signs of the Cultural Revolution had been erased. Shanghai was as modern as any metropolis, with highways above ground level and subways running underneath. It had become a tri-level, 3D city in the span of a decade. It had more skyscrapers than there were pine trees in Chapel Hill. I searched the street where my grandfather had bought his golden nugget, but the entire city block had been renovated with new apartment complexes and a shopping mall; I could not find anything recognizable. Although phone lines were still uncommon, no one needed them—now everyone had a cell phone. More impressive, I could get reception everywhere, even in elevators and parking garages.

From a business perspective, I discovered the extent to which China had learned from and largely adopted American and European corporate processes and practices. It made it easy for Geomagic and other companies to do business there. Chinese employees operated under work-for-hire contracts just like in the United States; employers and employees could come and go at will without paying stiff penalties. Chinese HR companies could handle payroll, taxes, and benefits at scale for smaller companies. I found only the banking system and currency conversion issues tricky. Overall, it was a full-blown free market economy operating within a one-party society.

For years, I had built up internal walls to protect myself from my ambivalent relationship with the birth country that had expelled me and yet was forever part of my identity. Now I observed a difference in my attitude toward China. In 1993, I had returned filled with nostalgia and longing to connect with my past. Memories of my childhood had overwhelmed me. On this trip, however, I arrived as a Chinese American entrepreneur. I found myself admiring and appreciating China's advances from afar, with emotional maturity.

I marveled at how ironic it was that over the past decades my two countries had grown closer together, becoming more interconnected and far more similar. China and the United States both were large nations whose people were capable of tremendous innovation and progress. How odd that, like twins separated at birth and raised by wildly different parents, the countries should turn out to be so alike when they grew up.

By 2005, revenue at Geomagic had grown on average 36 percent per year ever since I had taken over as CEO. We had more than one hundred employees across the globe. Yet managing our growing midsized global company turned out to be more challenging than I had anticipated. I felt confident about operating a start-up, securing financing, and managing global operations, but I started to feel that I wasn't as skilled at handling people problems or communicating effectively.

One of the common issues that I, like many other CEOs, faced was that I traveled frequently for business. Every time I returned to North Carolina, I would discover some fire burning. Such was the case at the end of the fiscal year in 2006. I came home from a business trip to find most of my employees up in arms about errors with their end-of-year payroll accounting. Geomagic's HR consultant had made mistakes with the number of vacation and sick days they had taken, and in some cases even their annual raises. Compensation is a sensitive topic. Concerned that the issue was harming morale, I jumped in without knowing any background information.

Usually, I would have turned to our director of finance, Gerrie, for an explanation. But Gerrie had recently left Geomagic to start her own company. So I walked directly into the HR consultant's office and asked what was going on. Her breath shallow and voice shaky, she assured me that while she had made a few mistakes, she would redo the calculations and get them right this time.

Just a few hours later, the HR consultant sent me the revised compensation spreadsheet. I spotted several errors immediately. Without pausing to consider my next move, I stormed into her office. "This isn't right," I said, eyes narrowing. I didn't expect what happened next.

"I quit," she said quietly. She gathered her things and left the building within the hour.

Now we were really in trouble. Not only were Geomagic's end-of-year compensation reports still a mess, but we also had no director of finance and no HR consultant to fix them. I knew I had screwed up. My habit from the start-up days of Geomagic was to leap in and fight fires myself. But these days, I often didn't have adequate knowledge of the situation. In this case, I had unintentionally ended up adding fuel to the flames. What I hadn't known was that Gerrie had always been the one to handle employment benefits; I had just assumed that HR did. But Gerrie was the type of person who would take out the garbage and never bother to tell you she had done it. She had helped HR with tasks requiring attention to detail, even though it wasn't Gerrie's responsibility to do payroll.

Fortunately, our CFO was able to handle the situation and our employees were patient with us while we sorted out their compensation in the following month. We provided transparency, admitting our mistakes and letting our staff know that we would correct the errors.

I learned from this experience that I could become a bottleneck at Geomagic if I were to attempt to make all critical decisions and be a firefighter myself. I needed to trust my team to handle the day-to-day operations and not interfere as a "helicopter CEO."

There is nothing like running and owning a business to challenge the most dearly held assumptions you have about yourself. I felt myself tested emotionally almost every day. In order to excel as a CEO, I realized, one must be committed to relentless self-improvement.

To facilitate teamwork among our different divisions and geographic regions, and to identify the management team's blind spots, we brought in a consultant to conduct a 360-degree review. This involved collecting feedback from supervisors, peers, and direct reports.

After pointing out a few strengths and areas for improvement to me, the consultant added, "You need to soften up a bit." He never would have said that to a man in a leadership position, I thought to myself crossly, recalling the affirmative action classes at Bell Labs. But, a small voice asked, what if he is right? The feedback piqued my curiosity.

In May, I was honored with a Woman of the Year award from *Business Leader* magazine. They offered me a scholarship to a four-day course for executives called Grinnell Leadership training. I had heard good things about the class and thought I should give it a try.

Six weeks later, I found myself lying on the floor of a retreat center in North Carolina with eight other business leaders for a guided hypnosis session. It was my first experience with such an exercise and I was skeptical. I rested my head on my crossed arms, listening to resounding drumbeats and sweeping music from the movie *The Last of the Mohicans*. We did breathing exercises for forty-five minutes while the instructor told us to visualize artifacts from a day in our past. At first, I saw nothing but black—no images. My mind refused to go back in time. I became irritated with myself as my thoughts jumped all over the place. I kept remembering things I needed to get done in the office and at home. This is bullshit, I thought. I should get up and leave. But my body refused to move. Slowly, I became conscious of my breath, deep and rhythmic, spreading down from my neck to my chest. I drifted away.

About thirty minutes into the session, I had the distinct sensation of falling, and the dam broke. The past rushed forth, scattering images across the screen of my closed eyes like an old movie I had forgotten I'd seen. Only I wasn't watching the film—I was starring in it. I panicked. I was trapped inside a void, a littered inescapable void that was Room 202. I saw blood. I saw the guts of my teacher splattered across a lawn. I saw my journals burning. Then, for the first time in my life, vivid details of the rape flooded my brain. I saw the faces of my attackers twisted into sneers. I heard them shouting, "Beat her!" I felt the sharp pain of something entering me between my legs.

Since arriving in the United States, I rarely had broken down crying. But all at once I was sobbing uncontrollably. One of the assistant teachers, a clinical psychologist, came over to where I lay curled up like a fetus on the floor.

"It's okay, let it out," she said, gently rubbing my back. "Let it all out." She handed me a box of tissues, but otherwise did not interfere. The warmth of her presence next to me felt safe and comforting, yet I could not prevent the tears from flowing. For over an hour, weeping, and with my knees hugged to my chest, I watched the most tragic moments of my youth play out on the private movie screen in my head.

By the time I had stopped, my face was a splotchy red swollen mess and the detritus of three boxes of tissues lay scattered around me.

"Ping, would you like to share what's happening for you?" Dr. Grinnell asked.

Strangely, I felt vulnerable and safe in that moment. The crying had offered much relief from the pain. For the first time, I felt open to talk to strangers about my ghosts. Everyone listened attentively as I shared the memories I had repressed for so many years. I talked about losing both parents at age eight, the atrocities I had witnessed at the hands of the Red Guard, and being a surrogate mother to Hong. I did not bring up the gang rape and beating.

One of the other participants moved over next to me. She held my hand while I was talking and hugged me when I finished. Then the others moved in for a group hug, and we all shared the tears. It felt liberating to know that I could talk about my past and feel so supported, so loved.

Dr. Grinnell ended the course by giving each of us assignments to complete in order to help us become better leaders. For me, he had an additional assignment. "Ping, you go home and lie in your husband's arms. Relax and feel the love," he said.

I was an emotional mess and took his advice literally. When I got home, I found Herbert and asked, "Will you hold me?" He nodded yes. I lay with him on our living room couch for hours, filled with tenderness.

"You've changed," Herbert said a week later. "You're softer."

I smiled.

A few weeks later, we visited Herbert's parents in the Austrian countryside. I found myself riding down a dirt road on the back of a bicycle with my arms wrapped around Herbert's waist, giggling like a schoolgirl. My mind was filled with images of my happy college days in China, when I had gone on delightful bike rides down country roads with my classmates.

"Your mother finds the funniest things romantic," Herbert told Xixi when we returned to his parents' home.

In the weeks that followed the Grinnell Leadership training, my mind was haunted by the past. It had been thirty-seven years since I had been raped. I had long hidden away that broken girl, especially after leaving China. I had been reconstructing my identity in the United States, treating it as a fresh start. I had built up an internal Great Wall to conceal the pain. Now the wall had been breached, and those old feelings of hurt resurfaced in my consciousness.

Around that time, John Brant, a reporter from *Inc.* magazine, flew to North Carolina to interview me for a half-page story on my journey as an entrepreneur. What happened next was a complete surprise. When John asked me to talk about my life, the combination of the way he asked, how safe he made me feel, and my wide-open state of mind inspired me to share the story with him. We talked for hours. I told him details about being taken away from my family, fending for myself and Hong, and I even shared with him about being gang-raped. John reminded me of Uncle W. He was a brilliant audience—caring, engaging, empathetic, and non-judgmental.

At the end of the interview, John said, "Ping, I'd like to come back and talk to you again tomorrow. Would that be okay?" I agreed.

John Brant stayed for three days, further interviewing me and speaking with others in the company. About a week later, *Inc.* sent a photographer to shoot pictures of me. When he appeared at my office door, he had the magazine's editor in chief, John Koten, in tow.

"Is it normal for you to fly down for a photo shoot?" I asked.

"No, but your company seems interesting," Koten answered. He didn't offer any further explanation.

A couple of months passed. Work was so busy that I didn't think much about the *Inc.* magazine article. In early December, I got a call from Paul Magelli, a former business professor I knew from the University of Illinois and my mentor when I'd first started Geomagic. "Congratulations, Ping!" he crowed enthusiastically when I picked up the phone.

"What for?" I asked.

"Don't you know? You've been named *Inc.* magazine's Entrepreneur of the Year!"

"I don't think so. That can't be true," I said.

Paul laughed. "Maybe I heard it wrong. But I don't think so."

A few days later, the magazine featuring me appeared at newsstands, airport kiosks, and Barnes and Noble shelves. *Inc.* sent me a couple dozen issues to share with my friends and family. The honor astounded me. Entrepreneur of the Year was an award given by *Inc.* magazine to just one person, one time each year. John Koten wrote in his editor's letter: "Ping Fu, who appears on this month's cover, is a moving example of what makes entrepreneurs so compelling. I have come to regard entrepreneurs as America's true heroes and most precious economic resources. I gradually fell in love with entrepreneurs because of their humanity and courage. They want nothing less than to change the world."

It felt surreal when I saw my own face staring back at me from the magazine rack. Who would have guessed it? I—Little Apple, the broken shoe, a black-blooded nobody—was a cover girl.

THE END OF AN ERA: 1976–1977

IN 1976, WHEN I was eighteen, Nanjing Mother received good news from her sister in Shanghai. The two had been exchanging letters rather frequently for the past few years, mostly sharing adult worries about their husbands and children. Shanghai Mama had written that four of my five cousin-siblings had returned home from the countryside; Shanghai Papa had already come back from a labor camp five years prior. Nanjing Mother asked if I would like to go visit them, saying that they would love to see me. I felt excited about reconnecting with my Shanghai family. I was curious to swap stories about our experiences.

The fervor of the Cultural Revolution had been dying down. People were allowed great freedom to travel where they wanted and take leaves of absence from their work. I notified my factory boss that I was heading off for two weeks, and he gave his approval. The next day, I eagerly packed up a few clothes, jumped on a train, and took off for my childhood home.

When I knocked on the door of the old Shanghai house, I heard footsteps running. All my family members came down to welcome me, their faces smiling warmly and hands waving in the air. (In Chinese culture, handshakes and hugs are less common between family members than they are in America.) I felt a surge of familiarity and joy upon seeing them. Shanghai Papa was regal and handsome, and Shanghai Mama was still beautiful. I wondered how the past ten difficult years had not put any wrinkles on their faces. My older brothers had grown into tall, handsome young men carrying an air of authority. My older sister, whom I still called Jie Jie, handed me an ice cream bar covered with chocolate. She had remembered all these years later that I loved that treat the most. Only my grandfather was missing from the family reunion. He had passed away.

We stayed together in Shanghai Papa and Mama's rooms on the second floor of the middle section of the house. The newspaper agency still occupied the first section of the house, and two families I didn't know lived on the third floor of our section. Shanghai Papa and Mama had gotten back an adjacent bedroom as well as a bathroom with a shower and toilet, in addition to the single room they had shared throughout most of the Cultural Revolution. Still, there were too many of us to fit comfortably inside. Shanghai Papa and Mama used the back room, which was smaller. The other five of us stayed in the front bedroom, which had a balcony, giving us space to stick our feet outside. We put blankets and sheets on the floor like a pajama party. It didn't matter to us how cramped the space was. We couldn't stop giggling, telling each other stories, and playfully fighting to use the toilet. At long last, we were reunited. As we talked, sang, and teased, my spirits took flight, like the finches that still darted about our garden. A smile illuminated my face, brighter than the sun.

On my second day in Shanghai, Jie Jie took me to celebrate our reunion by going to eat at the only Western-style restaurant in town, Red House. She had just received her paycheck, so the meal would be her treat. I had never tasted Western food before and was thrilled to try something new.

We walked over half an hour through the bustling streets of Shanghai to the elegant restaurant, which sported a bold red roof, and found a dozen patrons seated at tables inside. The waitress brought us bread and butter to start, followed by potato salad with mayonnaise and a breaded pork dish called "wienerschnitzel." We loved it, authentic Western cuisine or not.

Jie Jie and I were so enraptured by our conversation and the tantalizing food that we paid no attention to our surroundings. Suddenly, about an hour into our meal, she gave me a puzzled look. "There's no one left here," she remarked. I looked up from my plate and glanced about the restaurant. Not one other patron remained. Jie Jie summoned our waitress. "What's going on?"

Our waitress went to the kitchen, where she fetched a radio. When she placed it on our table, we heard the sound of foreboding music echoing around the empty room. It wasn't just any funeral march; it was the music the government played when someone very important died. Jie Jie and I gazed at each other with wide eyes. My hands started to tremble. Then the announcer's voice came on: "Our great leader Chairman Mao passed away today."

The piece of wienerschnitzel I had been chewing fell out of my mouth and onto the red tablecloth. I felt sick to my stomach. Blood rushed to my head, and I worried that it would trigger a migraine headache. I had been taught year after year to worship Chairman Mao. Even though I'd had my frustrations with our living conditions and the lack of freedom and choices, Chairman Mao was the absolute leader. It was hard to imagine that he was gone.

My mind raced, inventing a thousand different possible futures. Who knew what Mao's passing would mean for the future of China? Would our new leader crack down on recently implemented, more liberal policies? Or would we move in a direction of greater freedom of expression? Would we black elements finally be forgiven? Or would we be punished even more harshly for our ancestors' wrong-doings? I sensed that everything in my world would change, but I didn't know how.

"We'd better get out of here," Jie Jie said. We both sensed that it would be inappropriate to continue eating at a fancy restaurant at a time of tremendous national loss—people might think we were celebrating Mao's death. We paid our bill at once and practi-cally ran home through the now abandoned streets of Shanghai. Not even the streetcars were operating. It looked like a city frozen in time.

When we arrived at our rooms in the old house, panting from our jog and our brows damp with sweat, we found Shanghai Mama and Papa and two brothers huddled around their radio. Second Brother glanced up and waved us inside. Only after we had shut the door behind us did a smile appear on his face. "Mao died," he said, his voice elevated several notches above its usual deep, low tones.

"We heard," Jie Jie said.

My family started whispering about what might happen to China. I mostly just listened to what my parents and older siblings had to say. I didn't understand the intricacies, but I could sense that my brothers were well versed in the underground political news of the past few years. They felt certain that government policies would change for the better, allowing us greater personal and political freedom. I listened with intense interest.

"It's the dawn of a new era!" Second Brother exclaimed so loudly that we had to shush him, reminding him that listening ears might be surrounding us on all sides. He could be killed for saying such a thing—in the past he surely would have been. But at least we knew that our small room was a safe haven. Within its four walls, we could express our opinions freely. We shared hope for a brighter future.

The entire nation spiraled into chaos after Mao's death. Everyone went into grieving. Stores, restaurants, and even factories closed down for weeks. Nanjing Mother wrote that there was no need for me to return to work; I could remain in Shanghai until further notice. I was happy to stay. I was enjoying reconnecting with my adult cousin-siblings, being around the loving comfort of Shanghai Mama and Papa, and exploring the city, which was so much more sophisticated than Nanjing.

In early October 1976, about a month after I came to Shanghai, I returned to our shared rooms from a wander about town to find Second Brother grinning broadly. "Have you heard that the Gang of Four was arrested?" he asked. This was even more surprising news than that of Mao's death. Mao, after all, had been ill for some time. The Gang of Four—composed of Mao's wife and three of her close associates—had risen to power during the latter years of the Cultural Revolution. Now, Second Brother said, they had been accused of treason, labeled "counterrevolutionary forces," and officially blamed for the most damaging policies of the past decade.

We heard firecrackers going off and shouts coming from outside, and we raced into the street. There we joined thousands of Chinese celebrating. The Gang of Four's arrest was the first reliable sign that China was indeed setting off in a new, more liberal direction. I felt as though I had been trapped in a cage, and now the door had been cracked open. I could dare to pick up decade-old dreams from where they sat collecting dust on the shelves of my mind, brush them off, and pursue them proudly once again.

"The universities are going to reopen," First Brother announced later that day, as the family crouched around our single stovetop for a simple dinner of noodles. Papa then told us with pride that he had been asked to teach economics and accounting at Shanghai Jiao Tong University, and that he had been offered several jobs at companies that needed financial advisers.

Shanghai Papa looked at me. "You should apply to university," he said. "You are college student material, a bookworm."

I raised my eyebrows. "But how? How can I gain admission?"

Papa smiled. "You are smart, Ping-Ping. You always have had a clever mind. Study hard. That is the only way to get in."

I gulped. "I can imagine nothing I would rather do." I called to mind the mantra that Uncle W had given me years earlier: *I am precious.* I was determined to make up for lost time by sleeping less and working hard. Butterflies danced in my stomach, I was so nervous and excited at the same time. Yes, I would do it. I would find a way to go to school at long last.

Sure enough, my Shanghai family was right. The Cultural Revolution had ended. All at once, schools everywhere reopened—not only universities, but also elementary, middle, high, and night schools began to offer classes literally from six a.m. until midnight every day. They opened their doors to the general public, and anyone who wanted to could teach or study at will, free of charge. Here was a nation of over nine hundred million people starved for education. Thousands of teachers who had been persecuted, abused, and sent down to the countryside for the past decade came back to the cities. Paid or not, they were eager to share their knowledge.

I returned from Shanghai to Nanjing to live with Nanjing Mother and Hong in our dormitory room. Not long after that, Nanjing Father came home from exile. He looked dark and muscular, his face worn from years of exposure to the sun and open air. I learned that he had been chopping down trees and doing woodwork in the mountains along the snowy Russian border. Nanjing Father was an extreme introvert, and he spoke as few words as ever. But his mind had remained sharp. He returned to teaching aeronautical engineering at NUAA, and the university offered him a modest one-bedroom faculty apartment. Nanjing Mother took a job as the head of accounting at a large factory that made military vehicles.

We moved out of dreaded Room 202. Hong and I shared a bed

in the living room of our new place. I was delighted to have a desk with a lamp in the corner where I could study. I signed up for as many classes as I could fit into my schedule and studied day and night in a race against time. I quickly became known as "the girl who never turns off her lights." How could I possibly sleep? My mind was hyperstimulated by everything I was learning: math, physics, chemistry, literature, history, geology, geography. I felt like a sponge trying to soak up the entire ocean.

Nanjing Mother suggested that I study English. But I never imagined that I would need to learn a foreign language, and the only classes being offered were far from where we lived. Anyway, I didn't see the point. "Even if you don't learn your ABCs, you can still run machines," I quipped, citing a well-known Chinese expression. Although I made many wise choices that year, I lived to regret not taking my mother's advice.

Nine months later, in the spring of 1977, China held its first university entrance exams since 1966. Competition was fierce since no one had been able to get a higher education for the past ten years, and there were no more than a dozen colleges across the country open at the time. People of all ages, from eighteen to thirty, were eager to get in. I heard that out of every ten thousand applicants, only one was accepted to a university.

I raced to view the public bulletin board where the results were posted a few months after the test. I had done it! My score was above the minimum required for acceptance. Although I had been asked to fill out a form listing my preferences, I had no choice of where or what I would study. Ultimately, the government would make the assignment. But I was in. Out of the fifty or so children who had been in my study groups and taken the exams, I was one of only two people who made it.

I couldn't believe it: I was going to be a college student! I pinched myself to be sure it wasn't a dream and skipped home to tell my Nanjing parents and Hong. Although my Nanjing Father and

Mother had always been reserved, they couldn't help but grin when I shared the great news. "We knew you could do it, Ping-Ping!" they said, patting me on the back. I had never seen them more proud of me.

I was not accepted to an aerospace engineering program, even though all my life I had dreamed of being an astronaut. When the acceptance letter came in the fall of 1977, it said that I had been assigned to study literature at Suzhou University. Suzhou was a second-tier school, not as highly regarded as Beijing University or NUAA. My birth parents' faces fell when I told them.

"Maybe you shouldn't go," Nanjing Mother advised. "You can get in trouble so easily with a degree in literature. Wait half a year until you can take the entrance exam again. You may get into a science program."

But I didn't want to take a chance on my future. What if something happened and the government changed its policy, shutting down the universities again next year? What if I scored lower and didn't meet the minimum requirement to attend any program at any school? I was willing to accept any opportunity to pursue a formal education, even if it was less than optimal.

Anyway, I was nineteen and ready to strike out on my own. It would be sheer bliss to study in a new city, unburdened by the duties of cooking and cleaning for my family and working in the factory. In Suzhou, I would live with other students in a dormitory. The university was only forty minutes by train to Shanghai, so I would be able to spend breaks with my Shanghai family.

My decision was final: I would go.

I said my good-byes to my neighbors and colleagues. Ms. Lu, the teacher who had helped me so much by moving several bullies out of my study group years before, wept with joy when I told her. To my surprise, Wang, the former factory supervisor I'd become friends with, found me outside a night class one evening. "I heard from coworkers that you have been accepted to Suzhou University," he said. "I wanted to see you before you left, to tell you in person how happy I am for you." This time, I was the one who got misty eyed.

On my final day in Nanjing, I went to buy a few special treats for dinner to celebrate with my family. Fong, the boy whose "concubine" I had been, had set up a makeshift stall at the gates of NUAA. In typical Chinese entrepreneurial fashion, he and his mother were making money hand over fist selling her homemade dumplings and watermelons from a nearby farm. But when I got to the gate, I found so many people pushing their way toward Fong's stand that I couldn't squeeze in. Luckily, he caught sight of me in the crowd.

"I'll bring some food to you, Ping," Fong called out cheerfully. "Just go home."

I went back to our family's apartment and waited there, expecting Fong to knock on the door shortly. But hours passed and I didn't hear a sound. As dinnertime approached, I gave up hope, thinking he must have sold out of food or forgotten me. But when I glanced outside just to be sure, I discovered two big, ripe watermelons sitting on the ground by our front door. Next to them was a small pot whose lid had been left open a crack. The way the pot was positioned reminded me at once of that morning shortly after I had arrived in Nanjing, when I found two delicious steamed buns for Hong and me outside Room 202. Inside this pot, I discovered a dozen fresh, hot dumplings.

I understood at once that Fong was the mysterious benefactor who had been providing Hong and me with food all those years. If anyone had ever found out that he, a red-blooded boy, had been helping black elements, he would have gotten into serious trouble. Surely that was why he had kept his identity a secret until now. But instead of telling me to my face, the gentle, shy teenager had simply placed the food at our door in such a way that I would know he was the one. An indescribable emotion flowed from my heart, fresh and sweet like watermelon juice, tickling my tongue as it flowed down my throat and into my stomach.

When I look back on my childhood, I see that the shining spots of joy always resulted from random acts of kindness: Fong, my unknown benefactor, leaving a bit of food by my dorm room door; Uncle W sharing his wisdom and passion for Western literature; Wang's encouragement and praise in my factory jobs. People's openheartedness carried me through my darkest hours.

EIGHT

Life
Is a
Mountain
Range

PEAKS AND VALLEYS: 2006–2010

SOME POPULAR SELF-HELP books and articles depict personal and professional success metaphorically in terms of summiting a mountain peak, implying that we climb only in an upward direction. But reality isn't like that. It is more accurate to compare life to a mountain range. Sometimes we reach the top of a peak and then find ourselves unexpectedly tumbling back down into a valley again due to forces beyond our control. At other times, we ascend one peak, only to gain a view of many others all around us that we long to climb. In order to make it to the next mountaintop, we must first descend the one we are on. Either by choice or by circumstance, we find ourselves traveling up and down throughout our lives, traversing numerous peaks and valleys.

As soon as the *Inc.* article naming me Entrepreneur of the Year hit the shelves in December 2005, I was inundated with calls and e-mails—from old friends and colleagues who had seen my picture on the cover and wanted to catch up, from strangers who had read my story and were interested in learning more about me, and from people around the world who were eager to book me for speaking engagements. Offers began to come in from corporations wanting to buy Geomagic. We were, admittedly, in a sweet spot to be acquired: we had achieved consistent revenue growth and profitability, yet we were still small enough to be attractive to a variety of buyers. We also had a fantastic brand reputation for creating high-quality and highly differentiated products.

Some serial entrepreneur friends advised me to sell Geomagic and start over again. They themselves had gone on to successfully found multiple companies; doing start-ups was their area of expertise. I wondered if I should follow the same path. I had, after all, most enjoyed the early years at Geomagic, when the company had consisted of fewer than fifty employees. I knew everyone back then, and the decision-making process was quick and uncomplicated. People worked long hours and had fun together. We were like a big family. I saw clearly that it would not be easy for me to guide Geomagic forward, because most of what I had learned from starting the company would not apply to growing it. I would tumble into the valley of the unknown once again.

I looked at a couple of offers that presented good cultural fits and market synergies—the companies were also in the 3D design space and their users would find Geomagic software appropriate. Yet ultimately, I was uninterested in making a sale for several reasons. First, it was too early. Geomagic had not yet realized the vision that I had set out to achieve on the emerging space of 3D imaging and printing. I felt that I would let down some of our early investors, employees, customers, and partners. Second, I thrive on challenge. Taking the company to the next mountain peak excited me. Third, it seemed that most start-ups in our geographic area had sold early. I wanted Geomagic to stick around so that we could make a positive impact on the local entrepreneurial community. Last but not least, I didn't have a personal exit plan. I wouldn't know what to do without Geomagic, or what company to start next.

I had made many choices throughout my life that had me trekking down one mountain so that I could summit the next. I did not follow conventional measures of success. Instead, I always chose to move closer to my passion, traveling up or down, because I found that both peaks and valleys afforded me the joy of new challenges and interesting life experiences. In my twenties, I abandoned my well-paid programming job with Lane Sharman's start-up to join Bell Labs in an entry-level position because I wanted to work with innovators and attend graduate school. I later left my enjoyable and stable job at NCSA to found and run Geomagic. If I had pursued only a better title and bigger paycheck each step of the way, I definitely would not have ended up where I stood in early 2006: the founder and CEO of a global software company.

When I told our board that I had decided not to sell right now and shared with them the reasons, Paul Rizzo of Franklin Street Partners whispered in my ear, "Ping, I just knew you would make the right decision." I felt extremely grateful for the support that our first venture capital firm had given us over the past ten years. They had every right to push me to sell so that they could recap their investment sooner. When we later took on another VC investor, I realized just how lucky we had been with Franklin Street Partners. Their values aligned with ours; we both possessed a deep undercurrent of humanity. I could feel their pride in ownership of Geomagic. They were truly our partners.

Once I had the board's approval, I made an announcement to Geomagic employees that my goal was to continue to propel the company forward. The first slide of the presentation was a picture of a mountain range. "Let's move to another peak," I opened my talk, "and let's aim for one that is ten times higher."

Not everyone in the audience smiled; some employees were skeptical. But overall, the company mood was positive and energy levels high. We cheered when one person chimed in: "DROOM now stands for Don't Run Out Of Momentum." Indeed, we had come a long way from the days when our principal strategy had been Don't Run Out Of Money.

My intuition was right: the next phase was not easy. It felt as though we were always changing the tires while the car was still running. Doug Tatum, a fellow entrepreneur and personal friend, had just published a book called *No Man's Land: What to Do When Your Company Is Too Big to Be Small but Too Small to Be Big*. It resonated with me because Doug was so insightful about the issues that we were facing at Geomagic. More businesses die at this phase of growth than any other, the book points out. One of the reasons is that entrepreneurs underestimate the capital required to finance larger operations. Once the burn rate far exceeds the founder's ability to make payroll, many companies tank very quickly, faced with negative cash flow.

I was convinced that we needed to raise money, even though Geomagic didn't need any at the time. Experts had told me many times over the years, "The best time to raise money is when you don't need it." Paul Rizzo and Stuart Frantz, our two board members from Franklin Street Partners, were not thrilled—bringing another VC on board would dilute their investment. But to their enormous credit, they supported my decision and remained committed to Geomagic.

In May of 2008, I engaged an investment banker named Mir Arif, the founder of Madison Park Group in New York, to help us raise a round of venture capital funding. I had known Mir for a few years, and considered him one of the nicest and smartest people I knew. I trusted him because he had demonstrated the depth of his knowledge and given me sound advice in the past.

We felt fortunate to discover that there were many VC firms chasing a few great investment opportunities at the time. Our fund-raising process was made even more efficient because Mir had an excellent relationship with many of the midmarket firms. A few road shows and four weeks later, we had eight firms visiting our headquarters and meeting our team in North Carolina. We received six terms sheets. Mir ran the competitive matchmaking process, and I was flattered yet heartbroken to tell five of the firms no.

In the end, we chose Valhalla Partners from the Washington, D.C., area, mostly because the Geomagic team liked Scott Frederick, a Duke graduate and strategic adviser with an infectious smile. He came down to meet with our board members, and we felt good about the synergy. Scott made a funny comment during that visit, which later proved to be true: "The entrepreneur and VC relationship is like a marriage. Only it is a lot harder to divorce a VC than a spouse."

On September 10, 2008, investment bank Lehman Brothers announced a loss of $3.9 billion, and the U.S. stock market began falling like a rock. I realized that I had better get this Valhalla funding closed immediately. On September 13, which just happened to be a Friday, I asked our team to personally collect the required signatures from Franklin Street Partners early in the morning. Valhalla promptly wired us the $8 million at noon. At four p.m. that Friday, the Federal Reserve said that it would not bail out Lehman. The bad news put the entire nation into panic mode. Lehman Brothers filed for Chapter 11 bankruptcy just two days later. Our timing for closing the funding couldn't have been more perfect or our cash position more secure. Stuart said, "I always thought you were a visionary, Ping. You're also psychic."

In retrospect, I do not know if accepting the Valhalla investment was a smart move. We were financially secure before receiving their funding. I did not anticipate that the U.S. economic recession would dive so low or last so long. The manufacturing sector, Geomagic's primary revenue source, was hit hardest of all. We did not and could not achieve the high growth rate projected in our business plan. We also didn't anticipate Scott leaving Valhalla shortly after we signed the deal. Our relationship with Valhalla grew strained, and remains so to this day.

While we had raised the Valhalla capital intending to expand our business, we quickly discovered that under the new market conditions, there was no high growth to be found. We decided not to attempt to summit any new mountain peaks at the moment. We would be better off conserving cash.

Around the time that we closed the Valhalla deal, I fell unexpectedly into a dark valley in my personal life. A few years earlier, I had been deeply saddened to learn from Nanjing Mother that Shanghai Papa had passed away. Shanghai Mama had suffered a stroke shortly thereafter. She had spent the next three years in the hospital, paralyzed. Nanjing Mother told me that my beloved Shanghai Mama was miserable before she died in early 2006. Her children had done their best to help, but they were quite consumed with their jobs and caring for their own children. Most of the burden for her care rested with Nanjing Mother. I was filled with regret for not having spent more time in China or taken better care of Shanghai Mama.

A few months before Shanghai Mama passed way, I received a call from Nanjing Mother saying that Nanjing Father had suffered a massive stroke. He was now brain-dead. In China, people worship their ancestors and respect their parents, especially in old age. It was not permissible to stop life support, even knowing that he could not be revived. I hired two nurses to look after him night and day. I found it strange that Shanghai Mama and Nanjing Father, both having suffered a massive stroke, were staying at the same hospital at the same time. Nanjing Mother was now responsible for both her sister and her husband.

Nanjing Father passed a year later, in February of 2007. I rushed back to China because the funeral could not begin without me. Nanjing Father had written into his will that he wanted me to host the ceremonies and present his eulogy. Although I did not feel I had ever gotten to know him, I honored his wishes. I was, after all, a good Chinese daughter.

I felt saddened by Nanjing Father's death, and even more so by Shanghai Mama's and Papa's passing. Yet I had spent so much of my life without them, both as a child during the Cultural Revolution and as an adult in the United States, that I found myself able to mourn them and move on. My biggest concern was Nanjing Mother. Shanghai Mama's unhappy last few years weighed heavily on my shoulders. I did not want my birth mother to spend the remainder of her life alone and miserable in China.

That summer of 2007, Herbert took a sabbatical from Duke to teach at Berlin Technical University. He did so because Xixi was to attend the JFK International School in Berlin for a year. She was fourteen and, although only in the second year of middle school, remarkably independent. Having grown up with so little parental oversight in my own life, I always had granted her an unusual degree of freedom, compared with many Chinese and American parents. I allowed her to visit friends and go out on weeknights, manage her own schedule, and pursue whatever extracurricular activities she desired. She proved herself worthy of this liberal approach and always behaved responsibly. It made me proud to see how Xixi was blossoming into an articulate young woman who was both a talented artist and a top scholar.

During the summer of 2008, as we were seeking out venture

capital investors for Geomagic, I excitedly flew to Berlin. Xixi and Herbert's year abroad had come to an end, and I couldn't wait to bring them home. But when I arrived in Germany, Herbert told me that he was leaving me. Without giving me any warning or time to talk it over, he left for Paris with another woman. I packed up everything and came home with Xixi. That was it. Seventeen years of marriage dissolved in a flash. I felt as though I'd had the wind knocked out of me—disoriented and confused—but I tried hard not to show it.

Herbert appeared at home briefly at the end of August 2008 so that we could talk to Xixi together about our separation. A few weeks later, on the very same day that I was closing the investment with Valhalla, Herbert sent the movers. A year later, he returned to Austria and remarried. I became the primary caretaker of our daughter.

I was unprepared for the challenges of being a single mother and CEO at the same time, and didn't have any time to process what had happened with Herbert. Xixi, who was now fifteen, was having difficulties during her freshman year upon returning from Germany. Many of her longtime friends had gone to other high schools. As she headed into the awkwardness of adolescence, struggled to find her place, and dealt with her parents' divorce, she became very quiet, frequently withdrawing into her bedroom with the curtains closed. She also suddenly and inexplicably lost hearing in her right ear. To complicate matters, my body had me on a hormonal roller coaster, as I was premenopausal. I would wake up in the middle of the night drenched in sweat from hot flashes. I am usually calm and rational, so my uncharacteristic emotional state surprised me.

As Herbert moved out, I moved Nanjing Mother in to stay with Xixi and me. I wanted her to have an enjoyable time with her daughters and grandchildren, all of whom were in the United States. I found it ironic how Chinese our situation was: three generations living under one roof. The arrangement worked out well. Nanjing

Mother and Xixi got along and took good care of each other whenever I was on the road. I generally don't believe in fate, but sometimes life has a funny way of falling into place.

⌒

By March 2009, the U.S. market had hit a historic low. Almost everyone at Geomagic knew firsthand people who had lost their jobs, their homes, or both. As a nation, we had tumbled into a pit of hopelessness, and we couldn't seem to find our path forward.

During our quarterly company meeting that April, we conducted our usual survey of employee satisfaction using the Net Promoter Score tool. NPS asks only one question: "Would you recommend X product or company to someone else?" Independent surveys show a positive correlation between higher Net Promoter Scores and high-performance companies, such as Apple, Southwest Airlines, and Google.

At Geomagic, we used NPS to evaluate our products, training, and customer support services. Generally, great companies will receive an NPS of higher than 50 percent, and our scores were consistently within that range. We also adopted NPS to measure our employee satisfaction. For this, we asked: "Would you recommend working at Geomagic to someone else?"

When we collected the NPS ratings from our employees during the morning session of our company meeting that April, we got a surprising result. At lunchtime, the HR manager handed me the score: Geomagic had received its first negative NPS. There were more employees willing to openly complain about the company to someone else than employees who would recommend the company.

My hands began trembling, I felt nauseated, and I had trouble holding back my disappointment. I couldn't make sense of why this would be the case. Big companies were letting go of armies of people. Small companies were falling off the face of the earth. Yet we were financially secure and even hiring. How could our people be so miserable? If they didn't want to work here, why would they stay? Just for the paycheck? One of my goals in starting Geomagic had been to create an environment where people loved their jobs and enjoyed working together. Clearly, I had failed our people miserably.

After lunch, everyone gathered together again. It was time for me to announce the employee satisfaction survey results. When I gazed out at the tapestry of familiar faces, many of whom I considered dear friends, I could not hide my emotions. My voice shook as I spoke. "I feel ashamed that we have more detractors than promoters here. These results break my heart." I wanted to ask for our employees' help in turning this situation around, but words didn't come out. I cried instead.

Later that evening, over dinner with the Valhalla investors who had come to our annual meeting, a young associate scolded me. "Your speech was unprofessional, Ping," he said in a crisp, high-pitched voice. "You came across as defensive. Geomagic's employees won't feel comfortable telling you the truth."

I took his words at face value. Gazing down at my plate, I replied, "I'm sorry. I should have controlled my emotions better."

But thankfully, in the coming days many Geomagic employees stopped by my office to tell me that they appreciated what I had said during the meeting. They could tell from my voice and the pain in my eyes how much I loved Geomagic and cared for them. They told me that they very much enjoyed working at Geomagic. They suggested that their low scores might have reflected the bad mood brought about by outside factors such as the depressed economy, which was not fair to the company. Several people shared stories about their recent struggles: parents, partners, or friends who had lost their jobs and homes; lower than expected commissions due to missing revenue goals that were unrealistic, given market conditions; and the empathy they felt for customers who had been hit by hard times.

By expressing my genuine feelings to Geomagic's employees, I had opened the door for them to share theirs. Years later, I saw a video of a TED talk by Dr. Brené Brown, in which she said, "Vulnerability is the birthplace for connection, love, and change." Once again, I had found this to be true.

In the summer of 2009, at age fifty-one, shortly after receiving the negative employee Net Promoter Score at Geomagic, I looked around and realized that I was not okay. For the first time in many years, I was experiencing depression, isolation, and self-doubt, and starting to question the meaning of my existence. I couldn't sleep and was having trouble focusing at work. I couldn't grasp the reason for my divorce, which had been finalized at the end of 2008. I had difficulty controlling my mood swings. I was struggling with my relationship with my mother and our company's newest VC investors. In the prison of my own mind, I was once again a nobody— and I couldn't snap out of it.

I called Hong to vent. "It's just too much to handle all at once," I sighed.

Hong rushed to my rescue. "Come visit me. Let's go on vacation."

My team at work supported me. "Go, Ping," they said. "Take a long vacation. You need a mental break, and we will hold down the fort here."

A few days later, I hopped on a plane to Scottsdale. When I arrived in Arizona, Hong, forever spontaneous and supportive, was ready to take me on an American-style road trip. We threw one suitcase apiece in her car and off we went. Our first stop, we decided, would be at Hong's mother-in-law's vacation home in Durango, Colorado.

Driving through the desert and mountains raw and majestic in their red-hued glory reconnected me to my lifelong source of comfort: natural beauty. The saguaro cactus, tall and lean with branches sticking up like arms, reminded me of the cartoon character Gumby. Each time I caught sight of one, I smiled and waved, as if greeting an old friend.

Knowing my passion for rock collecting, Hong took me to the Petrified Forest National Park, where fossils, fallen trees the color of rainbows, had dotted the landscape since dinosaurs roamed the earth 225 million years ago. The world is so much bigger than us, I thought. How insignificant my petty problems seemed in comparison. Like a helium balloon released into the sky, my mind let go of its attachment to the negative thoughts that had tethered me for the past year.

I spent some downtime considering my divorce from Herbert. We had enjoyed a peaceful, supportive marriage for the past seventeen years, but how much time had we spent enjoying life together? Like most entrepreneurs, I had labored twelve hours a day, seven days a week, with barely a break since founding Geomagic in 1997. All my spare energy and loving attention I had devoted to Xixi. Even when I did have time for Herbert, I had often used it to consult him on business issues.

One aspect of our relationship that I had always appreciated was the freedom Herbert and I granted each other. We maintained independence, supporting each other's busy work schedules. But neither of us focused on cultivating our intimacy or sharing the joys of everyday life. Over the years, Herbert and I had grown into friends rather than lovers. The divorce, I realized, freed us both to pursue more authentic lives. In my heart, I was ready to let him go.

The trip with Hong did me so much good that the following summer, in 2010, I wrote to some good friends in Europe and asked if I could come spend a few days with them. In all my years of traveling for business, I had stayed in hotels, rarely having the time to stop by to see my friends, even if I was in their area.

My first stop was to see Sue and Peter Schmid in Lake Konstanz, Germany. They were a lovely couple, and Sue dressed my room with fresh flowers to welcome me. We visited stonecutters and a magnificent waterfall on the Rhine River. Peter, an artistic jewelry designer, worked with me to create a pendant made from African fire opal, green and red like a forest on fire.

Ever since reading *Jane Eyre* in China as a teenager, thanks to Uncle W, and then watching the movie based on the book at Suzhou University, I had longed to visit northern England. So for my last stop, I visited Chatsworth House, set in the heart of the Peak District of Derbyshire, which has had a long association with novels and movies. Jane Austen referred to there being "no finer country in England than Derbyshire." I, too, fell in love with the place. I found it comforting to resolve the reality with my youthful image of the English countryside. I loved being present with the verdant hills and quaint towns, the hauntingly desolate wet winds and gray skies.

I recalled a conversation during my college years in China. Discussing one of the central themes of *Jane Eyre*, I said, "It is about the clash between conscience and passion. Which one should we adhere to?"

My classmate replied, "Perhaps the key is to find the middle ground between the two."

Right now in my life, I realized, I needed to move toward my passion and away from the downward pull of my conscience. I had to let go of the feelings of guilt that plagued me regarding my divorce from Herbert, Shanghai Mama's lonely death, recent struggles to connect with my adolescent daughter and aging mother, and the dissatisfaction of my employees during this economic downturn. I had to rediscover my passion for being a mother, an entrepreneur, and a joyful person in the world. There at the Peak District

National Park, I found my resolve. The words of Viktor Frankl, Holocaust survivor and author of *Man's Search for Meaning*, came to mind: "Between stimulus and response there is a space. In that space is our power to choose our response. In our response lies our growth and our freedom."

I returned to North Carolina feeling ready to face anything. I had been experiencing an emotional low, but I recognized that my life was not at its lowest point—not even close. Like a rainflower stone buried in a riverbank, I had allowed myself to become caked with mud. Taking the time to connect with friends and myself was something that I rarely had done since starting Geomagic, if ever. Now I could see the myriad colors of my inner being sparkling brightly once again. Happiness, I knew, was my choice and responsibility.

The peaks and valleys, both professional and personal, that I experienced between 2008 and 2010 reminded me intensely of my university years in China. That, too, was a time full of surprising ups and downs. Looking back, paradoxically, I can see it was in those moments when I felt myself standing at the peak of achievement that I was least prepared for any emotional downturns.

UNIVERSITY: 1977–1982

SUZHOU IS KNOWN as the "Venice of the East" thanks to its picturesque canals; it is an old university town renowned for centuries as a center of culture and commerce plied on gondolas. The university campus had been built by American Christians in the nineteenth century and still retained its graceful lines. The year I arrived, its once grassy quads were dirt and the old brick buildings nearly bare. There was a scarcity of teachers. A Communist monitor sat in the front row of every class. Yet every step I took exhilarated me. I was nineteen, hungry for knowledge, and thrilled with my new-found freedom.

Our class, the product of ten years of pent-up demand for higher education, was one of the most intelligent and diverse in Chinese history, ranging in age from eighteen to twenty-six. I made friends quickly. There was JJ, the chain-smoking writer with the jumping mind who would go on to become one of China's most gifted news-paper columnists; Lao Han, the oldest student in our class, a white-haired genius who had spent the past decade firing terra-cotta roof tiles; and Jin Lin, the son of a Red Army family who charmed me with his dimples and easy laugh.

My friends and I often visited Suzhou's world-famous scholar gardens—intricate urban oases that had inspired my grandfather's backyard in Shanghai—to compose poetry and spend hours luxu-riating in intellectual banter. Accepting this radical contrast be-tween my present and past life circumstances was not easy. Sometimes, my young mind had to be coaxed with a long pause to accept that such changes were not a dream, but a new and unex-pected reality.

Walking through a Chinese scholar garden means taking a spiri-tual journey that unfolds like a painted scroll. As we wound our way over dragon bridges and through gateways decorated with hex-agonal windows, we encountered one unexpected view after an-other. It was in such a garden in Suzhou that the thought first occurred to me that my future might be utterly different from my past. I could be somebody someday. With my classmates, we dis-cussed how there are two kinds of people. A "sunrise person" goes through life open to the idea that the best may still be coming. A "sunset person," on the other hand, believes that the present is al-ways sloping downhill. We reassured each other that we would be sunrise people and prevent the past from contaminating our fu-ture.

I had wanted to major in aerospace engineering, but the government had decided that I would study literature. This turned out to be a blessing in disguise. Thanks to Uncle W, I had been exposed to great Western literature throughout my teenage years. Now I got to read novels, immerse myself in poetry, and even watch Western movies as homework—*The Sound of Music, Love Is a Many-Splendored Thing*, and *Jane Eyre*, among others. Zorro, a romantic "foreign devil" who rode with a sword on horseback, made me and my female classmates swoon like the young women in peril he rescued on the silver screen. That time was a high point of my life. I reveled in my creative activities and new friendships.

Halfway through our first semester, my friends and I formed a group called the Red Maple Society. We decided to publish a literary magazine composed of our essays and poems, as well as articles about events taking place across campus and in Suzhou. I was elected editor in chief, partly because I was the only woman in the group and the young men couldn't agree upon which one of them should be the leader, and partly because I was competent at handling administrative tasks like printing, accounting, and distribution.

Over the course of the next year and a half, our magazine grew quite popular—and not just among the university students or in Suzhou. The monthly issues were passed around among friends in different cities and mailed out to other universities as well. There still wasn't much reading material available in China since the publishing industry had yet to return. My classmates and I enjoyed writing and publishing immensely, with no sense that there was any risk involved in our poetic ruminations; our professors endorsed us, and the university itself printed the magazine. But it turned out that we were part of a nascent literary movement that was coalescing nationwide, which posed a threat to the Communist Party.

Toward the end of my second year at Suzhou University, our group was invited to attend a conference in Beijing with the publishers of literary magazines from ten other universities. Since we were not ranked a first-tier school, this was a tremendous honor. The Red Maple Society slaved for weeks to create what we considered our finest magazine yet. And in so doing, we took a huge risk: we chose to include an article written by a student titled "A Confession of a Communist Member," which compared Mao's Little Red Book to the Bible. The author claimed that the two books were similar in terms of popularity, accessibility, and their impact on human beliefs and behavior. He even compared their packaging, arguing that the books were the same size and weight, easy to hold and carry around every day.

We made a special cover for the issue, and I spent many nights hand printing copies. We then sent one representative from our inner working group to Beijing for the conference and distributed the publication around Suzhou. But the meeting never happened. The government decided at the last minute to ban the gathering of the ten universities, deeming it illegal. Instead, it was announced that China's de facto leader, Deng Xiaoping, would receive the representatives for a private meeting.

This was when things went terribly wrong. Every representative who attended the special meeting with Deng had a copy of the Red Maple Society's current magazine in hand. Deng asked to see what people were reading. One student from Beijing University passed him a copy of our magazine with its pages opened to the "Confessions" article, which was considered daring and controversial.

"A Communist member questions his own party?" Deng asked with his eyebrow raised after quickly skimming the article. It wasn't clear to our Red Maple Society representative or the other students in attendance whether Deng's comment was a condemnation or celebration of our work. Deng said nothing more.

The period from 1978 to 1984 was known as Deng Xiaoping's

First Reform. Although the Cultural Revolution had ended, tremendous freedom was nevertheless still mixed with uncertainty. Those in creative fields generally experienced some bumps in the road before becoming fully accepted. The local government continued to rule with people from the red-blood lineage, and they were incapable of following new directions from the central government. So when the news came back to Suzhou University of what Deng Xiaoping had said about our magazine, the authorities interpreted it as very bad news and took a preemptive strike against us.

The Red Maple Society was deemed an illegal underground society responsible for publishing anti-Communist propaganda. University officials arrested and interrogated all the students who belonged to our magazine group. For weeks, they pressed us to confess our counterrevolutionary activities. As the editor in chief, I was held most responsible for the trouble. For punishment, I was given a black mark in my personal file. I was labeled as a "Four Anti": anti-Communist, anti-socialist, anti-stability, and anti-China. This was the worst label anyone could receive. I knew full well that my hopes for a good life had been extinguished. In all likelihood, I would be sent into exile after graduation and be assigned to hard labor. I wondered if I would even be permitted to continue with my studies.

I also knew for sure that I now could not form a romance with anyone. Soon after my troubles, my dearest friend and classmate, Jin Lin, announced that his family had introduced him to a girl from a Red Army family whom he intended to marry after graduation. No one in our group of friends knew that he told me this with a deep sense of regret—not because the girl was an unsuitable wife for him, but because he had hoped that we might have a chance someday. I was touched and wished him well, encouraging him to proceed with the engagement and keep his distance from me. I had to push Jin Lin away to spare us both the trouble that would have come from his romantic involvement with someone as black as I.

For the rest of the semester, I endured relentless criticism by Communist Party officials and never-ending confession sessions. I sank into a deep depression. How could I have been so foolish as to jeopardize my college education and my entire future? I wrote to Uncle W asking for his advice. He counseled me to declare that I had "gone crazy" as an excuse for my lack of judgment—a tactic he himself had employed at one point to avoid punishment for having made inflammatory political remarks. Then, he said, I should drop out of school, returning only when the controversy had blown over.

I did not follow Uncle W's advice, but rather chose to stay on at Suzhou University and complete my education. It was the only hope I had left of pursuing my dream job: I wanted to be a newspaper reporter because I loved to travel and explore. I dared not reinvolve myself in the literary magazine, however. I felt lost as I struggled to find my place, now that I had been disgraced. I was blessed when a gentle and nurturing literature professor with a brilliant mind, Professor Xu, took me under her wing. She reminded me of Shanghai Mama and Nanjing Mother combined. She kept me out of politics and out of trouble, encouraging me to focus exclusively on my studies. To this day, I keep a melancholy poem that she wrote about mist settling over the canals of Suzhou hanging on my bedroom wall.

⌒

During my senior year, I selected a somewhat obscure research topic for my thesis: China's one-child policy. When I had been born in 1958, China was still encouraging large families. As Nanjing Mother had explained to me as a teenager, that was why she had given birth to two children when she had wanted none. Feeling that she couldn't burden Shanghai Mama with another child, Nanjing Mother had resorted to jumping off tables when she was pregnant to try to abort Hong.

But as China's population burgeoned, Deng Xiaoping's newly formed government reversed course and, in 1979, started enforcing its now infamous "one family, one child" rule. By 1982, regulations had grown so strict that they included mandatory IUD insertion for all women who already had one child, abortion for any woman who had an unauthorized pregnancy, and sterilization for couples with two or more children.

At our school, officials would confirm that all female students were menstruating each month by checking their sanitary napkins. When they discovered that some women were cheating by bringing in their friends' soiled pads, the officials began inserting their fingers directly into our vaginas to check for blood. The degrading practice made me wonder how the rest of China was responding to the one-child policy. Uncle W gave me his blessing, saying this sounded like a powerful humanitarian topic. Even the Communist Party leader at my school approved.

I spent a few months traveling around the Chinese countryside conducting research. I interviewed doctors and midwives, as well as farmers and government officials. What I discovered was shocking. Everywhere in rural areas, infant girls were being killed. In spite of decades of Communist propaganda about the equality of the sexes, ours remained a patriarchal society. Out of desperation, some parents chose unborn sons over born daughters. I witnessed the horrifying consequences with my own eyes: female infants drowned in rivers and lakes, umbilical wounds still fresh; baby girls flushed down the sewage system or suffocated in plastic bags and tossed into garbage bins. Women I spoke to sobbed hysterically as they told me how their husbands had taken their female infants away from them immediately after giving birth, or how local officials had forced them to have abortions even in their ninth month of pregnancy. I didn't think there was any way I could help, but at least, I thought, I could offer them an opportunity to unload their burdens and cry on a sympathetic shoulder.

When I completed my thesis in the spring of 1982, I never imagined that anything would come of my work. Unbeknownst to me, someone in my department sent a copy of my thesis to the Chinese press. My findings wound up as the editor's comment in the Shanghai newspaper, which called for an end to the madness. The editorial comment was then picked up by China's national paper, the *People's Daily* in Beijing. It was the first time a Chinese official newspaper acknowledged that peasants were killing baby girls. The news spread to the international press, who used this acknowledgment as evidence of China's violations of human rights, prompting cries from the UN for economic sanctions. I unwittingly had set off a chain of events that, like toppling dominoes, resulted in a worldwide shaming of my country and its new leadership.

One day in the fall of 1982, as I innocently walked across campus making preparations for graduation, someone sneaked up behind me, jammed a black canvas bag over my head, and bound my wrists together tightly. "Don't scream," a menacing male voice whispered as I was escorted into a nearby car.

We drove for hours. I had no idea what was going on, as I knew nothing of the international human rights pressure on China that had been traced back to my thesis. I did not ask any questions, either, as I had learned never to make inquiries in China, especially when the cops were involved. I simply remained silent as my mind raced, trying to guess what had gone wrong. The only thing I could think of was that the black mark in my personal file from my days at the Red Maple Society had caught up with me.

Eventually, we arrived at our destination. I was taken from the car and deposited in a pitch-black windowless room. My hood was removed but my wrists were left bound together in front of me. I heard the door close behind me. The stench of human excrement mixed with ammonia made me gag. I shuffled on hands and knees across the concrete floor exploring my prison. All I found was a thin mattress and a bucket, which I presumed would serve as my toilet. After what might have been many minutes or several hours, someone gave me a container of water and untied my hands. I received no food, but I did not feel hungry; my stomach churned with acid and fear.

The government officials did not beat me or even interrogate me. They ignored me completely. I was not given any information about why or for how long I was being held captive. The unknown was intolerable. I couldn't sleep. I could barely breathe. My mind started filling the darkness with vivid replays of the struggle sessions at NUAA, the rape, the burning of my journals, the murder of teachers and black elements. I tried to convince myself that my death would be quick and painless. I no longer had the responsibility of raising my little sister, so I could go. And yet it seemed cruel that I should meet with my end now, when I had survived the worst of the Cultural Revolution and finally gotten a chance at an education.

I thought about my Shanghai and Nanjing parents, my cousin-siblings, Uncle W, my college friends, and most of all Hong: Would they come looking for me? Would they ever find out what happened to me? Or would I, like so many others before me, simply disappear without a trace?

I lost track of time in the darkness. After what I later found out was three days, I had fallen asleep at last, so it startled me when the door to my cell slammed open. "Get up and come out!" cried a loud female voice. The small amount of light filtering in through a few high barred windows in the hallway nearly blinded me. Everything around me looked foggy and white. "You stink," the guard snarled. She handed me loose-fitting clothes and led me to a washroom where I could shower and change. "Go clean yourself," she said as she pushed me inside.

In the bathroom, there were just a few showerheads, no bench on which to put my clothes, and no dry towels. When I was finished washing, I stepped into the clean clothes, wrapping them over my wet body. The guard ushered me into the office of a burly fifty-something-year-old man in a police uniform. His eyeglasses made him look scholarly and less intimidating. "Sit," he commanded. He pushed some papers across his desk at me.

"You will go home now and await further instructions," the official said.

I was still blinking as my eyes adjusted to the light, my body weak from lack of food and sleep, my thoughts slow and fuzzy. Was I being placed under house arrest? I wanted to ask what offense I had committed, but once again I kept my mouth shut.

The guard escorted me out of the official's office and handed me over to a policeman with a round, soft, kind-looking face. As he drove me to my birth parents' apartment in Nanjing, we chatted a little. He told me that I had brought shame to our country because of my research on female infanticide, which had caused an international human rights uproar. Through him I learned that while my name had not appeared in the newspapers, I had been traced as the source of the embarrassment. I would have been in even more trouble, except no one had been able to find any evidence that I had done anything wrong.

"You are a lucky girl," he said before dropping me off at the gates of NUAA. "If this were the Cultural Revolution, you surely would be dead by now."

But I didn't feel lucky. I felt as though a thousand-pound stone had crushed my chest. I didn't know where I would be sent next or what kind of future I would face.

⌒

When I reached my Nanjing parents' apartment, I didn't tell them exactly what had happened, only that I had gotten in trouble with

Communist authorities once again for something I had written. I rarely ever talked to them about personal matters anyway, and I figured that in this case, the less they knew, the less the government would bother them.

"I want to leave university, claiming a nervous breakdown," I declared. My parents didn't question the decision; Uncle W had shared with them the advice he'd given me during the Red Maple Society scandal two years earlier. They feared that, given the black marks on my personal record, I would likely be sent to a far-off corner of China for some obscure job upon graduation. Such an outcome would force me to relinquish my residence in Nanjing, and I might never be able to return to a city again. It would be better if, by pleading mental illness, I could avoid losing my residency.

I stayed inside for weeks as my family tried to figure out some way of helping me. They had several contacts outside of China. Uncle W was able to convince an Australian friend to sponsor me for a student visa. One of Nanjing Father's former NUAA students had left two years prior to study at the University of New Mexico, and it was he who would secure my admission to the school as an ESL student. Nanjing Mother and Father were thrilled that I would have a chance to start a new life and get a graduate degree in the United States.

A few weeks after the house arrest began, I was called to the local police station and given my government orders. "You must leave China at once. You are not welcome back," a stiff-lipped officer told me. He instructed me never to talk about my arrest or my thesis research. "Don't embarrass your country again." After a short silence, he then added, "We know where your family lives."

I felt a deep sense of relief that I had a chance at a future, even if that future was unknown. Exile was, in my opinion, a far preferable fate to being sentenced to a hard-labor camp in Chinese Siberia. I was happy to know that my family had begun to make arrangements for me to live overseas. However, one major obstacle still remained: I needed to obtain an official passport from the Nanjing provincial government in order to leave the country. Chinese officials did not always communicate with one another or conduct thorough background checks unless an event triggered it. I was sure that when the Nanjing provincial passport office inevitably checked my personal record, they would discover the black mark from my Red Maple Society activities at Suzhou University. That might very well be enough reason for them to deny me a passport.

As I stood in the police station corridor wondering whom I could possibly ask for help, I was blessed with another stroke of good fortune. A beautiful young policewoman with a compassionate smile appeared and explained that she was in charge of my case. She called me into her office to talk about my situation. I don't know why—perhaps her warmth reminded me of Shanghai Mama—but I opened my heart to her. I told the story of the Red Maple Society's controversial magazine article, and about how my research on the killing of baby girls had gotten me into even more trouble. I had never intended to do any damage to my country, I said; on the contrary, I had only wanted to help.

The policewoman listened closely, tilting her head to one side. When I described what I had seen in the countryside as I conducted my thesis research—babies discarded in garbage cans and tossed into lakes—tears formed in the corner of her eyes. She had gotten married recently and was expecting, she told me. It pained her deeply to hear my stories. "If you are willing to risk your life to save baby girls," she said, "the least I can do is help save yours."

A week later, a handwritten note appeared under the front door of my Nanjing family's apartment, telling me to be at the Five Dragon Bridge at two p.m. When I arrived, I found the policewoman and her bicycle leaning against the bridge's intricately carved stone walls, where I had often played as a child. The young woman nodded for me to come close. With a glance over her shoulder to be sure that no one was watching, she pulled several dozen sheets of paper out of a thick brown envelope and handed them to me. She whispered softly in my ear, "If the officials see these 'Four Anti' black marks in your file, they will never let you leave China. Hold on to them while I go get your passport issued." Then she disappeared on her bicycle.

I glanced through the files from my official record. When I saw the labels I had been given—anti-Communist, anti-socialist, anti-stability, and anti-China—printed there in ink, I knew for certain that I must leave. I was lucky that the policewoman had risked her life to help me get the necessary documents. It was a brave and compassionate act.

For four hours, I waited nervously, the papers clasped tightly in my sweaty hands. Finally, the young woman returned. With a grin, she quickly took the papers from me and stuffed them back into the brown envelope containing the rest of my personal file. Then she jumped onto her bicycle, turned her head back toward me, and called out, "Make China proud, Ping. I know you will."

A few weeks later, my passport arrived in the mail. I traveled to Shanghai, where I was able to get my U.S. student visa at the American consulate without any difficulty. The only hurdle that remained was finding enough money to purchase my plane ticket to the United States. I converted my entire savings from my factory work and the sale of most of my personal items into U.S. dollars, and received an eighty-dollar cashier's check from China Bank in return. This would cover the flight from San Francisco to Albuquerque. But I still needed six hundred dollars to buy my one-way international ticket from Shanghai to San Francisco. Nanjing Mother offered to make the purchase for me.

"Where did you get the money?" I asked, eyes wide.

Mother lowered her voice and explained, "An old business partner owed your grandpa some money a long time ago. He recently settled his debts, and I got enough money to buy you a ticket. Don't worry about it."

I wanted to hug her with appreciation, but my feet wouldn't move; it didn't feel natural. I simply bowed my head.

⌒

Knowing that these were my last days in China, various family members began cramming my head with wisps of stories about my lineage. I learned sketchy details about Shanghai Papa's father, an illustrious business owner who had founded a bank and taken a second wife, who was not Papa's birth mother. As for Nanjing Father, he had been born into a political family. My great-grandfather had been killed during the uprising led by Sun Yat-sen, the founding father of modern China. Dr. Sun had raised my grandfather and grand-uncle as his own sons. Then, after the Chinese Civil War, my grandfather and his family had fled the Communists with the Nationalist Party to Taiwan. Nanjing Father ran away from his family somewhere along the escape route, choosing instead to remain in China. During the Cultural Revolution, Nanjing Father had been accused of serving as a spy and special agent for the Nationalists. No wonder I had been punished all my life. I was not only black; I was pitch-black.

There were few telephones in China in those days, but mail service was reliable. Still, I didn't know whether I would ever see my family and friends again, and I started to feel the weight of leaving. Due to the politically sensitive nature of my circumstances, I was unable to tell any of my classmates, including Jin Lin, that I was being exiled from China forever.

Into a tattered bag, I packed my small collection of rainflower stones, what few clothes I owned, and an English dictionary Nanjing Father had given me. The day before my departure, Nanjing Mother gave me a scrapbook she had made, which I had never seen before. It included photographs of her wedding to my father, her pregnancy with me, our family portrait, and a few of my baby pictures.

I bid my family farewell at the Shanghai International Airport and departed China on January 14, 1984. A few hours into the flight, it suddenly hit me that this was my first time on a plane, and that I was traveling halfway across the earth. I was the girl who had wanted to fly and live on the moon, the teenager who had longed for the same freedom that the characters in my favorite novels had enjoyed. Was this exile not, in many ways, the realization of my dreams? I took a deep breath, and much of my anxiety vanished.

I thought of a different parting, seventeen years earlier, when Red Guards had taken me from Shanghai Mama. Like a mountain range, I realized, life offers surprising views at every turn. Although the best views can be found on the peaks, it is the valleys that offer the most opportunities for growth and development. In valleys we farm, build roads, and formulate our visions for reaching ever higher. In valleys, we develop resilience and cultivate hope.

The World
Isn't
Flat;
It's 3D

In March 2006, shortly after I was named *Inc.* magazine's Entrepreneur of the Year, Thomas Friedman's book *The World Is Flat* rose to the top of the international bestseller lists. I was asked to give the closing keynote for the *Inc.* 500 Conference, celebrating the five hundred fastest-growing private companies in America. Friedman would be delivering the opening keynote.

During his talk, Friedman explained his theory that globalization has occurred in three phases. First, countries invaded other countries. Next, companies invaded other countries. Now, in the early twenty-first century, we were being personally invaded by global commerce. Thanks to the proliferation of computers and fiber-optic cable, multinational companies with global supply chains were making geographic divisions increasingly irrelevant. Friedman cited the simultaneous rise of India and China as examples of the leveling of the economic playing field—hence the emergence of a world that is flat.

Friedman's speech was insightful and entertaining. Mine was on an entirely different subject: I was to share my personal story about my journey from China to the United States, from a nobody to somebody, and how that experience influenced my leadership style at Geomagic. Yet when I took the stage, I couldn't resist spontaneously opening with the statement "The world isn't flat; it's 3D." This remark elicited a large burst of laughter and applause from the audience.

I was throwing in a little humor to engage the audience, but also I genuinely believed what I said to be true. The last thing I would ever claim to be is an expert in international trade, let alone economic policy. Yet in my opinion, it is possible to interrupt the cycle of painful and often shortsighted outsourcing that many people still accept as the inevitable outcome of globalization. Instead, we will move increasingly toward a modern version of localization, with local production marked by global interconnectedness and accessibility.

I marvel at the environmental and financial inefficiency of shipping millions of identical products or parts across the world. Today, we shop at Walmart, where most of the goods sold are made cheaply in China but carry no connection to the country or its culture. At the same time, my home state of North Carolina—once famous for its textile mills, woodworkers, and a whole village of potters—has been hit hard by this trend, losing jobs, industries, and heritage. I remember a day when Xixi was young and we visited Ben Owen, a master potter from Randolph County. He picked her up and sat her on his lap at the pottery wheel, guiding her hands to mold a lump of clay. These potters survived the industrial revolution, but now globalization is threatening to render their traditional handicraft obsolete. Unless, that is, technology not only preserves but also extends art into everything we make.

At Geomagic, we are passionate about the intersection of handcraftsmanship and technology, art and science, humanity and business. We believe that innovation can enable abundance in the future rather than scarcity—my original vision of a "personal factory" scaled up to a global system. I believe locally made, high-quality products that leverage technology can help make manufacturing in the United States efficient and price competitive once again. Businesses should be measured by more than mere numbers; they should strive to be good global and local citizens. We can start building sustainable business by creating socially responsible ecosystems. Common sense tells us that it is more efficient to build innovative products in our home countries. We should make more goods that people really want and need, and less stuff that people don't care about.

Humans are anything but one-size-fits-all; each of our bodies is unique, as are our tastes and styles. At Geomagic, we envision the day when individuals are invited to participate in the creation of products that have meaning for them on a fundamental level. With personal factories, there is no need to maintain a huge inventory; no costs or environmental degradation for shipping goods halfway across the earth by sea, rail, or air; no huge retail shops demanded for displaying wares; and far less waste from making products that nobody wants. Companies no longer need to spend hundreds of millions of dollars advertising fifty brands of shoes, many of which never sell, and consumers don't have to repeatedly waste time and become frustrated trying on dozens of jeans that don't fit their curves.

I have seen it happen already. Invisalign offered the first example of this paradigm shift in action: Geomagic has contributed to the mass customization of aligners to straighten teeth. Since 2009, it has also powered the creation of Bespoke prosthetics. Scott Summit was intrigued by a proposition that a friend put to him: While prosthetic limbs had come a long way in terms of mobility, comfort, and materials, they still created stigma for those using them. Could Scott, an industrial designer, find a way to make the devices more uniquely personal, while still keeping the process affordable? "I wanted to make people who had lost limbs feel beautiful again," Scott said.

In partnership with orthopedic surgeon Dr. Kenneth Trauner, Scott founded Bespoke Innovations. The team started to research ways to deliver a more customizable experience to patients with prosthetic limbs, and soon came across Geomagic. Today, Geomagic software enables Bespoke to manufacture customized prosthetic limbs, affording a great deal of individual expression. One woman wanted to wear cocktail-length dresses to evening parties and concerts without attracting undue attention to her prosthetic leg. Scott and his team developed a fairing that resembled fishnet stockings, which she could match on her other leg. Another patient, who had lost a favorite tattoo along with his leg, had the design etched into the leather of his prosthetic leg.

In just a few years, shoes will be made to perfectly fit the shape of our feet, chairs will be molded to provide optimal support for our backs, and artificial heart valves will be modeled on our own. With global accessibility through Internet technology, small companies and individuals will be able to make their unique local products, while also offering them on the global stage with pride and authenticity. Just as the democratization of the publishing industry opened mass communication for individual bloggers to offer their opinions to everyone, so, too, will the democratization of the manufacturing industry pave the way for people to enjoy and share personalized products and experiences across the globe.

During the summer of 2006, as Geomagic was expanding into China and the excitement from the *Inc.* magazine cover story about me was settling, I received an unexpected phone call. "Your middle school classmate is on the line," the Geomagic receptionist told me.

"Middle school?" I asked aloud, wondering who would make such a claim in order to reach me. Puzzled, I took the call.

I hadn't heard the voice on the other end of the line in thirty years. It was Winston, a leader of my study group and the son of a high-ranking Red Army officer. He had once slammed a door in my face and had shamed me on occasions by calling me "a stinky black element." He worked in Canada now, Winston said, and had seen my picture on the cover of *Inc.* He was pulling together a reunion of our study group as we were before we had all gone different ways at the end of the Cultural Revolution, and he wanted me to come to Nanjing to join in. Everyone wanted to get together, he said, and I would add a lot to the reunion. He also assured me that Zhang would not be invited.

"So you call that a middle school reunion?" I asked with a hint of sarcasm.

Winston chuckled. "What else would you call it?"

Curiosity and a newfound desire to confront the ghosts of my past piqued my interest. I decided to go.

Thirty years to the day since our study group had last sung "The East Is Red," I walked into a Nanjing restaurant for a gathering of former red leaders and black elements—the abused and their abusers. When I first entered the private banquet room, I couldn't recognize most of the people there or recall their names. Feeling alienated, I leaned uncomfortably against a wall, wondering where to sit.

All at once, Li, my Red Guard best friend whose mother had given me my first rainflower stone, appeared by my side. I hadn't even seen her coming. She greeted me with a smile and warm embrace typical of her ebullient personality. "Hey, everyone, Ping is here!" she shouted with a rollicking laugh that made the others turn their heads toward me. As she guided me to my chair, she told me that she was working as an accountant at a chemical company.

Thanks to Li's warm embrace, memories of those middle school years suddenly flooded back into my mind, and I found that I could put a name to almost every face at the table. I was excited to see that Fong had made it to the reunion, as well as the sympathetic teacher, Lu, who had rescued me from my tormentors. She told me that I had made a strong impression on her back then because I was so courageous and resilient.

I was shocked when a man named Huang, who I didn't think even remembered me, recited almost word for word an essay I had written when I was thirteen. He told me that he had always tried to imitate my clever reports.

"I know I beat you, and I'm sorry for that," a Red Guard with a red face said, raising his glass for a toast. He demanded that I drink to his apology. I wanted to decline: Chinese hard liquor deceives with its innocent clear color; it is 120 proof. But denying the toast would have been considered rude. Ever my quiet savior, Fong unobtrusively found his way to my side and switched glasses with me like a magician without anyone noticing so that I could discreetly drink water instead.

I was halfway through the sixteen-course feast before I realized that I was the star of this reunion. I had been dirt beneath my classmates' feet, and now I was their hero. I was the CEO of a successful high-tech company. In their eyes, I lived a glamorous American life of big houses, multiple cars, and other possessions they coveted. As the drinking went on and they started taunting Fong and me for the relationship we never had, I came to see that they didn't know me at all—not thirty years ago, and not now. I had not changed. What had changed was their perception of me. Prejudice, I realized, exists only in people's minds.

The highlight of the experience was getting to talk to Fong semi-privately for a moment in the corner of the banquet room, once everyone was standing up to leave and bidding their farewells. I grabbed his arm with my hand. "I never got to say thank you," I said, my eyes growing misty. "I brought so much shame to your name, and all you did in return was shower me with kindness. I can never repay you for your generosity."

Fong gave me his signature soft, shy smile. "I always wanted to protect you, Ping. I only wish that I could have done more," he said simply, dipping his head toward the earth. I wondered if life had been kind to him since the Cultural Revolution. I wished fervently that it had.

⌒

During the reunion trip, I was struck by two realizations. First, and most moving, was the change in my mind-set from nobody to somebody. Back then, I had feared even being friendly with Li, since my black blood would taint her and surely cause trouble for her. Now everyone, including those who had shunned me, wanted to associate with me because they thought I had an amazing life. They seemed genuinely happy for my success in America. Their acceptance and admiration healed some of my enduring wounds. I found the last clinging bits of bitterness fall away from my childhood armor, leaving me even more compassionate and vulnerable than I'd been before.

Second, I was struck by how much more American I felt than Chinese when I was with them. Naturally, in America I often feel the power of my Chinese roots. I still speak with a slight accent, dress with a Chinese flair, and cook Chinese food at home, and, most important, have a Chinese way of thinking about shared responsibility, humility, and the common good. But at the reunion, surrounded almost exclusively by people who had never left China, I felt dramatically American by comparison. I noticed that my former classmates talked with their mouths full and reached for food from the common plates with their chopsticks rather than using a serving spoon. They ordered the waitress around without a hint of politeness, which is typical in China—but given my many years of waitressing in the United States, I felt resentful of their rude behavior. I also noticed that they were uninhibited in discussing their private affairs, whereas I was more reserved. From time to time, I couldn't even find the right Chinese words to express myself; it was easier for me to describe many experiences and revelations in English.

In the twenty-five years that I had lived in the United States, I truly had become American in my attitude toward personal freedom and the power of individual expression. I had enjoyed incredible opportunities, been given the choice to study where and when I wanted, and stubbornly pursued my own path in education, marriage, family, and entrepreneurship. My Chinese counterparts had never been given such opportunities or had such rich experiences. I saw how difficult it was for them to imagine how many options we have in America. Even our ability to freely move from one city to another was not a concept they could comprehend.

When the 2008 mortgage crisis and stock market crash pulled the U.S. economy into a downward spiral, I contemplated what else—other than running a successful midsized technology company that hired locally and brought manufacturing back to the United States—I could do for my country. As with many blessings in my life, good fortune meant being ready to take action when opportunity came my way. In 2009, President Obama created the very first presidential National Advisory Council on Innovation and Entrepreneurship, and I was invited to be one of its inaugural members. I accepted the invitation because entrepreneurship and innovation are two topics dear to my heart and because it would provide a welcome opportunity for me to learn about policy making at the highest level. This was my chance to help guide America proudly forward through an era of uncertainty and change.

In February 2012, I was honored with an Outstanding Americans by Choice award. It is given each year to immigrants who have naturalized as American citizens and who have demonstrated outstanding service to the nation. I didn't choose to come to America; I had to leave China. But I did choose to become American. I have embraced this country as my adopted home, and I am fiercely loyal to it. I am humbly grateful every day that my life is an embodiment of the American dream, and I do everything in my power to offer others the same opportunities that I was blessed to have found here. After all, most Americans are immigrants, separated by only a few generations.

Life is full of surprises, and dreams come true in the most unexpected ways. As a little girl, I wanted to take flight and join the fairytale woman who lived on the moon. Later, sliding down airplane wings at NUAA, where my father had once taught aeronautical engineering, I dreamed of becoming an astronaut. I never did study engineering or soar into outer space. But in August 2005, I watched from the ground as Geomagic technology was used as part of the main mission for the space shuttle *Discovery*, commanded for the first time ever by a woman, Eileen Collins. Our software helped to detect and repair insulation tiles damaged in space, assuring the safe return of the astronauts. Nanjing Father watched the shuttle landing on CNN from his faculty apartment at NUAA. In one of the last conversations I had with him before his stroke, he said that I had made him happy and proud.

Around the same time, Geomagic software was employed by the U.S. Park Service to re-create a digital model and engineering drawings from 3D scan data of the Statue of Liberty. Three-dimensional digital documentation is a new application of Geomagic software, allowing us to help preserve our collective memories and national treasures. If the monument is ever destroyed or damaged, it can be reproduced as it stood at the time of the scan—with its original shape and artistry, right down to the details of wear and tear from time and weather. The *Wall Street Journal* called it "Digital Lady Liberty" in a front-page story. I felt amazed that I could play a role in preserving the symbol of freedom to which I had paid homage as a new American immigrant nearly two decades earlier.

Today, Geomagic continues to flourish. While I was writing this book, we completed a major acquisition that will advance 3D technology to the next level, incorporating the sense of touch into the digital environment. I have found great peace in my personal life as well. Nanjing Mother has continued to live with me since 2008. Slowly yet steadily over the years, like ice cream melting off a cone, my birth mother is softening. I am glad that we have had a chance to share a life together, and I know that I will not regret taking care of her. Hong not only helped me start Geomagic but also thrives as an entrepreneur, owning and running two successful specialty retail stores, Bischoff's Shades of the West and Bischoff at the Park, in Scottsdale. I am immensely proud of her. Xixi started college in the fall of 2012. She continues to impress me as an independent and thoughtful Renaissance woman, gifted in art and science and a maker in her own right.

I contemplated whether or not to write this book for several years. Initially, I was enticed by a well-known literary agent to share my life story. But it didn't feel right because I couldn't imagine why anyone would want to read about me. In addition, Xixi was young, and I wasn't sure whether she could face the brutality of her mother's youth. Finally, I am an introvert. I find sharing my life with people I don't know to be intimidating and uncomfortable.

Eventually, I became reconciled to the idea that others might find inspiration in my story. I write today not because of what I have become but because of the nobody I once was. I write because I wrote many pages long ago, more than these, in secret and at night, and they were burned in front of my eyes. I write because I am fortunate enough to have lived a life that I never could have imagined possible, and sharing the tale of how I got here seems to be the generous thing to do.

This book is not intended as a blueprint. I believe that all people should value their own pursuits, and even more so treasure their own life journeys. I do not wish for anyone to live the life I did. Millions of people in China experienced similar atrocities, and they passed away or have continued to struggle in the decades that followed. I do not think myself better than any of them. I was handed few advantages in life, and I possess no extraordinary talents. I simply was born with the curiosity to learn, the tenacity to make a better life, the desire to help others, and a great deal of resilience.

Perhaps I gained that resilience because of my particular life circumstances. I was raised by two different mothers, one nurturing and the other analytical; embraced two opposing ideologies, one socialist and the other capitalist; and lived an extensive life in two countries, China and America. I also journeyed through the most extreme valleys and have reached some remarkable peaks. I can relate to wild success, utter poverty, and everything in between. Bridging these gaps, I have developed flexibility and compassion for those experiencing the struggles we all face.

Life has been messy for me, as it has for most everyone. I have come to the realization that challenging experiences break us all at some point—our bodies and minds, our hearts and egos. When we put ourselves back together, we find that we are no longer perfectly straight, but rather bent and cracked. Yet it is through these cracks that our authenticity shines. It is by revealing these cracks that we can learn to see and be seen deeply.

True to my profession, I see my life in three dimensions, similar to the shapes that Geomagic software creates. There are three types of holes in topology. A tunnel has two openings that connect to the outside. A pocket has only one opening. And a void, an enclosed space like the inside of a ball, has no connection to the outside world.

My life has been composed of tunnels, pockets, and voids: a tunnel from Shanghai to Nanjing, and another from China to America; a pocket when I first arrived at NUAA, and another when I landed in the United States with no hope of returning home, both times knowing that I had to find my way to the opening of a better life. The voids still ache in my heart: the abuse I endured; my lack, for many years, of the parental love that most children take for granted; the nightmares that refuse to go away; and the loneliness that I felt for so long.

Yet as life comes to a full circle, I appreciate how all those spaces forced me to shape myself around them: I bent, but did not break. In spite of the challenges, I have created a reality that forms a whole. Even in the void, I made a womb where I nurtured my creativity and incubated ideas. Eventually, I gave birth to both a company and a child. It is in tunnels that we start our journey; in pockets that our imagination blossoms toward the opening; and in voids that we must face our naked, agonizing vulnerability.

ACKNOWLEDGMENTS

TO MY COAUTHOR, MeiMei Fox, whom I met at Burning Man in 2010. Working with her is a joy.

To our editor, Niki Papadopoulos. Her dedication, insight, and drive for excellence were instrumental in writing this book.

To our agents, Laura Yorke and Carol Mann. Their support and love of authors are unconditional.

To our publisher, Adrian Zackheim, for his integrity, intelligence, trust, and unwavering support of his authors.

To my assistant, Cecilia Gonzales. Without her, my life would be a total mess and I would not be able to write.

To Stuart Frantz, chairman of the board of Geomagic, and Fred Hutchison, our corporate attorney. They are my inspiration for treating people right while running a business with high integrity.

To all Geomagic employees, partners, customers, shareholders, and stakeholders. Without them, this book could not have been born.

To the four dear friends who pushed me from no to yes on writing this book: Chip Conley, Bo Burlingham, Alan Young, and Simon Sinek.

Numerous friends have had their hands in shaping the book, or have encouraged me directly or indirectly: Kathleen Maher, Jon Peddie, Ben Davis, Ana Fernandez, John Gage, Andrew Hessel, Grace Ueng, Jim Goodnight, Ann Goodnight, Art Padilla, Laura Lunsford, Yingbi Zhang, Martyn Day, Allan Behrens, Sue Barry, Peter Schmid, Ari Weinzweig, Sally Rosenthal, Scott Summit, Jack Stack,

Norm Brodsky, Elaine Brodsky, Steven Wilkinson, Doug Tatum, Carol Fox, Kiran Ramchandran, Mike Reilly, Lisa Burlingham, Donald Kurasch, Ken Morse, Jeremy Morrelli, John Koten, Marisa Koten, Bob McNeel, Ruel Joyner, Paul Spiegelman, Herbert Edelsbrunner, Joe Orr, Drew Banks, Brad Holtz, Laurie Becklund, Patty Geiger, John Grinnell, Roy Hefferman, George Gendron, Terry Wohlers, Amy Millman, Betty Kenan, Mir Arif, Peter Fuss, and many more. I am sure I've missed some.

Last but not least, to my family: my daughter, Xixi, who is my love and reason and everything in between; my mother, who takes care of our household and endures endless silence when I am busy; my sister Hong and her husband, Anselm, who financed the start-up of Geomagic and provide me with emotional support; my favorite nephew, Tien, with whom I enjoy our annual outings; and Uncle W, my siblings, and the younger generations.

—Ping Fu in Chapel Hill, North Carolina
September 2012